Neil Jordan

Contemporary Film Directors

Edited by James Naremore

The Contemporary Film Directors series provides concise, well-written introductions to directors from around the world and from every level of the film industry. Its chief aims are to broaden our awareness of important artists, to give serious critical attention to their work, and to illustrate the variety and vitality of contemporary cinema. Contributors to the series include an array of internationally respected critics and academics. Each volume contains an incisive critical commentary, an informative interview with the director, and a detailed filmography.

A list of books in the series appears at the end of this book.

Neil Jordan at work. Courtesy of Photofest.

Neil Jordan

Maria Pramaggiore

UNIVERSITY
OF
ILLINOIS
PRESS
URBANA
AND
CHICAGO

Manufactured in the United States of America
1 2 3 4 5 C P 5 4 3 2 1
∞ This book is printed on acid-free paper.

Library of Congress Cataloging-in-Publication Data
Pramaggiore, Maria, 1960–
Neil Jordan / Maria Pramaggiore.
p. cm. — (Contemporary film directors)
Filmography: p.
Includes bibliographical references and index.
ISBN-13 978-0-252-03325-4 (cloth : alk. paper)
ISBN-10 0-252-03325-6 (cloth : alk. paper)
ISBN-13 978-0-252-07530-8 (pbk : alk. paper)
ISBN-10 0-252-07530-7 (pbk : alk. paper)
1. Jordan, Neil, 1951—Criticisn and interpretation.
I. Title.
PN1998.3.J67P73 2008
791.4302'33092—dc22 2007024128

Contents

Acknowledgments

I wish to express my thanks to Neil Jordan for being so generous with his time. I am indebted to Diarmuid McKeown for making complicated transcontinental arrangements work smoothly.

Tom Desmond, Stephen Quinn, John Nulty, Liam O'Luanaugh, and the rest of the staff at the National Library of Ireland were gracious and efficient, ensuring access to materials quickly. It was an honor and a pleasure to work in their manuscript reading room. Marihelen Stringham and the Interlibrary Loan Services staff members at D. H. Hill Library at North Carolina State University were unfailingly cheerful in the face of my many requests.

The College of Humanities and Social Sciences and the English department at North Carolina State University provided time and travel support. Many thanks to Ron and Melinda at Photofest. Jim Naremore and Joan Catapano at the University of Illinois Press have been tremendously supportive editors.

Many colleagues and friends encouraged my work on this project, including Kevin Rockett, Brian McIlroy, Diane Negra, Joe Gomez, Deborah Wyrick, Elaine Orr, Nick Halpern, Jans Wager, Beth Hardin, Sheilah Zimpel, and David Kruidenier. Devin Orgeron, Marsha Orgeron, and Tom Wallis read chapters and shared their insights. Brian McIlroy's Irish Film and Genre conference in March 2005 provided inspiration for the home stretch, and Fidelma Farley and Dervila Layden made Dublin a home away from home. I am grateful for Jim Morrison's collegiality and continue to hope that some of his brilliance will rub off on me.

Loving thanks to Alfred Pramaggiore and Anne Pramaggiore, for being there in so many ways.

To Tom, my partner in all things, it goes without saying that this book exists primarily because of the emotional, intellectual, and material sustenance you provide, along with the companionship of our beloved mutual friends, Bob, Chloe, Claudia, Emmie, Fergus, and Tupelo.

Neil Jordan

Neil Jordan's Postmodern Gothic

In the era of the celebrity film director, Neil Jordan's movies are better known than he is. Outside his native Ireland, Jordan does not enjoy the name recognition befitting the creative force behind *The Crying Game* (1992), one of the most widely acclaimed independent films of the 1990s, or *Interview with the Vampire* (1994), a Hollywood blockbuster that earned more than $220 million. The status of the film director has changed over the course of Jordan's filmmaking career, which began in the early 1980s. In the wake of the corporate consolidation of a global film industry, and within an increasingly celebrity-obsessed popular culture, the film auteur celebrated by postwar French cineastes has morphed into the entrepreneurial producer-director, best represented by Steven Spielberg and George Lucas (Corrigan). In the age of the name-brand director, Neil Jordan has more or less preserved his anonymity.

One reason for Jordan's low profile is the diversity of his films; he cannot be linked to any particular genre or style. In 1988, having completed only four films, Jordan said: "Every one of my movies is quite different, each time the audience is a little thrown, because they expected something different" (Woodworth 12). He has maintained that eclectic approach, moving among projects of vastly differing scopes and sensibilities. Jordan adapts works of popular fiction and writes original screenplays. He remakes Hollywood comedies and French noir classics. He may be best known for his thrillers and his forays into gothic horror, yet intimate dramas and a historical biopic are among his most acclaimed films.

Jordan also seems to move somewhat effortlessly among production contexts. His first feature film, *Angel* (1982), was financed by the newly created Irish Film Board (Bord Scannán na hÉireann; IFB) and the Motion Picture Company of Ireland in conjunction with Britain's Channel Four television. Within a decade, he was working in Hollywood on *High Spirits* (1988) and *We're No Angels* (1989). In 1994, he directed *Interview with the Vampire*, a high-concept film made under the auspices of Geffen Pictures, and in 1999 he made *In Dreams* with Steven Spielberg's DreamWorks.

Although Jordan has worked with Hollywood moguls like David Geffen and Steven Spielberg, he also works independently, cobbling together international financing for small and medium-sized projects. Throughout his career, Jordan has maintained a close working relationship with the producer Stephen Woolley, who cofounded Palace Productions, the British production company that financed Jordan's early films and went bankrupt just after the U.S. release of *The Crying Game*. With Woolley as a frequent collaborator, Jordan has taken on the challenges of commercial projects and independent films alike.

Because of his eclecticism, Jordan seems to resist categorization as an art-cinema auteur for whom cinema serves as a medium of personal expression. Yet Jordan also deviates from the newer model of the auteur as a film-schooled entrepreneur because he came to filmmaking through writing, and he has remained a prolific fiction writer. He has taken a writing credit on twelve of the fifteen films he has directed to date and has published four novels since he became a filmmaker: *The Past* (1980), *Dream of a Beast* (1989), *Sunrise with Sea Monster* (1994), and *Shade* (2004). Jordan rose to prominence when he won the *London Guardian* prize for his first short-story collection, *Night in Tunisia* (1976), and an Irish Arts Council Award for his first screenplay,

Traveller, which was directed by Joe Comerford in 1979. Jordan got his break in film by writing dialogue for John Boorman's *Excalibur* (1981) and directing *The Making of Excalibur: Myth into Film* (1981). When the financing for *Angel* came through, he embarked upon his career in feature films with an original screenplay about a jazz musician who is ineluctably drawn into sectarian violence in Northern Ireland. *Angel* is one of several Irish-themed films in Jordan's oeuvre. It is also the first of many Jordan films to feature an autobiographical motif: characters who are musicians, actors, and circus performers. Jordan's father was a jazz musician, and Jordan played the saxophone professionally. During the 1970s, he performed in children's theater in Dublin, where he worked with the theater and film director Jim Sheridan (*My Left Foot* [1989]; *In the Name of the Father* [1993]; *In America* [2002]; *Get Rich or Die Tryin'* [2005]).

Since the release of *Angel,* the most consistent feature of Jordan's career has been an intense dedication to work, evidenced by the steady output of screenplays, novels, and films. Two films garnered early critical acclaim: *The Company of Wolves* (1984), which he cowrote with Angela Carter, and the neo-noir thriller *Mona Lisa* (1986), which he cowrote with David Leland. The latter won Jordan a British Academy Award (BAFTA) for best direction. On the tails of that success, Jordan made two Hollywood movies: *High Spirits,* a screwball ghost comedy based on an original screenplay, and *We're No Angels,* a remake of a 1955 Michael Curtiz–Humphrey Bogart escaped-convict farce. Both were widely panned.

Jordan redeemed himself in the eyes of many critics with a figurative and literal move back to Ireland to make *The Miracle* (1991), a coming-of-age drama based on his own short stories that he filmed in his hometown of Bray, south of Dublin. His next project, which was his first major success in the United States, was the political thriller *The Crying Game.* Like the contemporaneous films of Steven Soderbergh (*Sex, Lies, and Videotape* [1989]) and David Lynch (*Blue Velvet* [1986] and *Wild at Heart* [1990]), *The Crying Game* found a surprisingly wide audience. It became an indie phenomenon, partly because of a highly successful marketing campaign orchestrated by the new kings of the independents, the Weinstein brothers of Miramax. By encouraging critics to keep the film's second-act revelation a secret, the distributors created a buzz around the film and fostered a sense of community among viewers, whose word-of-mouth endorsement significantly broadened the audience for the film. *The Crying Game* was nominated for six Academy Awards, including best film and best director, and Jordan won the Oscar for his original screenplay.

Although he invariably earns critical praise for small independent films like *The Miracle* and *The Crying Game,* Jordan has never limited himself to low budgets or intimate dramas. His first project after *The Crying Game* was *Interview with the Vampire;* five years later, he made *In Dreams,* indicating his continued willingness to adapt the work of others and to make studio films. During the mid-1990s, he wrote and directed two smaller Irish films: *Michael Collins* (1996), a historical biopic about an Irish revolutionary that set off a storm of controversy in Ireland and Britain, and *The Butcher Boy* (1997), an adaptation of a 1992 Irish novel by Patrick McCabe that many critics have praised as his most powerful work to date.

Jordan's late twentieth- and early twenty-first-century works include two remakes, a short, experimental performance piece, a second Patrick McCabe adaptation, and *The Brave One* (2007). *The End of The Affair* (1999) is the second film version of Graham Greene's 1950 novel (the first was Edward Dmytryk's 1955 film), and *The Good Thief* (2002) is an arty homage to Jean-Pierre Melville's *Bob le Flambeur* (1955). "Not I" (2000) is a fourteen-minute filmed performance based on a Samuel Beckett monologue. *Breakfast on Pluto* (2005), adapted from Patrick McCabe's 1993 novel, is a film whose Irish subject matter places it squarely in a lineage that begins with *Angel* and continues through *The Crying Game, Michael Collins,* and *The Butcher Boy.* The protagonist, Patrick "Kitten" Braden—an orphan whose parents are the parish priest and the priest's housekeeper—embodies a number of Ireland's contemporary social traumas. Kitten is a transvestite whose coming-of-age memoir traces a personal and cultural identity crisis that is intertwined with Irish Republican Army (IRA) bombing campaigns and the escalation of the Troubles in Northern Ireland in the 1970s and 1980s.

With a slate of films that encompasses such a wide variety of subjects, genres, and industry contexts, it is not surprising that Jordan remains such an elusive figure. Even the fact that he is an Irish director, and therefore something of a rare commodity, has not increased his visibility. On the contrary: in the mid-1990s, after achieving commercial and critical success with *The Crying Game* and *Interview with the Vampire*, Jordan wrote, "I'm generally confused with Jim Sheridan and complimented for *My Left Foot*, which is fine with me" (Jordan, *Michael Collins Screenplay and Film Diary* [hereafter *MCFD*] 23).

The confusion between Jordan and Sheridan is no coincidence. In an increasingly corporate and global film industry, nationality has become one more branding mechanism. That makes it difficult to peg a director like Jordan; he is an Irish director who does not limit himself to making Irish-themed films. Like his contemporaries Ang Lee and Atom Egoyan, Jordan resists the implicit link between auteur and national context that has helped to make the work of other internationally known filmmakers, such as Abbas Kiarostami and Wong Kar-wai, more consistently recognizable. Although Jordan's Irish Catholic background is evident in his work, it would be a mistake to label him an Irish auteur and leave it at that. Jordan's work reflects the fact that being Irish and being a citizen of the world are not mutually exclusive identities. In this regard, his work resembles that of his Irish literary forefathers James Joyce and Samuel Beckett. Jordan continues to live and work in Ireland, however, which distinguishes him from Joyce and Beckett, who lived in self-imposed exile in Europe.

Until recently, "Irish film director" was an unlikely identity indeed. As a fiction writer and filmmaker, Jordan is acutely aware of the difference between joining the much-heralded tradition of Irish writers and helping to create an Irish visual culture virtually from scratch. When he began working in film, the cinema represented an uncharted territory: "Making films, in a way, was an escape from the weight of literature for me" (Interview in this volume, 153).

Jordan acknowledges that, more recently, film historians have begun to uncover Ireland's rich cinema history. When he was growing up in the 1950s and 1960s, however, that tradition was nowhere apparent. Until the 1970s, no indigenous Irish cinema existed. In 1907, James Joyce famously invested in Dublin's first movie theater, the Cinema Volta. Yet the First World War, the War of Independence (1919–21), the Irish Civil War (1921–23), and World War II (in which Ireland remained a neutral party) paralyzed the nation's economic infrastructure. The conservative values promulgated by the government and the Catholic church deepened the Irish Free State's and, later, the Republic's cultural isolation. In the postwar era, the Emerald Isle served primarily as a location for foreign filmmakers such as John Ford and David Lean, whose films popularized a clichéd notion of Irish pastoralism for viewers around the world. But international productions contributed little to the development of a local industry. Foreign filmmakers monopolized Ireland's national film studios at Ardmore, which opened in 1958, depriving the local industry of resources. This industrial context helps to explain the fact that Jordan, and many others, grew up believing that John Ford's *The Quiet Man* (1952) was an Irish film (Interview in this volume, 152–53).

The privileged status of foreign filmmakers in Ireland is clear from the history of the Irish Film Board. It was the American director John Huston (who became an Irish citizen in 1964) whose public pronouncements during the late 1960s spurred the government of the Irish Republic to support the development of a film industry. At the same time, Irish filmmakers such as Bob Quinn, Joe Comerford, and Pat Murphy forged ahead with low-budget projects such as *Lament for Art O'Leary* (dir. Quinn; 1975), *Poitín* (dir. Quinn; 1979), *Traveller* (dir. Comerford; 1979), and *Maeve* (dir. Murphy; 1982). When the government eventually established the IFB, the British director John Boorman became its head, a move that provoked controversy.

To make matters worse, the first project the board funded was Jordan's *Angel*, which aroused animosity because Jordan was seen as Boorman's protégé. After several contentious years, the government eliminated the IFB's funding in 1987, two years before Jim Sheridan's *My Left Foot* became a huge international success. The decision to defund the film board was reversed in 1993. Ireland's first minister of arts, culture, and the Gaeltacht (Ireland's Gaelic-speaking region) announced the IFB's revival in Dublin on the night that Neil Jordan won the Academy Award for *The Crying Game*. By the late 1990s, a thriving Irish film culture was producing a diversity of films including shorts, features, and Irish-language films; all of this activity was bolstered by the reinstated IFB and sustained by Ireland's booming Celtic Tiger economy.

This recent history of Irish cinema offers a useful reference point for examining Neil Jordan's work, not because his films epitomize Irish national cinema—however that term might be defined—but because his work has emerged from a tremendously vibrant period of Irish cultural production at the end of the twentieth century. Jordan's films reflect and have contributed to sweeping social, political, and aesthetic changes that have been taking place in Ireland. Over the span of Jordan's filmmaking career, Irish art and popular culture have emerged as important venues for a reassessment of Ireland's troubled sense of national identity, its colonial history, and its postcolonial experience. That process has been energized and complicated by the economic and cultural effects of globalization, which challenge the traditional frameworks of identity that have informed Irishness since the Easter Rising of 1916.

Jordan's films address the breakdown of modern institutions such as the nation-state and the nuclear family and hint at the disintegration of grand narratives of nation, religion, gender, and sexuality that underwrite those institutions. The French theorist Jean-François Lyotard has identified the breakdown of totalizing narratives as a central feature of postmodern culture. According to Lyotard, postmodernism "cannot exist without a shattering of belief and without discovery of the 'lack of reality' of reality, together with the invention of other realities" (*Postmodern Condition* 77). Neil Jordan's films focus on the destabilizing effects of these profound cultural shifts at the level of the individual character. In most of Jordan's films, characters' beliefs about themselves and the world are shattered in an instant: their realities suddenly become unreal. As they reconstruct themselves in newly surreal environments, they discover that they are empowered, perhaps even enjoined, to invent fictions, and often those fictions acquire the status of reality.

Jordan's iconoclastic approach to the political, religious, and cultural institutions that secure a sense of identity might suggest an indiscriminate embrace of the postmodern zeitgeist. Yet Jordan's work refuses any simple celebration of the schizophrenia, consumerism, and historical amnesia associated with postmodern culture. His intellectual and aesthetic perspectives grow out of the specific historical context of twentieth-century Ireland and its rapid transition from an insular and parochial culture rooted in traditional Catholic values to "the most globalized society in the world" (O'Toole, "Ireland" 23). That process did not occur overnight. Ireland's economic reforms of the 1960s and its entry into the European Union in 1973 inaugurated a period of internationalization that gradually undermined the hegemony of the Catholic church and loosened its stranglehold on government and society. Clergy sex scandals accelerated the process during the 1980s. During the 1980s and 1990s, matters of sexuality that the church had long deemed taboo moved to center of the public arena: referenda were held on the constitutionality of divorce (1985 and 1995) and abortion (1983 and 1992); legal restrictions on the availability of contraception were lifted (1985); and homosexuality was decriminalized (1993).

In politics, the practice of historical revisionism posed a challenge to another totalizing narrative that has played an important role in defining Irish identity: Irish Republicanism, which was linked to Catholicism throughout most of the twentieth century. Revisionist scholars and public intellectuals have adopted diverse political positions as they dispute and complicate the historical claims of Irish Republicanism. One common thread is their challenge to the Republican national narrative, which, they argue, exaggerates the importance of British colonial oppression and sectarian divisions within Ireland's long and diverse political, religious, and cultural history. The reassessment of Irishness taking place in contemporary Irish culture, and specifically the vociferous interrogation and deconstruction of Catholic and nationalist hegemonies, offers evidence for a breakdown in the Irish national narrative and for tangible shifts in political and economic power within the Republic.

Given the intense public debates in fin-de-siècle Ireland, it seems inevitable that Irish popular culture would speak to these dilemmas. Contemporary cultural and political concerns pervade the music of Sinead O'Connor and U2 and many of the films of Jim Sheridan and Neil Jordan. This reassessment of cultural identity does not merely respond to the seismic ruptures of the last thirty years; it also reflects long-standing anxieties regarding national identity. When the Irish Free State was established after the War of Independence from Britain (1922), the island was partitioned so that six counties in the north remained under British rule. The creation of the province of Northern Ireland, a legacy of the eighteenth-century British plantation of the north by Protestants and Presbyterians, contributed to political disputes over the geographical and symbolic borders of the Irish nation.

Historically, those political disagreements have been expressed through civil war and paramilitary violence. During the 1960s, the decade in which Neil Jordan (b. 1950) came of age, activists in Northern Ireland began demanding civil-rights reforms to improve the status of the working class and the Catholic minority. The British response was to impose direct rule and to send troops into the province, igniting a thirty-five-year guerrilla war known as the Troubles, waged by the IRA, the Royal Ulster Constabulary, Protestant paramilitary groups, and British military forces. The conflict has claimed several thousands of lives, and its effects have become a frequent subject for Irish filmmakers, including Jim Sheridan, Neil Jordan, Pat Murphy, Margot Harkin, Thaddeus O'Sullivan, and Orla Walsh. The Northern Ireland peace process, which produced the Belfast/Good Friday Accord in 1998 and culminated in the establishment of the Northern Ireland Assembly in 2007, offered some promise of a negotiated settlement to this seemingly intractable conflict. One indication of the immensity of the project of reconciliation was the announcement in January 2006 that the Historical Enquiries Team was beginning to investigate 3,268 killings that took place between 1969 and 1998 and expected to take five to ten years to complete its work.

Although Jordan's cinematic vision is rooted in this very specific, and very fraught, national context, his work speaks broadly to the anxieties of postmodern culture, where familiar frameworks of identity such as nationality, gender, sexuality, and race seem to be dissolving. The Marxist scholar Fredric Jameson characterizes postmodernism, the cultural dominant of the postwar period, as a depthless culture of circulating images. In postmodern culture, reality consists of a play of surfaces, where history and meaning founder. Unlike the anxious and alienated modern individual, Jameson writes, the postmodern subject is fragmented and decentered, possessing no identifiable inner self that can be distinguished from an outer reality (11–14). Identity is no longer understood as a grounded, inner essence but rather as a series of constantly changing roles.

Jordan's characters contend with their rapidly changing circumstances by treating themselves as works in progress and by enacting their fluid identities as performances. Most narrative films revolve around characters who grow and change. But Jordan's characters are often brutally deconstructed by the circumstances in which they find themselves, their romantic illusions shattered. They learn that their identities and their realities can be treated as fictional constructs, subject to continuous revision. Reflecting Jordan's cultural background, his characters remake themselves by resorting to the venerable Irish traditions of storytelling and performance, two aesthetic modes that also happen to have reemerged as central concerns of postmodern aesthetics.

Jordan's best-known film, *The Crying Game,* conveys his interest in the fragmentation of identity with specific reference to twentieth-century Ireland. At first glance, the film seems to endorse a view of Irish national identity as an unchanging essence rooted in centuries of nationalist struggle. But this complex thriller ultimately destabilizes stereotypes of Irishness and challenges assumptions about colonial and sexual identities as well.

The film revolves around Fergus Hennessy (Stephen Rea), a sympathetic IRA Volunteer. Fergus believes himself to be engaged in a heroic resistance movement against British forces occupying Northern Ireland. But Fergus's empathy for and growing attachment to his hostage, the black British soldier Jody (Forest Whitaker), forces him to reassess the tactics and ideology of the IRA. After British helicopters and Saracen tanks descend upon the remote greenhouse that serves as the IRA hide-out, killing Jody and several IRA comrades, Fergus recoils in grief and guilt. He also begins to question all political ideologies that rationalize such violence.

In the film's second act, Fergus relinquishes his romantic notions of Irish national identity as well as his assumptions regarding gender and sexuality. Escaping into the anonymity of London, a postcolonial metropolis that confirms the danger of relying on traditional notions of identity, Fergus hides from his former IRA cohorts. He honors Jody's dying wish to seek out his "special friend" Dil (Jaye Davidson) to tell her Jody was thinking of her when he died. Fergus falls in love with Dil and then, during their second sexual encounter, learns that Dil passes as a woman while possessing a penis. The disclosure shatters Fergus's already-fragile sense of himself, forcing him to reconsider his brief but intense relationship with Jody (which plays out in dreams) and, by implication, his sense of his own masculinity. Still reeling from Dil's revelation, Fergus encounters two former IRA comrades who have tracked him down. They demand that he carry out a suicide mission and threaten to involve the "wee black chick" (Dil) if he refuses. In the climactic confrontation, Fergus confesses his guilty secret to Dil (whom he has disguised to look like Jody), while IRA operatives descend on her apartment, merging the film's twin plotlines of romance and political intrigue.

The popular and critical affection for *The Crying Game* in the United States was partly the result of its beautifully orchestrated combination of nostalgia and novelty. Jordan conjures up traditional ideas about Irishness only to debunk them. Initially, *The Crying Game* seems to speak the language of America's best-loved "Irish" film, John Ford's *The Quiet Man.* Ford's melodramatic story concerns a guilt-ridden former boxer and American expatriate, Sean Thornton (John Wayne), who returns to Ireland to reclaim his ancestral home, a cottage called White-O-Morn. In the process, Thornton tames a shrew by marrying Mary Kate Danaher (Margaret O'Sullivan). In *The Crying Game,* after the botched political kidnapping, Jordan's guilt-ridden Volunteer leaves his homeland for foreign shores, an act that seems to resonate with Sean Thornton's travails. But whereas Ford privileges the American exile's return, Jordan brings to the foreground Ireland's history of *out*-migration, a phenomenon with deep roots in Irish culture, going back to Oliver Cromwell's land confiscations in the 1640s and persisting through the famine migrations of the 1840s and well into the twentieth century.

Ultimately, *The Crying Game* subverts Ford's sentimental notion of the exile's return and unsettles Ford's neo-Shakespearean romance plot. Unlike Ford's hero, Fergus can neither redeem his violent past nor claim his rightful place on an idyllic Emerald Isle. First of all, Fergus has no property to declare; he divests himself of everything, including his name and nationality. In London, he calls himself Jimmy, and although his employer derisively calls him Paddy—an ethnic slur that presupposes a generic Irish identity—Dil believes that he is from Scotland. In the film's concluding scene, the only territory Fergus occupies is a high-tech cell in a British prison. He is seated behind a transparent wall through which he converses with Dil. Like Orson Welles's character Mr. Arkadin, Fergus becomes a man without a country: this point is driven home by Jordan's adaptation of the scorpion-and-frog fable that first appeared in *Mr. Arkadin* (1955) and was later used by Wendell B. Harris Jr. in *Chameleon Street* (1989) to signify the instability of racial identity.

Perhaps most importantly, Jordan annihilates the Fordian image of a pastoral, backward, and atavistic Ireland. Unlike Ford's quaint and choreographed scenes of hand-to-hand combat, Jordan's violent sequences emphasize the sophisticated weapons and surveillance capabilities of the British military and its IRA antagonists.

As a political thriller in which an unconventional romance is embedded, *The Crying Game* is also indebted to the work of Alfred Hitchcock, an auteur who specialized in orchestrating multiple plotlines and destabilizing masculine identities. More specifically, Jody's early death and Fergus's mournful second-act exile function as Jordan's homage to Hitchcock's *Vertigo* (1958). Like *Vertigo*'s heartbroken detective Scotty Ferguson (James Stewart), Fergus seeks to assuage his remorse and grief over a lost love object but instead falls into a romantic obsession with a woman who links him to that guilty past. Like Scotty, Fergus learns that he has been pursuing a mirage. Hitchcock's Madeleine and Jordan's Dil are imposters; worse still, they are manufactured, man-made women. (Recognizing this fact, Scotty and Fergus make them over once more for their own purposes.) But whereas Scotty has been duped by Gavin Elster, a powerful man who successfully manipulates Scotty's all-too-predictable desire for the ideal woman, Fergus has been deceived by his own illusions about masculinity and femininity. Ultimately, he must accept the unpredictability of his own sexual desire and identity. In addition to demystifying Ford's exile plot, the film's unfolding love affair proves far more subversive than the spirited sexual tension that informs Ford's comedy. In the final analysis, Jordan denies viewers the standard heterosexual romantic coupling at the conclusion.

With its indictment of political violence and its exploration of alternative genders and sexualities, *The Crying Game* attacks the twin hegemonies of Irish nationalism and Catholicism. Jordan frequently trains his directorial eye on the excesses and hypocrisies associated with these political and religious agendas. An examination of his oeuvre reveals that, in aesthetic terms, Jordan's work also draws upon and often blends two other powerful Irish cultural traditions: gothic horror and satire.

The gothic literary tradition, with its gloomy metaphysics, is closely allied to Ireland's mystical brand of Catholicism, its bardic past, and its rich store of Celtic mythology. The gothic sensibility can be traced back to the novels of the British authors Horace Walpole (*Castle of Otranto;* 1764), Ann Radcliffe (*Mysteries of Udolpho;* 1794), Matthew Lewis (*The Monk;* 1796), and John Polidori (*The Vampyre;* 1819), as well as the gothic-revival writings of the Irish writers Sheridan Le Fanu ("Carmilla"; 1871), Bram Stoker (*Dracula;* 1897), and Oscar Wilde (*The Picture of Dorian Gray;* 1890).

Gothic works are concerned with death, decay, and sexual perversion. They explore states of heightened subjectivity through first-person narration. Gothic literature and one of its descendants, the horror film, rebel against Enlightenment principles of order and rationality by focusing on supernatural beings, distorted vision, and insanity (Schmitt 7). The political character of the gothic has been vigorously debated: often described as a feminine genre, the gothic challenges the idea of modern progress by suggesting that time is cyclical rather than chronological. The repressed past always returns, often in the guise of specters that haunt isolated mansions and ruins, passing down to subsequent generations an inheritance of sin and guilt. At the same time, the subgenre of the female gothic, in which women protagonists are entrapped by sexual predators and oppressive environments, offers a proto-feminist critique of corrupt authority based on gender and lineage.

In Jordan's novels and films, the gothic asserts itself through narratives of death and loss where male characters, for the most part, are terrorized by and transformed into ghosts, beasts, monsters, doubles, and alter egos. Jordan's human and inhuman creations obsessively narrate stories, attempting to rewrite themselves as they seek to shake off the sins of the past. In *The Crying Game,* Jordan draws from the gothic tradition by creating in Fergus an embattled protagonist who wanders far from home in search of way to exorcise the ghost that possesses him (Jody).

Several film scholars have remarked upon Jordan's penchant for the gothic. Brian McIlroy links Jordan's gothicism to his interest in race, gender, national identity, and sexuality ("Neil Jordan" 5). Keith Hopper limits his discussion of the gothic to Jordan's Irish-themed films, whereas Desmond O'Rawe maintains that a gothic outlook pervades Jordan's body of work (189–90). Each of these insightful critics offers a useful perspective on Jordan's gothic tendencies, but each one stops short of identifying the most distinctive aspect of Jordan's gothic vision. Jordan deploys traditional gothic elements in concert with a profound skepticism toward characters, narrative, genre, and the conventions of film realism.

In other words, although Jordan's films frequently invoke the supernatural, his flights of fancy are usually tempered by a savage and self-conscious use of irony. While the tradition of Irish satire can be traced back to Jonathan Swift's polemical writing in the eighteenth century, Jordan's ambivalent irony more directly reflects the lineage of Irish modernists and postmodernists such as James Joyce, Flann O'Brien, and Samuel Beckett. For one thing, Jordan lacks Swift's moral certitude; rather than engaging in polemic, he tends to leave questions of right and wrong ambiguous. Second, Jordan's authorial interventions often explore the aesthetic process itself; thus, his films exhibit the postmodern tendency toward citation and self-referentiality. Jordan's bemused skepticism toward his characters' journeys of self-discovery and his profound interest in pushing the boundaries of narrative form modulate and even deflate his operatic and expressionist tendencies.

In keeping with the gothic exploration of heightened subjectivity and the postmodernist fondness for breaking the representational frame, Jordan's films dispense with the conventions of cinematic realism. The director describes this tendency to flout realism as "particularly Irish in its impatience with reality" (qtd. in Glicksman 71). That impatience has roots in the Ireland of his youth, "a most irrational place" where the dominant Catholic and anti-British ideologies "bore no relationship to the reality that was around" (Interview in this volume, 159).

Jordan conveys the irrationality of such experiences using the ominous and often hyperbolic vocabulary of the gothic. Like much of contemporary popular culture, Jordan's films interrogate the constructed nature of identities, narratives, and reality. But it would be a mistake to characterize his work as a celebration of postmodernism. Instead, the anxieties of the gothic sensibility, which remind us that the past comes back to haunt us, temper the supposedly liberating implications of postmodernism's infinitely fluid and ungrounded identities.

Jordan's unique blend of gothic theatricality and postmodern irony is fully in evidence in one of his best-known films, *Interview with the Vampire,* where he frequently calls attention to the narrative process, exposing and exacerbating anxieties about the breakdown of the grand narratives of history. An excellent illustration of this principle occurs in an early scene, when the dour vampire Louis de Pointe du Lac (Brad Pitt) delivers a line intended to disabuse his human interviewer, Malloy (Christian Slater), of misconceptions about vampires that he may have gleaned from popular culture. Louis dismisses Malloy's questions about sunlight, crucifixes, and Count Dracula with a derisive snort. They are "the vulgar fictions of a demented Irishman."

This exchange does not appear in the novel from which Jordan and Anne Rice adapted the screenplay. Jordan's film introduces this reference, which acknowledges and pokes fun at vampire enthusiasts who religiously keep track of rules that change with each new iteration of the vampire saga. At the same time, Jordan comments on the elasticity and duplicity of narrative form. The director also seems to relish having a go at his fellow Irishman Bram Stoker, whose *Dracula* remains one of the most compelling vampire tales ever written and the primary source for most vampire films. By calling attention to the Irish heritage of the vampire legend, Jordan slyly addresses viewers who may recognize the director himself as another possibly demented Irishman whose vulgar fictions are implicated in the scenario unfolding on screen.

The remark serves as punctuation in several ways. Just before Pitt delivers the line, a shot/reverse-shot pattern builds tension between the interviewer and the vampire. When Pitt speaks, he seems to address the line directly to the film audience. Through framing, Jordan emphasizes the character's smirking delivery as he leans forward to discredit Stoker. The moment also marks a transition between the present-day interview and the vampire's reminiscences. After the statement, viewers are returned to the world of Louis's flashback.

Treating the line as punctuation reminds viewers that Louis is the film's narrator, but the comment undermines his claim to narrative authority rather than bolstering it. Louis has orchestrated the interview with Malloy to liberate the vampire image from trivializing misrepresentations. He seeks to wrest control from popular culture's cultish iconography and to expose the vampire's truly hideous dimensions. Yet, paradoxically, Louis's haughty dismissal of Stoker calls attention to the existence of other stories about vampires. Highlighting those vulgar fictions suggests that all narratives, including Louis's, consist of fabrication, a point underscored by the immediate return to Louis's flashback.

Louis's statement challenges basic assumptions regarding author, characters, and story—assumptions that the interview and the film require to proceed within the framework of realism. Louis denounces the fictions created by Stoker, a real mortal, and seeks to replace them with his truthful first-person account: the eyewitness testimony of not only a fictional character but a supernatural one. Clearly, this complex scenario raises representational dilemmas that go beyond the problem of choosing between competing versions of the vampire legend. Through this ironic and self-reflexive gesture, Jordan proposes that "vulgar fictions" of demented Irishmen, and those of other authors, do not merely reflect reality but may in fact help to constitute it.

Interview with the Vampire illustrates Jordan's fascination with central concerns of the gothic: death and decay, the breakdown of boundaries between reality and fantasy, and the properties of narrative form. Jordan is not the only writer and film director whose work reexamines the gothic; gothic themes and attitudes resurfaced in literature, film, music, and popular culture during the last two decades of the twentieth century. The renewed popularity of the vampire is a prime example. The vampire was reconceived from a contemporary perspective not only in Rice's bestselling *Vampire Chronicles* series (1976–98) but also in the vampire cinema of *Buffy the Vampire Slayer* (dir. Fran Kuzui; 1982) (later a hit television series), *The Hunger* (dir. Tony Scott; 1983), *Near Dark* (dir. Kathryn Bigelow; 1987), *Interview with the Vampire,* and *Nadja* (dir. Michael Almeyreyda; 1994). In 2005, Elizabeth Kostova's *The Historian* became a bestselling novel almost thirty years after Rice's breakout success with the same material.

Postmodern gothic works such as these can be distinguished from their literary and cinematic precursors in several ways. One important difference is their refusal to conform to the conventions of the horror genre, part of a more general postmodern tendency to blend genres. Deploying gothic elements in non-horror contexts is a critically important aspect of the postmodern gothic, according to the literary scholar Mark Edmundson. So, for example, *The Hunger* exploits the vampire's frightening qualities and sexual allure in equal measure, focusing on the romantic entanglements of chic bisexual vampires played by the French film icon Catherine Deneuve and the glam pop star David Bowie.

Neil Jordan's postmodern gothic sensibility, while most apparent in his monster movies, extends to his realist narratives as well. All of Jordan's films combine traditional gothic elements—including supernatural beings, morbid themes, a cyclical view of time, and an interest in states of heightened subjectivity—with a pronounced skepticism that acknowledges the breakdown of narrative authority, the constructedness of identity, and the disturbing tendency of fictional representations to assume the status of reality. Jordan's films propose that, in postmodern image culture, reality is merely another vulgar fiction, not far removed from the feverish musings of a writer like Bram Stoker. His characters grapple with the realization that their identities are effects of, not the basis for, narrative and visual representations. Jordan's films stop short of fully endorsing the supposedly liberating aspects of the playful, postmodern slippage of identity and meaning, however. They suggest instead that we treat our imaginative constructs with a measure of respect. Our identities may be fabrications, and they may be vulgar, but, in the postmodern society of the spectacle, they are all we have.

Gothic elements contribute to the narrative design and visual style of Jordan's films. Tropes of haunting and possession pervade his films. Unseen forces motivate characters' actions and shape their experiences. Those shadowy emanations may be represented in quasi-spiritual terms (*The End of the Affair*), but often they are linked to concepts of fate or chance (*We're No Angels, The Good Thief*). In some films, they assume the form of malevolent individuals (*Angel, Mona Lisa, In Dreams*). Often, Jordan's characters are possessed by the past for reasons they do not fully understand (*The Miracle, The Crying Game, The End of the Affair*).

The gothic emphasis on death and destruction articulates specific political concerns in Jordan's Irish-themed films; namely, an acute sense of national dispossession. In *Angel, The Crying Game, Michael Collins, The Butcher Boy*, and *Breakfast on Pluto*, haunting provides a framework for portraying the lingering effects of a long history of Irish deprivation and British colonial dominance.

Whereas classical works of gothic horror personify threats to identity in supernatural monsters that are easily vanquished by silver bullets or wooden stakes, postmodern horror films offer no secure resolution. Threatening creatures cannot be killed or quarantined because their similarities to their human victims outweigh their differences: in short, the monsters are us. Consider the threats to identity and meaning posed by postmodern horror films such as *Psycho* (dir. Alfred Hitchcock; 1960), *The Shining* (dir. Stanley Kubrick; 1980), *The Silence of the Lambs* (dir. Jonathan Demme; 1991), *Funny Games* (dir. Michael Haneke; 1997), and *American Psycho* (dir. Mary Harron; 2000).

Jordan's films expose the profound ambiguity of human identities—not only those of monsters—across a variety of narratives. Like the postmodern horror film, his films do not guarantee a return to normalcy and stability. Jordan's narratives defer resolution and closure, seeming to acknowledge the temporary nature of endings. In *The Crying Game*, an incarcerated Fergus converses with Dil, their romance indefinitely suspended; in *The Good Thief*, one fabricated autobiography begets another as the protagonist Bob's protégée learns the tricks of the trade. In the concluding moments of *Mona Lisa* and *The Miracle*, characters revise their stories about themselves, reflecting their own status as fictions and works in progress. In place of closure, Jordan's films offer the promise of new narratives or, perhaps, the invention of Lyotard's "other realities."

Jordan does more than imbue gothic narratives with postmodern ambivalence, however. He also merges mysticism and irony through his visual style. His films "start from realistic beginnings and proceed to very unrealistic, mythological territories" (Jordan qtd. in Glicksman 70). Subjective points of view distort space and time, as viewers share the dreams, hallucinations, and visions of characters. Jordan's talent for dramatic staging enhances the depiction of dream states and nightmarish realities. He is known for rendering scenes of radical destruction with flourish, such as the sequence in *The Crying Game* when British helicopters rain bullets on the IRA hideout, or the moments of fiery apocalypse in *Interview with the Vampire*. But Jordan just as often invokes a subtle sense of the Freudian uncanny, where the familiar (the *Heimlich*, or homelike) is made strange (*Unheimlich*, or unhomelike). Environments that should look familiar and unremarkable consistently defy those expectations. When he envisions the Dublin of *Michael Collins* as a shadowy, smoky abstraction, or presents the London of *Mona Lisa* as a carnival of women's bodies, he recasts well-known urban environments as strange and hellish places.

Although Jordan freely borrows from the theatrical sensibilities of directors such as Federico Fellini, Alfred Hitchcock, Max Ophuls, Michael Powell, Emeric Pressburger, and Nicholas Ray, he situates moments of heightened drama within realistic settings rather than on studio soundstages. He amplifies emotional intensity only to deflate it, joining gothic excess with irony. In *Mona Lisa*, he tethers a potentially magical white horse to a tree near a grimy roadside café. In *The Butcher Boy*, he casts the Irish musician Sinead O'Connor as the Virgin Mary. While O'Connor's angelic face resembles the image of Our Lady that graced nearly every Catholic household in midcentury Ireland, the singer's destruction of a photograph of Pope John Paul II during a television performance in 1992 (among other activities and statements) established her as a heretic and blasphemer.

Distorted vision—often manifested in characters' dreams and hallucinations—becomes part of everyday experience within the image-saturated visual field of Jordan's films. A case in point is *The Crying Game,* where the transparent panes of glass in the rural Irish greenhouse where Fergus guards Jody give way to mirrors in the Metro, the gay bar where Fergus meets Dil.

Given this repeated emphasis on the failures of vision, it is ironic that many of Jordan's characters, like Fergus in *The Crying Game,* initially attempt to view the world "at face value." They operate according to the rational terms of the Enlightenment, where clarity equals truth, and seeing is believing. Jordan signifies the impossibility of seeing clearly by layering the frame with translucent fabric, glass, mirrors, portraits, paintings, photographs, and religious imagery.

Jordan develops motifs of distorted vision by composing shots through fog, smoke, and water. He often stages action on bridges, near water, in water, and under water, capitalizing on the bridge as a symbol of transition and the way that water reflects and absorbs light. He uses rain, fog, and smoke to give weight and texture to the atmosphere in *Michael Collins,* undermining any stable reference point from which to view the world objectively. In *The End of the Affair,* he inundates his characters with rain, overwhelming them with a literal deluge of lucidity that only serves to obscure their vision, and ours.

Jordan's frequent display of figural images such as portraits, photographs, and posters invokes the uncanny double of gothic literature and Freudian theory and also points to the postmodern theorist Jean Baudrillard's concept of the simulacrum. Like the gothic double, the simulacrum undermines the uniqueness thought to be embedded in an original work of art or an individual person. This concept takes form in *Mona Lisa,* where multiple Mona Lisas populate Jordan's mise-en-scène: the Da Vinci painting appears as a kitschy refrigerator magnet, while the Nat King Cole song saturates the soundtrack. Within the context of the film, these multiplied Mona Lisas are likened to the host

The poster for *The End of the Affair* emphasizes its ghostly atmosphere. Courtesy of Photofest.

of strange objects sold in large quantities by Thomas, the protagonist's best friend. Thomas's glowing Madonna statues and plastic spaghetti are mass-produced simulations that have ceased to refer to any original, whether that would be an idea (romance), an emotion (love), a belief (the Virgin Mary), or a plate of food. Similarly, the plot of *The Good Thief* turns on the difference between original paintings and fakes and involves a mock casino heist and a real one.

In Jordan's films, theatrical performances often eclipse reality. Whereas a number of Jordan's characters perform professionally as actors, magicians, musicians, and circus performers, at some point, many of his characters find themselves performing in one way or another. Even in films where performances are carefully distinguished from daily life—as they are in *Angel, The Miracle,* and *Interview with the Vampire*—they eventually encroach upon and colonize reality. Examples of such moments include a stage set that comes to life in *High Spirits* and the Parisian vampire theater in *Interview with the Vampire.* Theatrical performances spill over the proscenium arch and become real, implying that performances can upstage reality. They are not easily controlled, not even by those who create them.

In this world where images and performances overtake reality, Jordan's characters lose their grounding through experiences that the director describes as "dangerous, frightening, [and] terrifying" (qtd. in Glicksman 70). Brian McIlroy writes that Jordan's horror films evoke "an exalted state that induces awe and terror" ("Neil Jordan" 15). I would extend McIlroy's observation to suggest that moments of overwhelming and contradictory emotions occur with great regularity throughout Jordan's oeuvre. What saves Jordan's characters from these exalted states and from potentially paralyzing ambivalence is their self-conscious reconstruction of themselves and their realities. Jordan's characters rescue themselves by creating vulgar fictions, fashioning new identities, and experimenting with new meanings.

Jordan's troubled, ambivalent, yet resourceful characters provide a model for Jordan himself as a film director. He is a contemporary auteur who rejects the mantle of art-cinema auteur and the persona of the entrepreneurial producer-director, but partakes of each construct. Although Jordan contends that the golden age of the European auteur cinema is long gone (Interview in this volume, 151), his films suggest otherwise: they speak to a consistency of narrative interests and aesthetic preferences as well as revealing an idiosyncratic worldview. Jordan is just as wary of being defined as an Irish maverick as he is of accepting the label of the commercial cinema craftsman whose identity is as important as, if not more important than, the work itself. Yet both models inform his work in contemporary international cinema.

Neil Jordan's postmodern gothic vision informs the fifteen feature films and one short film he has directed to date. Jordan's monster movies,

The Company of Wolves and *Interview with the Vampire,* are explicitly gothic in that they rely on the convention of the supernatural monster. Yet they also exhibit postmodern tendencies to bend and blend genres (drawing from the fairy tale and the literary autobiography) and reflect the gothic interest in narrative form by linking storytelling to the formation of identity. *The Company of Wolves* foregrounds the development of a feminist counternarrative to the traditional fairy tale, whereas *Interview with the Vampire* proposes that Enlightenment vision—and its all-seeing, authorial "I"—is anything but enlightened, particularly when it comes to defining differences. In both films, characters confront the distinction between monster and human being and ultimately embrace sexualized monsters that defy the boundaries of identity.

In several other films, Jordan uses another unmistakably gothic figure—the ghost—as an avatar of national identity. In *High Spirits* and *Michael Collins,* ghosts evoke Irish historical traumas and destablilize monolithic notions of Irishness. Instead of functioning as sources of terror and dread, the literal ghosts in *High Spirits* and the metaphorical ghosts in *Michael Collins* emphasize competing constructions of the Irish nation.

Monsters and ghosts personify the uncanny: they embody the notion of something familiar made strange. Jordan works with the concept of the uncanny in other ways as well. Throughout his oeuvre, Jordan uses popular songs as intangible specters; like ghosts, they challenge the linear notion of time. Jordan exploits the paradoxical ability of popular music to fix a specific place and time and also to transport listeners to other places and times. Through their lyrics and their historical context, popular songs also play a role in the formation of identity. In *Angel, Mona Lisa,* and *The Crying Game,* Jordan uses popular music to "[endow] present reality with . . . the spell and distance of a glossy mirage" (Jameson 21). Jordan chooses songs that underscore a common theme in these films: each protagonist must contend with radical challenges to his masculinity and his national identity.

The uncanny assumes tremendous importance at the visual level as well. In a number of Jordan's films, dreams assume the status of reality. In *The Miracle, The Butcher Boy, In Dreams,* and *Breakfast on Pluto,* young male characters have visions that imaginatively reiterate their personal and cultural traumas growing up in postwar Ireland and America. More specifically, their dreams speak to the loss of a culturally determined ideal of home and mother, and these traumatic experiences are linked to their national and sexual identities. Jordan's use of dream states reiterates the traditional gothic emphasis on distorted subjectivity. These films imply, however, that the subconscious and symbolic world of dreams may have become indistinguishable from the image-driven reality of postmodern culture.

Jordan refuses to limit the gothic uncanny to characters' dreams, however. Several of his films explicitly link the uncanny double to postmodern practices of repetition. *We're No Angels*, *The End of the Affair*, "Not I," and *The Good Thief* are film remakes whose narratives involve doubles and cases of mistaken identity. The disturbing implications of the gothic double—a mirror image, a copy, or a counterfeit self—play out at the story level in terms of characters and plot. At the metatextual level, these films comment on aesthetic practices of repetition. More specifically, these four films engage in postmodern parody and pastiche, terms that have been much debated in postmodern theory. Whereas Fredric Jameson defines pastiche as the empty, ahistorical recycling of familiar signifiers, Linda Hutcheon describes repetition in less critical terms, holding that postmodern parody has the capacity to reconsider the relation between original and copy.

Throughout these analyses, I consider the way that Jordan's films merge traditional gothic concerns with subjectivity, the cyclical structure of time, narrative form, and the disintegration of boundaries with a postmodern skepticism toward the tools of representation, including genres, identities, and narratives. Jordan's postmodern gothic films challenge discourses of nationalism, sexuality, and aesthetics by exposing the fictional status of all identities. Yet they simultaneously assert the necessity of continuing to generate vulgar fictions, with their tenuous promise of meaning. Maintaining the powerful sense of ambivalence that is central to the the gothic worldview and to postmodern culture, Jordan's films diagnose and delve into the pleasures and perils of postmodern identities.

Monster Movies: *The Company of Wolves* and *Interview with the Vampire*

> I wouldn't be a good social realist.
>
> —Neil Jordan

Neil Jordan's commitment to the gothic tradition is clearly apparent in *The Company of Wolves* and *Interview with the Vampire,* two horror films in which supernatural creatures claim their human victims using seductive and brutal techniques. But these films do not repudiate their monsters, as traditional gothic literary works and classical horror films do. Instead, they revel in the perversity of monstrosity and conclude with scenes where their protagonists are willingly transformed into monsters.

These films exhibit two classical markers of the gothic: supernatural monsters and a focus on narrative form. Yet they also feature several important characteristics of postmodern horror cinema: the monsters are sexualized human hybrids whose threat can never be eliminated, and thus the narratives fail to provide closure. In horror films prior to 1960, supernatural monsters represented an external threat to the community and were vanquished by the proper combination of male ingenuity and violence (Piñedo). But postmodern horror films such as *Psycho, Night of the Living Dead* (dir. George A. Romero; 1968), *Rosemary's Baby* (dir. Roman Polanski; 1968), and Jordan's werewolf and vampire films take the gothic critique of rationalism to a new level by depicting humans *as* monsters (thus completely undermining the distinction between the rational and irrational) and rejecting the ideological certainty of narrative closure.

Jordan's monsters embody forms of eroticism that depart from conventions of gender and sexual difference. His werewolves and vampires do more than raise the specter of alternative sexualities, however; ultimately, they destabilize categories of male/female, human/inhuman, and heterosexual/homosexual altogether. In *The Company of Wolves,* a young woman's dreams unleash the erotic potential of familiar fairy tales. Fascinated by the sinister and seductive werewolves she encounters while dreaming, Rosaleen (Sarah Patterson) embraces the sexual beast within her. Through her dream alter ego, Red, she defies the patriarchal model of sexual difference and its presumption of feminine passivity. Rosaleen reshapes Little Red Riding Hood's cautionary narrative as one of sexual awakening: a journey that encompasses power, pleasure, and danger.

In *Interview with the Vampire,* the world-weary vampire Louis de Pointe du Lac (Brad Pitt) recounts a saga that emphasizes the sexual alterity of the undead. From the initiatory moment of violent sexual frenzy, during which Lestat de Lioncourt (Tom Cruise) makes Louis into a vampire, to the formation of their unconventional family with the child vampire Claudia (Kirsten Dunst), these immortals reject heterosexual dualities. Instead, they openly exhibit polymorphous desires for blood and companionship, flouting traditional "family values." But Louis fails in his attempt to deliver a cautionary tale that paints vampires as depraved and amoral creatures. At the conclusion of his oral memoir, the fearful and fascinated interviewer Malloy (Christian Slater) begs Louis to make him into a vampire.

Both of these films are founded on a profound ambivalence. The monsters are as enticing as they are despicable, and their victims' fear is matched by an equally compelling desire to give themselves over to the powerfully transgressive energies associated with creatures who defy all boundaries. In *The Company of Wolves* and *Interview with the Vampire,* human characters acknowledge their own sexual monstrosity and, in doing so, they summon the Sublime. Described as "rapturous terror" by the eighteenth-century Irish political philosopher Edmund Burke, the Sublime calls forth "strong and equivocal emotion" (Lyotard 29). The concept of the Sublime frequently has been linked to horror films because they evoke extreme, contradictory emotions in their viewers. According to Cynthia Freeland, viewers process "ineffable and painful feelings" by distancing themselves ("Sublime" 68). They "shift into another mental mode, [and] conceptualize the film's deep emotional intensity as part of an artistic rendering of a viewpoint on its subject" (68).

Jordan's characters in these films process their sublime experiences through acts of aesthetic creation, not distancing and judgment. They generate new narratives of self, working within and against familiar genres. *The Company of Wolves* fractures the form of the fairy tale, whereas *Interview with the Vampire* rewrites the vampire saga and the literary autobiography.

As they become something different from human beings, Jordan's characters defy models of difference that not only underlie gender and sexual identities but also supply the conventions of narrative and visual representation. Thus, in *The Company of Wolves,* the narrator loses control of the story, challenging the idea that the teller is the driving force behind the tale. In *Interview with the Vampire,* vampire vision reveals the blind spots of Enlightenment vision, with its ideal of an all-seeing "I" that has the authority to frame the world in either/or terms. Both films explore the distinction between reality and fantasy—a theme that pervades gothic works and postmodern aesthetics alike—and finally suggest that the difference between the two may be academic.

Postmodern ambivalence toward conventions of representation is apparent in the subject matter and the form of both films. For both projects, Jordan collaborated with women writers whose work not only questions traditional sexual ideology but also challenges narrative and generic frameworks of authority. *The Company of Wolves* is based on Angela Carter's short stories, which self-consciously rewrite fairy tales from a feminist perspective. In developing the screenplay, Carter and Jordan established the linking device of Rosaleen's dream and conceived of a nested organization for the various dream stories. These choices establish a resonance between form and content. The dream stories recount familiar fairy tales after they have been processed by a young girl's dreaming imagination, not as delivered "straight" by an authority figure. As such, they are uncannily familiar and new at the same time. The film turns the form of the fairy tale inside out, just as the werewolves—who are uncanny because they look like human beings but are "hairy on the inside"—turn the human form inside out when they undergo their physical transformation.

Like Carter's stories, Anne Rice's *Vampire Chronicles* rewrite a specific narrative tradition, that of vampire folklore. By using the vampire's first-person narration, Rice reverses the familiar angle of vision on this creature, who is best known from Bram Stoker's *Dracula* and its numerous film adaptations, which include F. W. Murnau's *Nosferatu* (1922); Carl Theodor Dreyer's *Vampyr* (1931); Tod Browning's *Dracula* (1931); Alan Gibson's Hammer films *Dracula A.D. 1972* (1972); Dan Curtis's *Dracula* (1973); Werner Herzog's *Nosferatu* (1979); John Badham's *Dracula* (1979); Francis Ford Coppola's *Bram Stoker's Dracula*

(1992); and Mel Brooks's *Dracula Dead and Loving It* (1995). In contrast to Stoker's novel, which is an assemblage of diary entries, testimonies of the creature's victims, and newspaper reportage, Rice foregrounds the voices of the vampires, presenting their oral histories. The decision to rely on first-person narration is consistent with the emphasis placed on the human-monster's point of view in the postmodern horror cinema; examples include *Peeping Tom* (dir. Michael Powell; 1960), *Halloween* (dir. John Carpenter; 1978), *The Hunger, Near Dark* (dir. Kathryn Bigelow; 1987), the *Blade* series (1998–2004), *Shadow of the Vampire* (dir. E. Elias Merhige; 2000), and the stage musical *Lestat* (2005), which is based on the Anne Rice character.

By embracing their own monstrosity, Jordan's characters travel "beyond the end of the fairy tale and [see] its true terrors" (Jordan qtd. in Jones, "Company" 4). Jordan's sexual monsters propose new ways of conceiving difference and reiterate several lessons of the postmodern gothic. First, they reveal that human identities are irrational and unstable, plagued by perverse desires that respect no boundaries. Second, they self-consciously refuse to endorse the distinction between reality and fantasy. Finally, Jordan expands the monsters' defiance of difference to include representation itself. Although his monsters most obviously pose a challenge to oppositions of gender and sexuality, their threat to binary structures ultimately encompasses narrative form and cinematic representation.

The Company of Wolves draws upon the female gothic subgenre, whose good-versus-evil plotline involves the liberation of a woman from an oppressive environment and, most important, her delivery from sexual predators. Jordan imbues the traditional female gothic with ambivalent irony. First, the oppressive environment is the protagonist Rosaleen's own dreaming imagination, a psychosexual mise-en-scène where fairy-tale narratives concerned with coming of age play out. By exploring Rosaleen's unconscious wishes and fears, the film exposes the instability of the cultural categories that conventionally define sexuality rather than endorsing those categories, as a traditional telling of fairy tales would do. Finally, rather than being rescued, Rosaleen embraces the sexual monster that resides within her. This gesture dissolves any distinction between the innocent female victim and the monstrous evil other, offering the heroine an ambivalent sense of liberation at best. The film fails to provide narrative closure, and, although it documents the power and the perils of sexual desire, it refuses to endorse the view that women should be protected from sexuality.

In the film's frame narrative, a middle-class British couple return home to find their daughter Rosaleen in her attic bedroom dreaming, a copy of the magazine *Shattered Dreams* at her side. Viewers then enter Rosaleen's dreams, which depict a medieval village that is being terrorized by werewolves. Rosaleen's alter ego, Red, is fascinated by these monsters rather than repulsed by them and, eventually, acts on her curiosity and her desire. In the final dream scene, she unleashes the werewolf within her, an act that is as painful as it is cathartic. The film returns to Rosaleen's attic at the conclusion, where she hovers on the brink of consciousness, neither dreaming nor awake.

By adopting a dreaming girl's perspective, the film marks itself as a female gothic, but it also invokes the distorted subjectivity of German Expressionist films such as *The Cabinet of Dr. Caligari* (dir. Robert Wiene; 1919). Instead of treating Rosaleen as a horrific figure, akin to the gothic madwoman in the attic (*Jane Eyre*) or to *Caligari*'s insane narrator, Jordan's film endorses Rosaleen's bizarre dreams, emphasizing the way that they draw from and undermine realist representation.

The opening scenes make evident the film's refusal to obey realist conventions that distinguish waking reality from dream states. In this film, these supposedly oppositional modes are forced to share the same space and time. The film begins with a German shepherd sniffing around an old stone well and running through the woods. The camera cuts between the fluid tracking shots of the wolflike dog and shots of a car speeding down country roads carrying the adult couple home. Wide-angle lenses and slow motion distort the space shared by the dog and the car, suggesting that the mystical and the mundane are moving along parallel tracks to the same destination: a stately old home. The isolated rural setting recalls the Big House of Anglo-Irish gothic fiction (and of British colonists in Ireland) and the dangerous forest of fairy tales. Yet when the couple emerge from the Volvo sedan to greet their eldest daughter, Alice (Georgia Slowe), their demeanor alludes to the confident, status-conscious era of the Thatcher 1980s. The characters are clearly satiated by the activity of consumption, as they carry bags of groceries and other items into the house.

Baroque wolves evoke the uncanny in *The Company of Wolves.* Courtesy of Photofest.

In a similar way, real and imaginary spaces merge in Rosaleen's dreams. The forest outside her attic window becomes the abstract, theatrical setting for her dreams. Although the dream forest looks distorted, it subtly recalls the woods surrounding the house because the dream is motivated by a shot that moves out of the attic window into the trees. This repetition with a slight difference was intentional. Jordan and the production designer Anton Furst "tried to build each set so that it reminded you of something you had seen but weren't quite sure what it was" (Taylor and Jenkins 266).

The parallel lines of action in the film's opening scenes and the repetition of the forest setting produce a feeling of déjà vu by combining realist and expressionist techniques. By blending real and surreal, Jordan implies that reality and fantasy are not spatially or temporally distinct. As the film continues, Rosaleen's dreaming perspective refuses the supposedly fixed boundary between reality and imagination, producing the uncanny—the feeling of dread experienced when the familiar becomes something other than itself. The important point to note is that the uncanny arises because the spaces of reality *resemble* the spaces of the imagination, and vice versa, not because they are radically different.

The film's producer, Stephen Woolley, has compared the film's surreal style to *Un Chien Andalou* (dir. Luis Buñuel and Salvador Dalí; 1927) and to the melodramatic fantasy films of the British director Michael Powell. In Rosaleen's dream world, Jordan reproduces the stark visual poetry of *Beauty and the Beast* (dir. Jean Cocteau; 1946) and *Night of the Hunter* (dir. Charles Laughton; 1955) as well. The familiar fairy-tale theme of innocence yielding to experience appears in the symbolic use of red and white. Several lyrical moments combine the two colors, underscoring the notion of oppositions merging to produce something completely new. For example, as Red stands outside Granny's cottage, knowing that the wolf awaits her, the white moon turns red. Jordan offsets such graceful interludes with dramatic physical transformations that are as grotesque as those found in films such as *The Howling* (dir. Joe Dante; 1981) and *An American Werewolf in London* (dir. John Landis; 1981).

Although many critics focus on the film's fairy-tale origins, its most relevant cinematic precursor may be *The Wizard of Oz* (dir. Victor Fleming; 1939), with its dreaming, adolescent girl protagonist, its character doubles, and its parallel yet interpenetrating worlds of Kansas and Oz. But Jordan turns the positive munchkin mantra of "follow the Yellow Brick Road" into Rosaleen's Granny's (Angela Lansbury) prohibition—"don't stray from the path"—and reveals its basis in the patriarchal desire to control women's sexuality. These parallels evoke the uncanny on a metatextual level. Jordan offers the viewer a well-worn path through cinema history—the path traced by the yellow brick road—and then strays just far enough to make it even stranger.

For unlike *The Wizard of Oz*, in *The Company of Wolves* there is no return home. The nested stories do not resolve neatly at the film's conclusion. "You are led through one sequence, and think you are at home," Jordan explains in an interview, "and then someone tells a story and you go into another world, and so on" (qtd. in Taylor and Jenkins 266). Jordan replaces Dorothy's sentimental simile, meant to express her maturity—"there's no place like home"—with Rosaleen's frightening realization that no place *is* home. This idea confronts her at the film's conclusion, when she is left suspended between worlds, neither fully dreaming nor awake. She remains suspended in the uncanny, an unhomelike space that lacks the categories of girl/woman, human/monster, self/other, or reality/representation.

The film's refusal to sustain a clear-cut opposition between reality and fantasy mirrors its storyline of female sexual exploration. In her dreams, Rosaleen/Red refuses to endorse conventional distinctions that maintain hierarchies of power. In her embrace of the monstrous, Red substitutes intersubjectivity for the "old-fashioned sublime of domination" (Yaeger 204). In the final dream story, which is a direct parody of "Little Red Riding Hood," Red's sympathy for the injured Huntsman/werewolf (Micha Bergese) seems to be drawn equally from her sexual attraction to him, her wish to help him, and her desire to become him. But the film is not a prescription for a utopia based on embracing similarities rather than differences. Instead, it questions the underlying configuration of those categories.

The Company of Wolves acknowledges the threat posed by proximity and mutuality as well as the problems associated with distance and domination. Rosaleen rejects the presumption of sexual sameness—for example, the notion that all women share certain affinities—along with the supposedly radical otherness of the werewolf. She responds to the danger of assimilation into a homogeneous ideal of femininity by generating violent wish-fulfillment dreams: a werewolf dispatches her sister Alice in the first dream, and the Huntsman/werewolf consumes Granny in the final dream story, in a partial endorsement of the traditional conclusion to the Riding Hood tale.

Within the dream stories, Red challenges traditional categories by exploring which differences matter. When her father returns from a hunt with a human hand that, prior to his shooting it, had been a wolf's forepaw, she struggles to organize this newly dangerous world. Using the classic fairy-tale structure of three questions, she first asks, "Was it someone you knew?" then, "Was it a wolf or a man you killed?" and, finally, "Do we bury or burn it?" She seeks guidance about oppositions that seem to be dissolving: between friend and foe, between human and nonhuman, between social ritual (burial) and natural force (burning the limb). Later, Red's mother explicitly rejects the binary paradigm of sexual difference when she tells Red that the beast within men is matched by a beast within women.

The film sketches the promise and the perils of straying from the path: to dismantle sexual hierarchies is to relinquish the oppressive aspects of the masculine-feminine binary as well as those that confer privilege. Red must learn to defend herself, for example, rather than relying upon her father or the village boy who admires her. The fact that Red must make her own way in this ever-changing landscape is made clear in a scene where she embarrasses the village boy who wants to walk with her. She assures him of her ability to defend herself by displaying a much larger knife than the one he carries.

Red explores the exercise of phallic power in other ways as well. Jordan adopts a spatial metaphor that equates vertical height with power. In several scenes, women literally occupy a higher ground. Before Rosaleen's dreams begin, Alice follows the German shepherd as it bounds up the stairs to the landing outside Rosaleen's room. High camera angles and crosscutting emphasize the effort expended as they ascend the narrow stairs and underscore the height and isolation of the dreamer's inner sanctum.

In several dreams, women take to the treetops. In two different dream narratives, Red and an Irish witch climb a large tree and occupy its upper branches. The disparity between the claustrophobic living structures in the village and the openness of the tree's upper limbs was carefully planned: "[M]uch of [the film's] budget was spent on eight three-dimensional model trees, with assorted stumps and root structures, which were designed to create the illusion that they soared to a sky that could barely be seen" (Finney 71). In keeping with the film's deconstruction of difference and hierarchy, height may grant women power, but they don't always use it to dominate others. In the treetop, Red looks into a mirror, puts on lipstick, and envisions herself blossoming into a woman (she also encounters tiny baby figures that suggest both maternity and rebirth). By contrast, the witch rocks her baby to sleep, serenaded by a pack of aristocrats that she has turned into wolves. Having bewitched the rapacious former aristocrats, one of whom had abandoned her, she uses her power over them to create a peaceful environment for her child.

In the dream stories, women express their ambivalent desire for the werewolves, who become sympathetic and enthralling monsters. In her classic 1981 essay on horror, "When the Woman Looks," Linda Williams argues that women and monsters share a nonnormative status within patriarchal culture. In Jordan's film, that connection is made visible throughout Rosaleen's dreams, where women look at the monstrous body of the werewolf with empathy and terror. They also gaze at the werewolf with fascination and desire. In the first story, a village woman marries a traveling man, only to be abandoned on their wedding night after he answers the "call of nature." When he returns years later, she has married again and borne three children. In a spectacular special-effects scene, the returned traveler becomes enraged and turns into a werewolf as tears flow from his eyes. In the next shot, a close-up of the woman's face registers her reaction, as she expresses conflicting emotions of awe and desire.

A moment of rapturous terror occurs in the final dream story as well, when Red empathizes with and desires the Huntsman/werewolf. She discovers that he has killed Granny, and she shoots him, only to witnesses his agonizing transformation from human to wolf. His transition has an orgasmic quality to it, with its "undulating, thrusting flesh against a black background" (Rockett and Rockett 48).

Yet the stages of his transformation also depict an alternative, and potentially enticing, sexual economy. A wolf snout emerges from the Huntsman's human mouth, reversing traditional sexual imagery by showing a phallus emerging from (rather than entering) a vaginal cavity. In another sexual reversal, the Huntsman's male body turns inside out, giving birth to a wolf. Jordan wanted this special effect to invite and endorse Red's desiring look: "The imagery in films like *Alien* and *The Thing* conveyed a very deep hatred of sexuality, a pathological disgust with the human form. . . . *The Company of Wolves* was to be about sex, not about hating it" (qtd. in Finney 70). A critical point is that Red's desire is unleashed in a moment of extreme ambiguity. She risks losing herself to her fear and fascination at the precise moment at which the sex, gender, and species of the transitioning werewolf are indeterminate.

The encounter between Red and the werewolf represents a dramatic moment in Jordan's film as well as in the history of the horror film. Red's transformation challenges traditional cinematic representations of the werewolf as a beast that articulates "our culture's concept of masculinity" (Dyer 71 n.29). In fact, it is possible that Carter and Jordan's work contributed to the subsequent feminist reclamation of the wolf in popular books such as Clarissa Pinkes Estes's *Women Who Run with the Wolves* (1996).

Despite its graphic depictions of the wolf, the film refuses to portray Red's transformation. In contrast to the scenes involving the traveling man and the Huntsman, Red's rebirth as a wolf occurs off-camera. This failure or refusal to represent this moment may suggest that conventional structures of representation cannot account for the both/and identity of the human monster. A counterexample would be the penultimate shot of Hitchcock's *Psycho,* where superimposition is used to suggest the twoness of the monstrous protagonist. In Jordan's film, Rosaleen's dream world has eliminated distinctions between self and other, and Red's embrace of the eroticized monster places her in a liminal position where her identity eludes representation.

Just as it refuses to provide a visual representation of Red's transition, *The Company of Wolves* undermines the oral narrative tradition that serves as its primary structuring device and guarantee of authorship. As the dream stories unfold, it becomes more and more difficult to locate the narrator. Using direct cuts as transitions, Jordan treats all of the narratives equally, so the origin of the various stories becomes increasingly difficult to ascertain. In one sense, Rosaleen's psyche contains all of the dream stories, and therefore she controls them. But the film's basic structure—wherein Rosaleen's dream contains embedded stories that are organized by Granny's narration—disintegrates when both Granny and Red tell stories within the dream, and when stories are told without a designated narrator. Stories told within the dream disrupt the hierarchy between reality and dream: they suggest that characters in dreams have the ability to dream as well. Eventually, the proliferating narratives elude the grasp of any narrator.

In keeping with the film's self-conscious exploration of form, the narrative concludes without resolution. The final scenes leave Rosaleen in a state of near-wakeful agitation that attests to the impossibility of fully leaving the dream behind. As Rosaleen dreams of her own transformation—unseen by viewers—wolves crash through the windows of her attic bedroom. The dream metaphor has penetrated the film's reality, preventing Rosaleen from ever returning to a state of normality, if, indeed, one had ever existed.

Some critics have argued that the final scene does not represent a happy ending because it signifies Rosaleen's entry into adulthood and concomitant loss of innocence (Zucker, "'Sweetest'" 70). The more important point, however, is that Rosaleen never fully awakens into adulthood. Instead, she remains suspended in her own imagination, which respects no boundaries. Her embrace of her own sexual monstrosity prevents her from returning to the waking world as a child or as an adult.

In the film's concluding moments, Rosaleen's voice recites lines from Charles Perrault's "Little Red Riding Hood," closing with a phrase that, characteristically, marries attraction and repulsion: "Sharpest tooth has sweetest tongue." Some critics have suggested that the recitation indicates that Rosaleen has asserted control over the story (Hopper, "Hairy" 23). I would argue that the narration represents one more ambivalent merger of self and other that cannot yield a single, controlling figure: Rosaleen's voice recites someone else's words.

In addition, the idea that Rosaleen has taken control of the narrative is contradicted by her thrashing body and the pack of wolves invading the house. Keith Hopper attributes the calm quality of the voiceover to the fact that Rosaleen "finds a soul-mate—her *animus*" ("Hairy" 23) and views the invading wolves as bringing together her divided psyche. But Rosaleen's dream self has rejected traditional models of sexual difference all along, and thus she cannot be paired with the wolf as her better half. The marauding pack of wolves also undermines the heterosexual couple as the ideal social unit.

In her liminal state, Rosaleen simultaneously experiences dream and reality, pain and pleasure, fear and desire. Rosaleen's monstrosity has turned her inside out, deforming the rules that organize sexual identity and that police the borders of reality and fantasy. My claim that the film's conclusion suggests the ambivalent power of Rosaleen's imagination differs from the views of other critics. Some have seen this sequence as "an attack on passive femininity and the 'lies' and illusion produced by art" (Rockett and Rockett 50). In my view, Rosaleen's dreams are shown to be powerful fictions: they are akin to the lies and illusions of art. They have the power to engulf and eclipse reality.

The ending that Jordan planned for the film, but was unable to achieve because of technical constraints, depicted Rosaleen dissolving into a rippling pool in the floor of her bedroom (Rockett and Rockett 51). This proposed conclusion supports the idea that the narrative and visual frames have been irrevocably broken. It also imagines another scandalous merger of opposites, wherein *The Wizard of Oz*'s Dorothy joins her nemesis, the Wicked Witch, in a puddle on the floor.

Rosaleen's gothic dreams are not the antithesis of realism. On the contrary, the film's conclusion reiterates the interconnectedness of dreams and reality. In keeping with the lessons of the postmodern gothic, the threat posed by the dream is not that it is radically different from reality but that it is continuous with it, just as monstrosity is coterminous with humanity. In a similar fashion, Jordan's second gothic horror film questions the distinction between human and monster as part of a larger challenge to binary differences. Jordan's vampire film, like his werewolf film, links sexual indeterminacy to alternative ways of seeing.

David Geffen offered Neil Jordan the job of directing *Interview with the Vampire* after the director's success with *The Crying Game* and after a series of ill-fated attempts to make Rice's 1976 novel into a film. (In 1977, it was reported that a film would be made with Peter O'Toole or Jon Voight in the lead role.) As it happened, Jordan's "foppish, *fang de siècle* costume drama" (Kempley) became one of the biggest blockbusters of 1994. With a reported budget of $50 million, it grossed more than $220 million worldwide. Because of its commercial caché, its presold audience of Rice fans, the casting of the A-list Hollywood hunks Brad Pitt and Tom Cruise (not to mention Antonio Banderas), and Anne Rice's initial public repudiation of the choice of Cruise as Lestat, it would be easy to lose sight of the film itself and its allegiance to the gothic tradition. Jordan wrote that the project represented a "return to the gothic world I found I loved so much in *The Company of Wolves*" (*MCFD* 9–10). As he had done with *The Company of Wolves*, Jordan cowrote the screenplay with the work's original author.

Whereas *The Company of Wolves* explores a monster that refuses conventional notions of heterosexual difference, *Interview with the Vampire* openly courts the idea of a queer monstrosity. Through its vampires, the film unleashes myriad polymorphous desires that disobey heterosexual and reproductive norms. Its centerpiece—the vampire—is the most eroticized monster in the gothic pantheon. The film portrays encounters between mortals and vampires, and those between and among vampires, as sublime mergers that deconstruct gender, sexuality, and identity.

Like *The Company of Wolves, Interview with the Vampire* highlights the process of narration, a traditional gothic concern that dovetails with Jordan's tendencies toward irony and narrative experimentation. A frame story depicts Louis de Pointe du Lac delivering an oral testimony to the journalist Malloy. Louis recounts experiences that span two centuries, from the 1790s in Louisiana to the 1990s in San Francisco. Louis's flashback narration details the afterlives of a community of vampires, focusing on his relationship with Lestat (the one who made Louis into a vampire) and their "daughter" Claudia.

But whereas *The Company of Wolves* uses dreaming to explore the way that fantasy and reality mutually construct one another, Jordan's vampires approach the question of sexual difference from another vantage point. The film openly challenges the supposed naturalness of heterosexuality through its characters and plot and also through a metaphor on vision that drives home the notion that sexuality is a construct. Jordan develops a motif that exposes the limitations of Enlightenment vision, of the human eye, and of the narrating "I." In this film, Jordan makes it clear that the sexualities that can be seen are produced by particular conventions of representation; they are not preexisting, natural, or essential identities. *Interview with the Vampire* links queer sexualities to the dynamics of visibility and, ultimately, to questions of representability. Jordan thus embellishes the traditional gothic interest in sexuality with a postmodern perspective that emphasizes the way visual codes determine our sense of reality.

Clearly, Jordan's film owes a great deal to Anne Rice's novel, which recasts the gender and sexual dynamics of Bram Stoker's classic vampire saga by shifting the focus to relationships among male vampires. *Dracula*'s gender anxieties center on the New Woman, a threatening upstart of the modern age who rejects the domesticity associated with the Victorian Angel in the House. She is exemplified by Mina Harker, an aspiring journalist, and Lucy Westenra, who laments the fact that she cannot accept more than one marriage proposal. While Mina survives her encounter with Dracula and goes on to become a wife and mother, Lucy succumbs, becoming a lascivious vampire who must be dispatched with a wooden stake wielded by her former fiancée. Male characters are central to the story, but once Dracula's threat is understood, their role is to protect the women and defeat the menace.

By contrast, Rice's book and Jordan's film focus on two male couples: Louis and the interviewer Malloy, and Louis and Lestat. Louis's narration imparts the latter couple's two-hundred-year-long love-hate relationship. Critics disagree about whether Jordan's film enhances the novel's homoeroticism (Maslin, "Rapture") or downplays it (Johnson). Either way, the film emphasizes the heterogeneity of masculinity and vampirism. For example, the performances of Pitt, Cruise, and Banderas draw sharp contrasts: the contemplative Louis versus the action-oriented alpha-male Lestat versus the worldly and mysterious Armand.

Jordan's vampires challenge codes of masculinity and heterosexuality in a number of ways, building on connections between vampirism and queerness that became overt within popular culture in the late twentieth century. Richard Dyer wrote about the "gay gothic" genre in 1988 (50), and Carolyn Brown has contended that, by the 1990s, "[t]he connection between death/queer/vampires/other others, [was] very much a historical *a priori*" (120).

Rice and Jordan's vampires reject the equation of masculinity with phallicism and heterosexuality. They are New Men, shrugging off traditional roles that tie them to business or family. Their relationships with mortals and other vampires are nongenital and nonreproductive, the most obvious deviation being the displacement of genital sexuality by oral eroticism. Genital sexual practices become irrelevant to vampires, who express their desire using fangs that penetrate bodies to withdraw blood. The oral paradigm encompasses a number of intimate acts, including draining victims, the mutual exchange of blood that creates new vampires, and simple conversation. When dealing with creatures whose organ of choice for intersubjective encounters is the mouth, any verbal act takes on added significance, from Lestat's grandiose speeches to Louis's morose narration to Claudia's bratty rants. Louis's interview with Malloy is also an oral exchange: it realizes one form of social intercourse and leads to other forms of mutual interpenetration. (In the novel, Louis drinks from the interviewer; in the film, Lestat does so.)

In depicting the relationship between Louis and Lestat, Jordan not only highlights their oral exchanges but also emphasizes moments of rapturous and terrible intimacy. These moments challenge the borders of self and other. Lestat first approaches the mortal Louis by rescuing him from a New Orleans prostitute and her pimp. (These predators, along with two *commedia dell'arte* performers, are the only representatives of heterosexuality in the film, and both couples suggest that such relations are as violent and exploitive as polysexual vampire relationships.) As Lestat bites Louis, a sweeping crane shot tracks them as they rise together in agony and ecstasy. From that great height, Lestat drops Louis into the Mississippi River—a proverbial cold shower. After Louis accepts Lestat's "dark gift," the actors depict extreme physical states that suggest various roles and relationships: Lestat gives Louis his blood and strength, like a mother in childbirth, yet their thrashing bodies and vocalizations also suggest sexual pleasure. The merger of progenitor and lover in the same figure is echoed later in the film when, after a period of estrangement, Lestat asks Louis, "You've come home to me then?" as if he is an abandoned lover or a neglected mother.

Louis discloses their complex, polymorphous bond when he mourns Lestat, whom he and Claudia have tried to destroy. "He was all I knew," Louis laments. This statement subtly undermines the concept that nature determines emotional bonds and sexual desire. Instead, Louis's experience of knowing an other, of knowing the one that made him—with its implications of sexual, psychic, and even spiritual congress—defines his identity. Lestat made Louis, and he continues to possess him, although those terms cannot be defined within the framework of binary gender or genital heterosexuality.

The queering of gender and sexuality extends to the vampire family unit as well. Here geography offers a perverse genealogical model, one based on replication rather than reproduction. Paris is progenitor and sister city to New Orleans, her offspring and uncanny double. That relation mirrors the vampire family composed of Lestat, Louis, and Claudia. Lestat has made Louis and Claudia vampires; to them, he is father, mother, brother, and lover. Claudia treats Lestat and Louis as parental figures but also becomes possessive of Louis when the seductive Armand threatens their bond. Madeleine (Domiziana Giordano), the companion Louis makes for Claudia, further embodies the vampires' multiple desires. Claudia not only craves her company but also wishes to be an adult woman like she is.

The film's most visually compelling example of sublime merger is an image of Claudia and Madeleine physically joined in death. Unsettled by the existence of a child vampire, the Parisian vampires invade Louis and

Claudia's home, kidnap Claudia and her companion, and consign them to a stone tunnel that resembles Dr. Frankenstein's tower turned inside out. A harsh beam of morning sunlight strikes and destroys them.

Jordan worked with the production designer Dante Ferretti to design their statuelike remains, which recall the intertwined limbs of the Pietà. The director envisioned an apocalyptic event to help create the effect: he imagined the vampires were victims of a nuclear blast (Jordan, *Interview with the Vampire* commentary). The shell of their bodies is preserved in brittle gray flakes. When Louis touches the figure, it crumbles into a single pile of ashes. Throughout the film, Jordan has graphically depicted characters who lose themselves in fearful embraces, beginning with the "shocker of a neck-biting embrace" (Maslin, "Rapture") and culminating in this mingling of identity at a granular level. Claudia and Madeleine are lost in a final embrace, made anonymous and invisible in death.

At any time, however, vampires can make themselves invisible to mortals. Along with their mantle of invisibility, vampires acquire new ways of seeing. "Vampire vision" is the term Jordan uses to describe the special visual effect that conveys Louis's point of view immediately after his transformation. As a newly born vampire, Louis sees movement in a graveyard statue—a laden image that cites pagan and Catholic traditions, the gothic writers Horace Walpole, Ann Radcliffe, and Henry James, and the sighting of moving statues in Cork, Ireland, in the mid-1980s. This brief eyeline match is merely one small contribution to a complex motif of vision and visibility that Jordan weaves throughout the film. The film's broader notion of vampire vision links the vampire's sexual monstrosity to the creature's challenge to all kinds of categories. Ultimately, vampire vision exposes the fact that representation constructs categories of difference, including the difference between seeing and not seeing. In other words, no preexisting reality accounts for the organization of the world; instead, aesthetic and social codes govern our experiences of reality.

Vampire vision implies that the dialectical relationship between visibility and invisibility is determined by rules of representation rather than by natural laws governing vision. By implication, "[t]he invisible . . . is what makes the visible possible" (Wolfreys 85). By using vampires to explore the way visibility and invisibility are mutually defined, the film challenges a central tenet of the Enlightenment, namely, that vision equals knowledge, or that seeing is believing.

Vampires queer the dynamics of visibility because they are visible and invisible at the same time. The initial encounter between Louis and the interviewer introduces this paradox. Louis has orchestrated the meeting with Malloy in a parody of a gay pickup. Louis wanders through San Francisco by night, observing mortals while remaining invisible. During the opening-credits sequence, a camera moves at eye level among the masses of humanity swarming the city streets. Louis is invisible in the crowd: the camera's first-person perspective never invites a look back from the people on the street. Yet Louis secures the interview by allowing the interviewer to see him. "I watched you watching me," Louis tells Malloy.

Once inside the room, Louis's invisibility provides the evidence that he is a vampire. When Louis turns on the light, he moves so quickly that Malloy cannot see him. He confirms his status as a supernatural being through his invisibility. Once he is illuminated by the light, Louis's pale visage and prominent blue veins are readily apparent, providing additional clues. In these opening moments, Jordan highlights the fact that Louis is capable of being seen and unseen. He manipulates the dialectic of visibility, the social and aesthetic rules that govern vision. It is important to note that Jordan's presentation contrasts with Rice's treatment: in the novel, Louis's face alone confirms his status. "And the boy, staring up at the vampire, could not repress a gasp. . . . 'Dear God!' he whispered, and then he gazed, speechless, at the vampire" (3).

The challenge that vampire vision poses to normal mortal practices of looking becomes apparent during the performance of the *Théâtre des Vampires.* In this Theater of Cruelty, Parisian vampires pretend to be humans performing the roles of vampires. These "actors" stage the destruction of mortals for a mortal audience. Only other vampires, including Louis and Claudia, can see beyond the theatrical artifice to comprehend the violent reality of the performance. Whereas the Aristotelian concept of catharsis holds that spectators experience real emotions when confronted with representations, here a mortal audience becomes captivated by a display of real violence but sees it as representation. The illusion of safety provided by the performance context ensures the spectator's complicity in the violence.

In this scene, the camera initially adopts the perspective of the onscreen audience, which is primarily composed of fascinated mortal spectators. But Jordan intervenes to suggest that visibility is determined by the angle of view and context of the representation. At the outset, point-of-view shots and reverse shots link the camera's line of sight with the mortals and with Louis and Claudia, who are seated in the audience. But as the mortal woman is consumed onstage, an abrupt cut to an overhead shot reveals a new angle on the violence: film viewers are treated to a horrific image of black-clad vampires scuttling around their mortal prey like rats or roaches (a reference to Murnau's *Nosferatu*). This reframing—which cannot be associated with any character's perspective—reminds film viewers that vision is circumscribed by the rules of a particular mode of representation. Acts of seeing always imply acts of not seeing, and this relationship obeys a medium-specific configuration. Furthermore, as this performance makes evident, mortal vision is not synonymous with knowledge or truth.

Vampire vision also points to the destructive aspects of unfettered visibility. In several scenes, Louis is responsible for setting fires that illuminate the night sky as they destroy parts of his plantation, the city of New Orleans, and Paris. Even the design of the DVD incorporates the idea that enlightenment has dubious implications. Transitions between menu pages are marked by a blinding light aimed directly at the viewer. The effect reinforces the notion that enlightenment possesses a "dark side" because it reproduces the beam of light that destroys Claudia and Madeleine.

In contrast to these scenes of piercing vision, the film's overall visual texture evokes a sense of sedimentation that tends to obscure vision, even through Jordan's baroque mise-en-scène offers plenty for viewers to look at. Jordan dresses interiors with tapestries and paintings, treating the vampires' richly decorated rooms as mausoleums. He consulted the paintings of Nicolas Poussin to capture a sense of historical grandeur. The film's surface acquires the sheen of an oil painting, reflecting layers of saturated reds and golds. The repeated use of these hues magnifies the importance of certain settings and events, including the Golden Gate Bridge, which appears in the opening and closing scenes. But these saturated colors provide an ironic commentary as well: they are vibrant hues capable of warming the vampire's afterlife in aesthetic terms only.

Vampire vision: Louis (Brad Pitt) and Claudia (Kirsten Dunst) watch as New Orleans erupts in flames. Courtesy of Photofest.

The dazzling beauty of the mise-en-scène—which earned Dante Ferretti a British Academy Award for production design—is matched by Sandy Powell's ornate costumes and glamorous makeup. The film's male characters, writes Janet Maslin, "may be undead, but they're drop-dead, too" ("Rapture"). Harry Benshoff argues that this effect undermines the film's critique of sex and gender: "[T]raditional models of gender inversion are invoked to suggest the vampire's queer Otherness; the male vampires are feminized through lighting, make-up, and costumes" (271).

But the glamor of these vampires goes beyond a simple gender inversion or feminization of male characters. The focus on beauty serves to extend the film's ironic commentary on visibility by linking the vampire's existence to the contemporary culture of celebrity. Jordan explains the connections between vampires and movie stars in practical terms. "The world of the vampire is not that different from the world of a massive Hollywood star. You're kept from the harsh daylight; you live in a strange kind of seclusion. Every time you emerge, a tremendous kind of ripple runs through people" (*Interview with the Vampire* commentary).

These somewhat prosaic comparisons mask another, metaphorical connection between vampire and celebrity that informs the film's motif of vampire vision. Traditionally, celebrity has depended upon a secure boundary between invisibility, which is tantamount to anonymity, and visibility, which is the province of the celebrity, a manufactured persona that exists to be seen. But postmodern popular culture has confounded that opposition. Cultivating a star image—also referred to as branding—has become the ultimate expression of self, the most obvious way to assert an identity. With the rise of reality television, digital technology, and the Internet, all of which allow "ordinary" people to become "stars," the boundary between celebrity and identity has eroded. Through the gothic vampire, who confounds all binaries, Jordan presents a commentary on the fashioning of identity in the postmodern era and its dependence upon a particular aesthetic and social regime of visibility. In the ultimate irony, the human interviewer Malloy begs Louis to make him a vampire so that he can live the glamorous life of the undead. In a culture where appearances often eclipse reality, immortality is equated with the unchanging vampire-celebrity body. (This theme is revisited in a later Rice novel, *The Vampire Lestat* [1985] where the vampire Lestat becomes a rock star.)

Although Louis's beautiful and powerful vampire body may insure his dominance over his mortal interviewer, his position as narrator does not. Louis may mock the pretensions of the autobiography by mentioning Charles Dickens's *David Copperfield,* but he fully intends to control the meaning of the story he tells. Yet the dialogic nature of the interview challenges his authorial ownership, particularly since Malloy creates a recorded text by taping their exchange. (In emphasizing the recording device, the film mimics the multitextual character of Stoker's *Dracula.*) To Louis's chagrin, even the supposedly neutral recording device cannot guarantee the transmission of his story on his terms: Malloy misreads Louis's cautionary tale as an enticement to join the (after)life.

By repeatedly undermining Louis's status as narrator, Jordan emphasizes one postmodern concern: "[T]he essential precariousness of the aesthetic order itself" (Mishra 256). As in *The Company of Wolves,* it is difficult to know whether the teller (Rosaleen, Louis) has control of the tale, or vice versa. At the film's conclusion, as Malloy flees the scene of the interview and drives across the Golden Gate Bridge, listening to Louis's narration, the vampire Lestat descends from above to join Malloy in his vintage red Mustang convertible. After complaining vociferously about the doleful quality of Louis's version, which by now has assumed the somewhat diminished status of a book on tape, Lestat pledges to rewrite Louis's account of vampire existence. The conclusion serves as an ironic deflation of Louis's sober tale and, at the same time, promises to perpetuate the vampire saga thorough replication. From the film's conclusion emerges another narrative of vampire identity, this one in Lestat's voice. The final scenes also hint at the creation of a new monster—the vampire Malloy.

Jordan's two gothic horror films use the traditional device of the monster to explore the boundaries of narrative, identity, and reality and, in the process, reveal the director's fascination with irony and ambivalence. Rosaleen remains suspended in a state of being that makes it impossible to tell whether she controls, or is controlled by, her culture's fairy tales, which are now indistinguishable from her own dreams. Jordan's vampire extravaganza subverts narrative authority and refuses to endorse the singular "I" of Enlightenment vision. Its discourse on visibility proposes that queerness, vampirism, and celebrity, when "seen" within conventional frameworks of narrative and visual representation, cease to be queerness, vampirism, and celebrity. Challenging the tenets of Enlightenment vision and realist aesthetics, the film suggests that visibility and transparency are merely criteria designed to produce a certain image of reality.

The culmination of these two films' efforts to probe the relation between reality and fantasy is the dismantling of film representation. This occurs in the concluding scene of each film. In *The Company of Wolves,* Rosaleen's calm voiceover contradicts the visual evidence of her troubled body writhing on the bed. She is neither awake nor asleep, neither present nor absent, but her voice can be heard. The disjunction between image and sound suggests two fractured subjectivities: that of Rosaleen, and that of the film medium.

The conclusion of *Interview with the Vampire* also alludes to the failure of representation through a shift in the relationship between sound and image. The film concludes with a rock-and-roll song, a cover of the Rolling Stones' "Sympathy for the Devil" recorded for the film by the U.S. band Guns 'N' Roses. The song is heard after Louis has disappeared from view, angered that the interview has backfired, when Lestat replaces Louis's taped narration with rock music.

"Sympathy for the Devil" displaces the film's primary narrator and also offers an audio summary of the film. The song's stated purpose is to document the shadowy world of a monstrous creature from a first-person perspective. One film critic has referred to the Rolling Stones as the vampires of rock and roll. "Sung by an imposter," he writes, "their satanic majesties' signature tune has a counterfeit ring to it" (Johnson). A counterfeit object is a sham, an imitation made with the intent to defraud. The counterfeit ring of the performance may be due to the fact that the iconic Rolling Stones version of the song has been slightly, strangely modified in the hands of another band, provoking the strange familiarity of the uncanny. Another explanation is that the song repeats the events just witnessed onscreen, condensing them and returning them in a different aesthetic form. In other words, a sense of déjà vu or disorientation may arise from the fact that the song reiterates and defamiliarizes Jordan's gothic saga. It offers a competing version, but in the form of a musical narration that avoids the complex snares of cinematic representation.

In these two films, Neil Jordan employs the supernatural, the perverse, and the macabre in a self-conscious manner that addresses specific postmodern concerns. Like many postmodern horror films, monsters in his films cannot be vanquished, mainly because they reside within, or are synonymous with, human beings. These monsters are explicitly, often graphically, sexual and violent, which contributes as much to their appeal as it does to their repulsiveness. The threat they pose to binary structures extends to the very narratives that create them. Finally, the monstrous transgressions in Jordan's films speak to a defining characteristic of postmodern culture: they undermine boundaries that differentiate fantasy and reality, rationality and irrationality, visibility and invisibility, and self and other.

In pursuing his interest in gothic gloom, Jordan has made use of another popular gothic figure, the ghost. In keeping with the postmodern tendency to detach gothic elements from horror per se, Jordan's ghosts become prominent elements in the farcical comedy *High Spirits* and the historical biopic *Michael Collins*. Jordan employs ghosts in these films not to evoke fear but to serve as spectral embodiments of national identity and, more specifically, to suggest competing notions of Irishness. Ghosts take center stage in these two films by addressing the contentious nature of Irish national identity.

Ghosts of the Nation: *High Spirits* and *Michael Collins*

> I grew up in Ireland, where statues walked. There seemed to be more dead around than living. . . . Ireland is a country formed from ghosts.
>
> —Neil Jordan

Whereas Neil Jordan's horror films feature monstrous werewolves and vampires, two of his less obviously gothic films employ the supernatural figure of the ghost in unexpected ways. Jordan plucks the ghost from its horror-film context and inserts this spectral figure into a comedy—*High Spirits*—and a historical biopic, *Michael Collins.* In the process, Jordan draws out certain implications of ghostliness within Irish culture and, more specifically, explores its relevance for Ireland's contested national identity.

The title of this section is a play on Frank O'Connor's well-known short story, "Guests of the Nation," published in 1931. The story follows events in the lives of two IRA men who are guarding British hostages during the War of Independence (1919–21). The narrator Bonaparte is "struck too silly to speak" when he and his comrade Noble are ordered to kill the hostages, Belcher and Hawkins, because British forces have executed their Irish prisoners (7). The camaraderie the four men have developed through their late-night card games cannot trump the rules of warfare, to Bonaparte's chagrin. The story inspired Denis Johnston's 1935 film adaptation, the first IRA film in the post-independence era to "question the prevailing orthodoxies of heroic nationalism" (Barton 46). It also served as source material for *The Crying Game,* which opens with an IRA hostage scenario and explores the interpersonal dimensions of national conflict. An early draft of the screenplay for *The Crying Game* has the guard playing cards with the captive British soldier, echoing the O'Connor story.

"Guests of the Nation" sheds light on the question of Irish national identity in Neil Jordan's films because it examines the way personal connections sometimes temper political ideology. The story also suggests that divisions within a nation can remain intact, even under circumstances that should insure a united front against a common enemy. In the story, Bonaparte and Noble question Irish nationalist imperatives and resist the order to shoot their hostages because they remain loyal to an older code: the Irish tradition of hospitality. That cultural ideal defines their Irish identities as powerfully as political independence defines Irishness for their IRA cohorts. Bonaparte and Noble are confused by the oppositional logic that political nationalism depends upon. The structure of us versus them eliminates ambiguity and pits citizens of the nation against its enemies. Ultimately, that ideology prevails in O'Connor's story, and Bonaparte becomes an unwilling witness to the execution of his British chums.

In several of his films, Neil Jordan uses ghosts, rather than guests, of the nation to suggest the diverse and contentious character of Irish national identity. Ghosts haunt the Irish national imaginary in explicit ways in the farcical *High Spirits* and in the somber *Michael Collins*. In these films, ghosts are not deployed as traditional gothic devices designed to elicit terror; instead, they represent the return of a repressed and unresolved national past. They actively disrupt monolithic notions of Irish identity and, in particular, the dominant narrative of Irish nationalism.

Ghosts and other supernatural creatures are pervasive elements in Jordan's work, appearing in *The Company of Wolves, The Crying Game, Interview with the Vampire, The Butcher Boy, In Dreams,* and *The End of the Affair.* Jordan's early notes on *The Crying Game* suggest that the story depends upon the idea of haunting: "[I]t should have all the atmosphere and terror of a horror story, without actually being one . . . the dead man covers the story like a cloak. He inhabits it through his absence" (National Library of Ireland [hereafter NLI] Accessions 4761, box 1). A number of observers have noted Jordan's penchant for spectral gloom. The Irish journalist Hugh Lineham has written that "ghosts and the shadows of the dead hang over Jordan's work" ("Greene" 15). The *New York Times* critic Caryn James dubbed Jordan "Mr. Dark" ("Mr. Dark's" 13). And the director himself has offered his own appraisal of his morbid fascinations: for example, he labeled *High Spirits* a "necrophiliac romance" (qtd. in Jones, "High" 16).

Yet in *High Spirits* and *Michael Collins,* ghosts do more than dispense gloom; they reveal that Irishness has long been, and continues to be, a contested identity. Literary critics often link ghost stories to historical trauma; they are "a means by which repressed histories can be brought back to the surface" (Huggan 354). In the case of Jordan's ghost stories, however, disputes over the literal and figurative borders of the Irish nation are not merely a matter of repressed trauma: the ongoing conflict over the status of Northern Ireland is a present-day reminder of the critical importance of unresolved historical events.

Like most ghost stories, *High Spirits* and *Michael Collins* portray history as a cyclical process: through ghosts, the past continues to inhabit the present, often invisibly. By connecting past and present, Jordan links contemporary questions of Irish nationality—in particular, the existence of an Irish diaspora (*High Spirits*) and Ireland's continuing legacy of political violence (*Michael Collins*)—to the history of British colonialism as well as to the postcolonial Irish state.

In *High Spirits* and *Michael Collins,* ghosts reveal the discrepancies between Ireland's long tradition of cultural diversity and the narrow terms of its identity as a modern nation-state. In *High Spirits,* ghosts and humans together explore the notion of an Irish diaspora. This concept, which embraces multiple cultural and geographical contexts for communal identity, gained prominence in the late twentieth century as a way to characterize the dispersion of Irish people around the globe after centuries of migration, the most well-known being the famine migrations in the mid-nineteenth century.

High Spirits concerns an Irish castle that is in danger of being foreclosed upon by an absentee, Irish-American landlord, a scenario Jordan uses to revisit a specific historical concern: the prohibition of property ownership by indigenous Irish Catholics under the British penal laws that were in place from the seventeenth century to the nineteenth century. Jordan reanimates this historical concern over Irish people owning land in Ireland with a decidedly postmodern twist on the notion of property. He incorporates a subplot dealing with a contemporary struggle over the commodification of Irish identity.

Michael Collins reframes the question of political violence—a prominent feature of twentieth-century Irish culture—by returning to the War of Independence and the Irish Civil War (1916–22). The film resurrects and, arguably, exorcises two ghosts of Irish history: Michael Collins (Liam Neeson) and Eamon de Valera (Alan Rickman), leaders of the early twentieth-century movement for Irish independence. Collins, a banker, businessman, and organizer, developed the urban guerrilla tactics that forced the British empire to the bargaining table. He turned farmers and working-class youth into a trained Irish Republican Army. Collins was killed in an ambush in 1922 after the treaty he had negotiated with the British government was ratified by a popular referendum but was rejected by his comrades.

His former "chief," Eamon de Valera, led anti-treaty IRA forces against Collins's newly established Irish Free State. De Valera's "Irregulars" objected to provisions that demanded an oath of allegiance to the British crown and the partition of the island, which left six northern counties under British rule. A decade after Collins's death, de Valera became president of Ireland and dominated the nation's politics for more than three decades. His vision for Ireland—which wedded the power of the Catholic church and that of the new Irish state—became the defining feature of Irish politics and culture well into the 1970s.

By resurrecting these dead revolutionaries, who are metaphorical ghosts rather than the literal mischief makers of *High Spirits,* Jordan's film examines divisions within Ireland before, during, and after the War for Independence. The contentious issues that arose in the 1920s—guerrilla tactics, the partition of the North, and the legitimacy of British rule—have long defined the course of Irish politics and culture but have escaped public scrutiny as history.

Ghosts do more than highlight the question of Irish national identity in these films. They also allow Jordan to address his interest in the relationship between reality and representation and, more specifically, the way representations can acquire the status of reality and even affect the real world in ways their authors might not have been able to imagine. In most films, ghosts are treated as real entities or as figments of a character's imagination. If ghosts are "real" supernatural beings, then their existence entails a loss of human control. If they are merely constructs of the human psyche, then they imply a profound destabilization of an individual's identity. In *High Spirits* and *Michael Collins,* spectral figures are both real and imagined, they possess the power to affect reality, and they evade the grasp of those who attempt to control them.

Ghosts of the nation play an important role in the storyline and the visual style of these films, but they also inform their production and reception. These films provide excellent examples of the exigencies of corporate filmmaking in a global market. During the development of *High Spirits*, the perceived need to address an American audience became an important factor as Jordan, the producer Stephen Woolley, and the film's American producers disagreed about the way the film should represent Ireland.

The question of how to represent Ireland also became an issue with the release of *Michael Collins*. The film's historical content was received very differently by audiences in the United States, in Ireland, and in Britain. In the United States, *Michael Collins* met with mixed but positive reviews and was nominated for two Academy Awards. In Ireland, the film broke box-office records: it took in $4 million and remains that country's second highest-grossing film after *Titanic* (dir. James Cameron; 1996). In Britain, the film made £7 million amidst an acrimonious debate that extended across the Irish Sea. The controversy over *Michael Collins* in the press in Britain and Ireland drives home the fact that representations have enormous power to shape reality. The film is not merely about history; it also made history.

As Jordan's first Hollywood-financed project, *High Spirits* had a reported budget of $15 million, yet it grossed less than $9 million at the box office in the United States. Critics attributed the film's weaknesses to a culture clash between Jordan and American producers that resulted in the elimination of important Irish elements in the film. The *Manchester Guardian Weekly*'s Derek Malcolm wrote of "an American takeover of style and content" ("Hands" 25). Janet Maslin of the *New York Times* argued that the film needed an injection of Irish humor: "In small roles, the actors who play the Plunketts' Irish retainers do the muttering, grumbling, and modest clowning that the film badly needs in larger doses" ("Ghostly" C10). Jordan himself claims that he made *High Spirits* "in a fit of madness or desperation" brought on by the apparent collapse of his *Michael Collins* project (*MCFD* 7). (David Putnam, who had encouraged Jordan to work on the Collins screenplay in the early 1980s, became head of Columbia Studios and then gave the green light to Michael Cimino to direct his own Collins film. That project never came to fruition.)

As a story of encounters between Irish ghosts and American tourists, and as an Irish-Hollywood project, *High Spirits* grapples with the question of who may legitimately define Irishness and how rival definitions might be deployed, for better and for worse. In many ways, Jordan's film presages the commodification of Irish ethnicity that took place during the 1990s, when "the lifestyling of Irishness [became] a *bona fide* cultural phenomenon in the U.S." (Negra 54). Made in 1988, the film is surprisingly prescient in its treatment of real estate, tourism, and entertainment as the growth industries of postindustrial global capitalism.

In *High Spirits,* whose screenplay was originally entitled *Ghost Tours,* Peter Plunkett (Peter O'Toole) concocts a scheme to attract American tourists to his dilapidated castle by advertising that it is haunted. Plunkett seeks to avoid foreclosure and the wholesale removal of the castle to Malibu, California, where the lien holder, an unsavory Irish American financier named Jeb Brogan, plans to establish a new theme park called Irish World. Plunkett's motley staff impersonates ghosts and banshees, but their antics fail to impress the tourists. At the same time, a romance involving two actual ghosts transpires. Mary Plunkett and Martin Brogan (Darryl Hannah and Liam Neeson) have spent the last two hundred years reliving their wedding night, when Martin murdered Mary in a fit of jealousy. Two American tourists, Jack and Sharon Crawford (Steve Guttenberg and Beverly D'Angelo), who have serious problems in their own marriage, interrupt the cycle of violence and become romantically involved with Mary and Martin, respectively.

The romance plot pairs the ghosts and the humans in a spouse-swapping scenario. Jack intervenes in Mary's murder, freeing her ghost from its gothic time loop. They pledge their love for one another and plan a tryst for the next day, which is All Hallows' Eve, the night when all ghosts assume fleshly form. In the meantime, the obstreperous Sharon is outed as Jeb Brogan's daughter; he sent her to spy on Plunkett. She announces her support for her father's plan to foreclose on the castle. She inadvertently doses herself with Valium instead of Vitamin B, however, and loses all her inhibitions. Her intense physical attraction to the roguish ghost Martin offers a neat solution to the plot's romantic disequilibrium.

But when the exasperated American tourists threaten to leave, thus jeopardizing the castle's future on Irish soil, a profusion of ghosts stages an irate return. Numerous spirits and Plunkett ancestors, including Peter's father, Plunkett Sr. (Ray McAnally), are emboldened by All Hallows' Eve and proceed to unleash chaos. The tourists are ravished in a variety of ways: Malcolm, a skeptical parapsychologist from Duke University (a reference to Robert Wise's *The Haunting* [1963]) finds his instruments overwhelmed by the level of paranormal activity; a seminarian, Brother Tony (Peter Gallagher), is repeatedly thrown into the arms of a beautiful young woman, Miranda (Jennifer Tilly); and the nautical stage set in the castle basement comes to life.

By the next morning, the evening's activities have united the various romantic couples and secured Castle Plunkett's future as a tourist attraction. An epilogue serves as *mise en abyme*, reframing the film's central dispute over Irish real estate. Jack and Mary (now both alive) and Martin and Sharon (now both ghosts) have chosen to stay on at the castle. The final scene depicts them squabbling about their time-share arrangement in the great hall, where each couple has designated hours of use.

The *High Spirits* project evolved as a compromise between Jordan's vision of a film based in a comic and fanciful Irish literary tradition and the producers' interest in an Irish *Ghostbusters* (dir. Ivan Reitman; 1984) or *Beetlejuice* (dir. Tim Burton; 1988). In interviews publicizing the production, Jordan links the film to the writing of James Stephens, Flann O'Brien, and Oscar Wilde, as well as to British antecedents such as *The Old Dark House* (dir. James Whale; 1932), *Blithe Spirit* (dir. David Lean; 1945), and Shakespeare's *Midsummer Night's Dream* (Jones, "High" 16). Jordan's goal was to showcase indigenous Irish traditions of fantasy and satire: "Ireland is a country with almost no cinematic tradition," Jordan wrote, "and the challenge here was to see what riches this literary tradition could glean" (NLI Accessions 4761, box 4).

The final version of the screenplay represented a collaboration between Jordan and Michael McDowell, who cowrote *Beetlejuice*. The story was based on reality: Jordan's discovery of an Irish tour operator who specialized in "haunted and spooky graveyards of Ireland" and "ghostly weekends with Irish country house tours." This savvy entrepreneur rehabilitated the Anglo-Irish literary genre of Big House fiction to capitalize on the growth of tourism, an industry whose importance to the Irish economy only become apparent a decade later. Between 1990 and 2000, the number of overseas tourists in Ireland doubled.

This basic premise of the film remained consistent throughout many versions of the screenplay. Over time, however, many specifically Irish references were modified or eliminated, the first of which was the setting. The earliest draft of the *Ghost Tours* screenplay available in the Neil Jordan papers at the National Library of Ireland is dated October 21, 1986 (NLI Accessions 4761, box 4; subsequent page citations refer to this version). In it, the film opens with a view of a castle looming over a bog. This original conception of the bog landscape is significant, particularly given the film's focus on the ghosts that emanate from the past. Bogs preserve human remains, ossifying them while also hiding them from view. The bodies of the past remain, yet they are submerged and invisible, until they come back unbidden. Bogs may preserve the past, but they also return it in an uncanny form. The bog is a wholly appropriate setting for an Irish ghost story: more than eighty-nine "bog bodies" have been discovered in Ireland since the 1970s. The bog also offers a metaphor for the dialectic of historical continuity and rupture that informs this ghost story; the bog's delicate balance of past and present can be sharply contrasted with the apocalyptic discontinuity implied by the earthquake-plagued terrain of Malibu, where Jeb Brogan seeks to relocate the castle.

The bog location does not appear in the completed film, however. The bog has been replaced by a lake, another natural setting with numerous symbolic implications. The lake contributes to a motif that links water to character transformation. *High Spirits* opens with a scene of a torrential downpour. The establishing shot reveals the castle perched at the edge of a lake. As the image cuts to interior shots, Plunkett attempts to negotiate with Brogan on the phone as the camera tracks down hallways that are dripping wet because of numerous leaks and gaps in the stone walls. When a busload of American tourists arrives, the bungled attacks by the ghost impersonators cause the bus to careen out of control and plunge into the lake, which metaphorically baptizes the newcomers. Later, Brother Tony and Miranda are pursued by nun ghosts and must leap into a mossy swimming pool to escape them. On All Hallows' Eve, Martin resurrects the bus and drives it through the air, chasing Sharon. And when the stage set in the castle basement comes to life, several nautical disasters occur, including a shipwreck and an attack by a giant squid. In the process, the tourists and staff are drenched with sea water.

The lakeside setting and water motif convey a significantly different view of the relation between past and present than the bog location does. Water connotes transformation and rebirth, whereas the bog merely offers the deforming but hardly transcendent effects of the earth on human bodies. Water supplies a metaphor for continuous change and forward movement, whereas the bog is a static location that both preserves and changes the past, returning it in surprising and disruptive ways. The generic water motif eliminates the geographical and cultural specificity of the bog setting and offers little support for the film's underlying implication that it is possible and preferable to preserve and transform cultural traditions. No evidence suggests that this shift was part of a self-conscious move toward Americanizing the screenplay, but its effect was to eliminate one specifically Irish motif.

In addition to the migration of the central action from the bog to the lakeside, the original balance of the screenplay shifted during the process of development from the Irish to the American characters to favor the presumed tastes of an American audience. In the early version of the screenplay, Peter Plunkett and Jeb Brogan embody the film's central conflict, pitting Irishness against Irish-Americanness. The hybrid Irish American Brogan is equal parts mercenary capitalist and sentimental Irishman, representing the worst of both worlds. He has made himself rich by exploiting stereotypes of Irish pastoralism (marketing tap water as "Irish Spring" water) and contributing to international terrorism (selling missiles to Libya).

Through this character, Jordan satirizes American acquisitiveness. Brogan tells Plunkett Sr., "It's why I worked eighteen hours a day for thirty years to get rich. I knew that someday I'd live in Haughlin [pronounced 'howlin'] Castle" (104). His plan to relocate the castle to the United States is a contemporary rendition of the exile's return. Brogan claims to want to preserve the Irish past, but in reality he merely seeks to simulate it elsewhere. Brogan's theme park is a textbook example of Jean Baudrillard's concept of hyperreality, a simulation of a reality that never existed. Brogan's Irish World promises Americans the pleasure of an identity based on an imaginary past. In Brogan's hands, Irishness becomes a profit-making proposition, a commodity for nostalgic identity tourists.

Jordan had originally devised a compromise solution to the conflict between Plunkett and Brogan: Brogan arrives at the castle and is killed by Plunkett Sr. Instead of profiting from the relocation of the castle, he becomes another of its ghostly inhabitants. Thus, this representative of the Irish diaspora comes home to reclaim his castle but finds that he must share the space with humans, ghosts, and other creatures, all of whom have as legitimate a claim to the place as he has.

Brogan's character was all but eliminated from the final version of the film; he is never seen and can only be heard as a voice on the telephone. By removing the Brogan character, the clash between the Plunketts and the Brogans becomes a zero-sum game of pure competition with clear winners and losers, rather than a conflict whose surprising reconciliation reflects one potential rallying point for diasporic identities: the importance of shared access to a common past that, like the bog, must balance preservation with the inevitability of change.

Successive drafts of the screenplay gradually eliminated other Irish references. Subplots involving American tourists assumed prominence at the expense of stories about the Irish hotel staff, and the romance between the two ghost-human couples gained emphasis. Notes that refer to a late draft of the screenplay but are not attributed to an author read: "We now have an American focus that our audiences can identify with" (NLI Accessions 4761, box 4, p. 2).

Although Jordan described the project as "an affectionate lampoon of both American and Irish eccentricities," his initial approach to the material clearly privileges an Irish sensibility. In his production notes, he examines the cultural implications of the Ghost Tour scenario: "What struck me was the metaphorical possibilities of this enterprise, how it encapsulated in a nutshell two of our great attributes. First, the unsurpassed ability to conjure up alternatives to that awful condition—The Way Things Are. And second, the absolute indifference to their practical application" (NLI Accessions 4761, box 4). Jordan goes on to make connections between his farcical screenplay and the deadly serious issues of defining Irish national identity. "Once one frees an institution or an enterprise from the tyranny of usefulness or fact, one does come up with all sorts of intriguing results. For instance, a 32 county republic whose writ runs in only 26. Or, a national language spoken by nobody" (NLI Accessions 4761, box 4).

Jordan's interest in a story that explores Irish national identities is evident in the early draft of the screenplay, which includes historical references that are absent from the final cut of the film. In one, Peter Plunkett claims that the castle's Unicorn room is "haunted by the ghost of a priest strangled by Oliver Cromwell himself" (9), Cromwell being the notorious Puritan leader who ventured to Ireland after the English Civil War to kill and deport Irish Catholics and confiscate their land. In another version of the screenplay, an American tourist has come to Ireland to contact a great-grandfather who died in the 1798 rebellion (16). This uprising represents an important moment in Ireland's history when the United Irishmen, led by the Belfast Protestant Wolfe Tone, attempted a coordinated insurrection to throw off British rule. The United Irishmen exemplify a nonsectarian brand of Irish nationalism: the organization welcomed Catholics, Protestants, and Presbyterians. The failure of the rising led to the Act of Union in 1801, which brought Ireland under the direct rule of the British crown. These important historical ghosts were excised from the final film.

References that draw upon Irish supernatural traditions were eliminated in the development process as well. A wide variety of creatures and spirits appear in research notes on the film, including the Madrallan (an enormous dog), the Cluricane (a loner ghost), the Banshee (a wailing mourner), the Pooka (a trickster), the Dullahan (a malicious goblin), and the Fir Darrig (a merry red man). Only the Banshee, the Cluricane, and the Pooka are mentioned in the film, and none is explored with specificity. Here it becomes apparent that, to the film's American producers, the Irish supernatural tradition offers great potential for exploitation, as long as the range of references is circumscribed to suit the presumed short attention span of American audiences.

Other evidence speaks to the aim of Americanizing the project. A set of notes whose authorship is unclear discusses the possibilities that the film's argot might become popular. The model for this process was *Ghostbusters:* the term "sliming" had entered the American vernacular and was thought to have prolonged the popularity of the film. "Tupping," which is the ghosts' euphemism for sex—a term that may have been drawn from animal husbandry or from Shakespeare's *Othello*—was seen as having similar prospects. Moreover, the casting of A-list American actors such as Steve Guttenberg, fresh from his success with the *Police Academy* series (1984–87), and Darryl Hannah, who had a hit with *Roxanne* (1987), confirms the importance of attracting an American audience.

Whereas the evolution of the screenplay reveals numerous revisions aimed at simplifying the story for American audiences, the film that was released reflects the tension between Irish and American perspectives during production. Jordan's creative control seems to have been compromised. When Pauline Kael contacted him to inquire about a director's cut, Jordan hadn't assembled one (Jordan, *Donal* 46). The Irish press reported that Shepperton Studios had refused to release a print to him because producers had defaulted on payments (Rockett and Rockett 75).

Ironically, the tension between Jordan and American producers over representing Irish culture mirrors the struggle within the film over who owns, controls, and defines Irishness: the nation's inhabitants (living and dead, human and supernatural), or wealthy exiles returning from distant shores to reclaim, rename, and remove their cultural inheritance.

High Spirits is a case study in the politics of representing Irishness on two levels: the film's production history and its narrative design. Within the film, the struggle occurs primarily within the real-estate plotline. Yet the romance between the ghost-human couples highlights the potential to navigate and potentially redefine cultural differences.

Ghosts themselves disrupt binary categories. "Neither alive nor dead," they are subversive figures that "eras[e] the limit which exists between the two states" (Cixous 543). The relationships between the flesh-and-blood Americans, Jack and Sharon, and the Irish ghosts, Mary and Martin, not only erase limits between life and death, past and present, but they also merge Irish and American cultures. A scene between Jack and Mary suggests the comic and grotesque implications of erasing some limits, only to encounter others. After they have "tupped" on All Hallows' Eve, "the powers" return Mary to her actual physical age, and she becomes a desiccated corpselike figure. As she chases Jack, begging for the kiss that will restore her youth, their physical juxtaposition produces dismay, not because one character is a ghost and the other human, but because one is old and the other is young. The scandal of illicit mixing materializes in a tangible way: the distasteful specter of Mary's withered flesh joined to Jack's youthful body. (Later, Mary is restored to full vitality after she and Sharon mysteriously exchange places.)

High Spirits. To an American (Steve Guttenberg), Irish beauty is synonymous with decay. Courtesy of Photofest.

These ghost-human pairings and transformations point to diasporic identities: states of being that are neither one nor the other, but both. One of the film's tag lines, played for comedy, is Jack's despairing statement to Mary, "You're a ghost and I'm an American: it will never work." The humor is provoked by the lack of commensurability between these categories as well as the absurdity of resorting to nationality in the context of life and death. The line also hints at the problem of simply establishing the proper terms for comparison.

Ultimately, Jack and Mary are able to breach the divides of culture and corporeality. They "skelp," which involves a physical and erotic joining that is completely different from human sex. Skelping acts as a metaphor for new forms of connection across seemingly unresolvable differences—in this case, the difference between humans and ghosts.

These possibilities for developing new forms of cross-cultural intersubjectivity may seem to be overshadowed by the film's Hollywood ending, which returns to binary categories by pitting the now-human couple (Jack and Mary) against the ghost couple (Martin and Sharon) as they vie for time in the great hall. Kevin Rockett and Emer Rockett see the scenario as reiterating the notion of Ireland as backward: "[T]he fact that Jack . . . chooses to remain in the realm of magical mysticism, rather than return to capitalist America, emphasizes America's outdated perception of Ireland as pre-modern" (85). (Jack's nostalgic tendencies are underscored by his repeated citation of the Big Bopper and 1950s American pop music; in the final scene, Mary wears a puffy skirt that recalls the era.) But an argument could be made that, given their ability to form bonds across differences, the two couples have the capacity to explore productive cultural exchanges. They appear to have an eternity in which to do so. This foursome represents a new community, albeit a fractious one composed of ex-wives and -husbands. But what could be more postmodern? The resolution suggests that Ireland has been, and should be seen as, a land of the living *and* the dead, and of the foreign *and* the familiar, and that its future depends upon negotiations among diverse, and potentially conflicting, elements.

Finally, and in keeping with Jordan's interest in the relationship between representation and reality, *High Spirits* links questions of social difference to the politics of representation. He focuses specifically on performance, an Irish cultural tradition and one of postmodernism's privileged aesthetic forms. The connection comes to the foreground in the basement scene during All Hallows' Eve when the theatrical stage set comes to life. The notion that film editing creates false geography takes on an entirely new meaning in this scene: shot/reverse-shot sequences establish the fact that the cardboard representation on stage has become real. The camera cuts between shots of the painted seascape on the stage and reverse shots of water and wind lashing out at the tourists and staff, who are gathered in the basement hoping to avoid the rampaging ghosts outside. The raging sea becomes real only through its effects, not when it is shown on camera. When the camera cuts back to the stage, the set always appears as a cardboard representation.

Malcolm's son is snatched by a giant squid, and the group is forced to go on the offensive and participate in this parodic theatrical representation. After the squid grabs the boy with one of its tentacles and pulls him onto the stage, the boy is transformed into a cardboard cutout. When Eamon (Donal McCann) tosses him a life preserver, the reverse shot reveals that the preserver has become a cardboard cutout, now encircling the cardboard boy. The assembled onlookers haul the boy off the stage with a rope that also moves back and forth from real to representation. In this highly imaginative sequence, the onscreen audience responds to the demands of theatrical performance: they act "as if" the supernatural events on stage are real. If they do not, they risk losing the boy. (This scene predates a similar sequence in Jane Campion's *The Piano* [1993], where Maori audience members appear to confuse literal reality and figurative representation. They storm the stage in protest when they believe the axe-wielding actor playing Bluebeard is about to kill the actress playing his wife. Later, this joke about Maori naïveté becomes ironic, because the Scottish settler Stewart becomes a Bluebeard, chopping his wife Ada's finger off with an axe.)

In the basement scene and throughout the film, Jordan's ghosts and creatures signify the inherent impossibility of fixing meanings of place, of national history, and of individual and communal identities. Like many ghost-comedy films, *High Spirits* dramatizes "an inherently masochistic process" that entails the surrender of mastery (Fowkes 163). The film specifically addresses the loss of control associated with competing narratives of Irish national identity, including the conflict between home and diaspora. It explores states of being that defy binary categories—neither alive nor dead, neither Irish nor American—and explores the surrender of mastery in a number of contexts, including romance. Traditionally, lovers are expected to lose control of their emotions and their physical states. In this film, surrendering to romance is taken to an extreme and involves states of life and death.

Ultimately, neither the Americans nor the Irish are able to definitively assert the meaning of Irish national identity. In the final analysis, Plunkett's scheme is a success; his plan secures his continued ownership of Castle Plunkett and ensures that the structure will remain on Irish soil. Yet it also presupposes the continuing commodification of Irish culture for the amusement of paying customers.

That history and identity will remain contested issues is further apparent from the fact that, despite Plunkett's success, no strategy frees the tourists and staff members from the mischievous ghosts. (The end of All Hallows' Eve forces the ghosts to return to their former state of being.) The preferred tactic of the Irish characters is to deny the ghosts' existence. By contrast, the Americans, at least initially, are interested in raising the dead for purposes of entertainment. Both approaches are shown to be misguided: the specters of the past refuse to be ignored or contained. Yet the tourists and staff successfully do battle with supernatural elements when they are confronted by the stage performance because they are forced to treat the representation as reality. By acknowledging that such representations affect reality, they are able to deny the potentially dangerous designs of the past (the spirits) on the future (the young boy). The specters of the nation, whether they emanate from the past or take hold in the present, cannot be ignored. Instead, they must be engaged through performances, perhaps because ghosts and performances alike represent the intersection of fiction and reality.

In contrast to the diasporic dilemmas of *High Spirits, Michael Collins* directly addresses the "internal" politics of Irish national identity. What may be considered internal to the Irish nation remains a contested issue, however, given the border established by the Anglo-Irish Treaty of 1922. Since that time, successive generations of Irish Republicans have declared the goal of uniting Ireland, merging the six counties of Northern Ireland with the Republic. Not all Republicans endorse violence as a means to that end, but the tradition of using violence as a political tool has, until recently, dominated efforts toward a settlement.

Ghosts of the nation are significant to *Michael Collins* in several ways. First, the very existence of the project raised hackles in Ireland and Britain, reviving long-suppressed disputes and instigating a rancorous debate in the press. Some objections were related to the historical events depicted, others to the film's potential impact on contemporary events. In other words, the film provoked an "involuntary return to the same situation," an aspect of the repetition-compulsion that Sigmund Freud defined as the need to imaginatively return to past traumas to gain control over them ("Uncanny" 144).

Ghosts also assume prominence as a critical element of the film's visual style. Jordan paints Collins and his IRA comrades as ghostly figures in a borderless landscape. These stylistic choices resonate with the idea that the Irish nation may be a spectral figure in its own right. Centuries before the establishment of the Irish Free State in 1922, the Irish nation existed only in political and literary representation. More than most nations, Ireland may deserve Benedict Anderson's designation of "imagined community." Fintan O'Toole has written eloquently about this subject: "For most of its history, Ireland has been a contested space, fought over not just with arms, but also with ideas and symbols. It has always been possible to imagine it in different, sometimes opposite, ways. . . . And for most of its history, the presence of opposing imaginations has been a source of conflict and cruelty, as well as richness and complexity" ("Ireland" 25). Since the late nineteenth and early twentieth centuries, during constitutional efforts to secure Home Rule and during the War for Independence, the question of contested space has focused on which configuration of Ireland's thirty-two counties constitutes the nation-state. The partition of the North was rejected by Eamon de Valera's anti-treaty forces as one of two unacceptable provisions of the 1922 agreement that Michael Collins negotiated.

Yet even in 1922, the border was a preexisting condition, if not a foregone conclusion. The Government of Ireland Act in 1920 had already established the Parliament and Government of Northern Ireland. And even this political declaration merely formalized the legacy of the British colonial plantation of Ulster in the eighteenth century, when Protestants and Presbyterians settled there. Thus, the geographic borders of the

Michael Collins. In a film about tangible and intangible borders, it is difficult to discern land's end. Courtesy of Photofest.

Irish nation that Collins negotiated were already compromised. Jordan's film visually evokes the difficulty of defining borders in Ireland through smoky, grainy, low-contrast images that blur spatial coordinates.

Political developments in the late twentieth century have continued to focus on defining the physical and symbolic borders of the nation. The 1985 Anglo-Irish agreement between the Thatcher government and the Republic of Ireland stipulated that no constitutional changes would occur in Northern Ireland as long as a majority there wish to remain part of the United Kingdom (Coogan, *IRA* 507). The Northern Ireland peace process—which was unique in bringing together governments of Ireland, Britain, and the United States as well as Northern Unionists (who support British rule), Sinn Fein (the political wing of the IRA), and the IRA—eventually turned the question of the legitimacy of British rule in Northern Ireland over to voters in the North and South. In a 1998 referendum, 94 percent of voters in the Republic and 71 percent in Northern Ireland approved the Good Friday/Belfast Agreement, which effectively eliminated from Irish politics the nationalist demand that Northern Ireland be recognized as an integral part of the Irish state. The agreement also paves the way for a fluid notion of national identity, because it proposes that Irish and British citizenship need not be seen as mutually exclusive.

This historical context is important to understanding why Jordan's film was such a flash point for audiences in Ireland and Britain. With *Michael Collins,* timing was everything. The film was released shortly after the IRA violated a 1994 cease fire with the London Canary Wharf bombing and plunged the peace process into jeopardy. The film was excoriated (in some cases, sight unseen) by members of the British and Irish press who leveled charges of historical inaccuracy (the film anachronistically depicted the IRA detonating a car bomb in the 1920s), of an unduly hostile representation of the British, and of implicit support for violent tactics. The fact that Sinn Fein approved of the film lent credence to claims that it was mere propaganda (Cullingford, *Ireland's* 94).

The furor over *Michael Collins* makes clear that the issues in contention in Collins's time remain salient, including the ethics of guerrilla warfare and the stalemate over partition. Jordan wrote, "[T]he process was eerie in the way a whole series of contemporary events paralleled the ones in the past we were filming" (*MCFD* 10). The refusal of de

Valera's IRA to recognize the legitimacy of the new Irish government in the 1920s and his group's armed struggle against Collins's forces seem to be replayed in events occurring on the contemporary political landscape, with the resurgence of the Irish National Republican Army and the splintering of the Real IRA from the Provisional IRA as well as the estrangement between the IRA and Sinn Fein over the likelihood of a negotiated settlement (Cullingford, "Reception" 17).[1]

Whether or not it was motivated by the dynamics of the repetition compulsion (the need to repeat past traumas to overcome them), the film casts several historical parallels in high relief. Jordan's film dramatizes Bloody Sunday, which took place at the Croke Park stadium in 1920. In retaliation for the IRA's assassination of fourteen special British agents called the Cairo group, who were brought in to crack Collins's intelligence network, British government forces fired on a peaceful crowd assembled for a Sunday afternoon soccer game. The film's depiction of British troops firing on unarmed civilians from an armored vehicle (the latter a historically inaccurate detail) brought to the foreground Ireland's more recent Bloody Sunday, which occurred in Derry on January 30, 1972. In that incident, British paratroopers killed thirteen peaceful civil-rights marchers.[2] In another parallel between past and present, Gerry Adams, like Collins, engineered a transition from IRA leader to Sinn Fein politician. Jordan's film has been interpreted as implicitly endorsing Adams by championing Collins as a man whose ultimate goal was to remove the gun from Irish politics, a phrase Adams has used.

Jordan's film not only revives debates about Irish history; it also intervenes in Irish history. The film narrates a story that has been suppressed in Ireland. Jordan wrote, "[T]his particular part of Irish history was an embarrassed secret for so long, told in metaphors, never told straight" (*MCFD* 55). In the television documentary *The South Bank Show: Michael Collins* (1997), the critic Tom Paulin refers to the events depicted in Jordan's film as a "buried part of Irish history." According to the producer Stephen Woolley, Collins's story "had been lost, forgotten, and buried under 40 years of de Valera" (38). That burial may have been motivated by the goal of national unity. David Ervine, a member of the Progressive Unionist Party (which supports the maintenance of British rule in Northern Ireland) argues that, in a bid for national cohesion, the War of Independence has been highlighted and the Irish Civil

War has been suppressed. "Homogeneous Ireland now has elevated its common enemy to paper over its own divisions," he observes (*South Bank*). But, as Frank O'Connor's "Guests of the Nation" implies, not even a common enemy can cement together every fault underlying the bedrock of the nation-state.

The ghosts of history remain tangible to many Irish and British people, but are not as accessible to people elsewhere, which may explain why the film was not a major box-office success in the United States. Jordan recognized that *Michael Collins* depicts a complex scenario of internal division that does not easily translate to audiences outside Ireland: "For us the divisions within the island are as fascinating as those across the Irish Sea. The wider world, though, wants to see it in more simplistic terms" (*MCFD* 7). Still, Jordan's film may have paved the way for Ken Loach's *The Wind that Shakes the Barley* (2006), a highly acclaimed account of the turbulent years between 1919 and 1922 in Ireland.

One way that Jordan satisfies the need for a somewhat simplistic representation of history for international audiences is through genre and style. *Michael Collins* evokes the gangster genre and the ghost story in equal measure, suggesting the gothic haunting of Irish history through its visual design. Not surprisingly, discussions of the film's style have been shaped by political considerations as well as by aesthetic concerns. In their insightful reviews of the film for the *Irish Literary Supplement*, Luke Gibbons and Elizabeth Butler Cullingford arrive at diametrically opposed conclusions. Gibbons describes *Michael Collins* as documentary realism. He mentions the film noir atmosphere of urban scenes, but only after establishing the film's "matter-of-fact depiction of urban terror [and] the absence of the grand gesture" ("Demisting" 16). Cullingford, by contrast, argues that "Jordan is creating a highly mediated representation of events, not a documentary" ("Reception" 17).

It is difficult to support Gibbons's contention that the film favors documentary realism. Jordan tells Collins's story by citing a specific genre: he adopts the visual shorthand of the Warner Brothers crime films of the 1930s (*South Bank*). In costumes, lighting, and setting, Jordan renders Dublin as a shadowy underworld populated by ghostly assassins. The structure of *Michael Collins* borrows from the gangster genre as well, with its focus on the rise and fall of a charismatic leader who is done in by former allies. That narrative arc resonates with Irish political mythology, namely, "the tragedy of the betrayed lost leader, the hero cut down in his prime" (Cullingford, *Ireland's* 95). Jordan's use of cross-cutting between scenes of violence and domesticity has been compared to the distinctive editing pattern at the conclusion of Francis Ford Coppola's gangster classic *The Godfather* (1972).

The gangster genre infiltrates the film through an oedipal subplot as well. Eamon de Valera emerges as a father figure to Collins, an effect that was enhanced by the actor Alan Rickman's decision to read de Valera's prison letters to Collins in a voiceover. Jordan states, "[de Valera] somehow becomes a father to the Republic and a father to Collins. A father who will betray him" (*MCFD* 60). At the film's conclusion, however, their oedipal struggle is overshadowed by another intergenerational conflict. Jordan's ironic historical footnote suggests that both of these leaders will be replaced by "a new, harder, more brutal generation of Republicans," as represented by Collins's young assassin (Jordan qtd. in Schruers).

The film tempers its rendition of the gangster saga with the narrative and visual hallmarks of a ghost story. The story opens after Collins's death. One of the slain leader's junior associates, Joe O'Reilly (Ian Hart), offers Collins's fiancée Kitty Kiernan (Julia Roberts) a postmortem summary of Collins's life, telling Kitty to "think of him the way he was." That exhortation to remember introduces the extended flashback that depicts the events that take place between 1916 and 1922. With its retrospective structure, its shadowy protagonist, and its interest in solving the mystery of Collins's death, the film may bring to mind Orson Welles's *Citizen Kane* (1941).

Not unlike *Citizen Kane,* the film's key visual and narrative trope is the ghostly shadow. Here, treating the human figure as a shadow establishes a visual metaphor that also reflects a historical reality. The ability to remain invisible to the authorities became a critical weapon in the IRA's campaign of resistance against the British. The anonymity that enabled Collins's effectiveness as an agent is manifested in the film's lighting design, cinematography, sets, and costumes. Each component emphasizes the tactile aspects of Dublin, which becomes a steely blue, murky urban environment in which dangerous men materialize out of "thin air" and disappear back into the fog. The texture of the atmosphere becomes palpable. Grainy, molecular images of Dublin present the city as a gray blizzard of fog, smoke, and particles of ash.

Michael Collins. A ghost town: Dublin, 1916.
Courtesy of Photofest.

Collins's IRA remains a ghostly and a deadly army because it is invisible. In the scene of the failed Easter Rising, the faces of Collins, de Valera, and Harry Boland (Aidan Quinn) are covered in plaster, soot, and ash, a motif that returns during the failed attempt of the IRA to take the Customs House. Assassinations take place under cover of darkness and in broad daylight, carried out by a faceless, swift-footed, silent, and invisible army. In a guerrilla war, unseen forces such as secrets, spies, plots, and informers drive the events as much as uniformed armies, weapons, and occupied territory do.

The darkened silhouette is the film's most prominent visual feature (one that Jordan puts to use again in *The End of the Affair*). The "boldness of the silhouettes," Jordan wrote, is "like a signature for the film" (*MCFD* 50). The most important silhouette is that of the notoriously anonymous Collins himself. In one scene, he walks unnoticed into Dublin Castle, posing as an informer. His anonymity makes him a spectral figure to the British. When the elite Cairo group comes to Dublin with the express purpose of eliminating Collins, their commanding officer asks, "Doesn't he have a face, this Collins? Doesn't he have corporeal form?" Collins acquires the mythic status reserved for gangsters and ghosts, or ghosts of gangsters. When Harry Boland returns from the trip to the United States, Collins greets him by telling him he looks like a gangster, to which Boland replies, "You look like a ghost."

Michael Collins suggests that we ignore ghosts at our peril. This is the lesson the British forces learn, with respect to the IRA's shadowy assassins and its imagined republic. Irish Republicans, de Valera wrote to Collins, must "act as if the Republic is a fact." They unseat the British empire by denying its political legitimacy and by substituting their own belief in and performance of a mythical Irish Republic. By performing—by acting as if the Republic is a fact—these ghosts of the Irish nation "ghostify" the British empire itself, causing it to vanish into thin air.

In *High Spirits* and *Michael Collins,* ghosts of the nation destabilize notions of Irish national identity. In the former, a ghost comedy, an agreeably chaotic carnival arises from the antics of troublemaking spirits. Metaphors for cultural encounters across difference—which entail the mixing of ghost and human and of American and Irish—suggest that there are pleasures and dangers associated with losing control over one's identity in a diasporic and globalizing world. Those encounters also suggest the impossibility of fully controlling individual or collective identities, because they must be negotiated through performances that merge reality and representation. In *Michael Collins,* Jordan uses the ghosts of national heroes to explore numerous unresolved traumas associated with the Irish nation, an entity that grafts an imagined community and a global diaspora onto a modern nation-state. These ghosts exploit the power of invisibility as well as the political value of performance. Failing to see the enemy, and refusing to recognize the political fiction that sustains the enemy, result in death, which is the ultimate surrender of mastery.

Julian Wolfreys writes that "[t]he haunting process puts into play a disruptive structure" (6). The specters that haunt Jordan's ghost films are not simply reminders that no one fully controls an identity or inhabits a national narrative. Like his werewolves and vampires, Jordan's ghosts disrupt the very frameworks of difference that are used to establish identity. Finally, Jordan's ghosts suggest that performance—which might be characterized as the surrender of mastery to a collective articulation of the "as if"—takes into account the reality of representation and creates new possibilities for enacting individual and collective identities. Thus, the gothic ghost proves useful for understanding postmodern dilemmas of identity and difference.

While monsters and ghosts provide tangible connections to the gothic in *The Company of Wolves, Interview with the Vampire, High Spirits,* and *Michael Collins* because they personify the transgression of boundaries, Jordan frequently makes use of less obvious formal devices to conjure the gothic sensibility. In three films whose narratives focus on profound challenges to masculine identities, he uses popular music to confound the past and the present, endorsing a gothic view of time as cyclical. Throughout each film, Jordan emphasizes that these songs are performances, hinting at the way that, in contemporary culture, individuals often construct and enact their identities through multiple iterations of popular songs.

Gothic Cycles: Popular Music in *Mona Lisa, Angel,* and *The Crying Game*

> I thought of the question, as I played, of why music soothes the restless soul.
>
> —Neil Jordan, *The Dream of a Beast*

In *High Spirits* and *Michael Collins,* Neil Jordan exploits the ghost's immateriality to comment on the elusive character of Irish national identity. In three other films, Jordan relies upon an equally intangible form—the popular song—to challenge the ideologies and practices of masculinity.

Jordan peppers the soundtracks to *Mona Lisa, Angel,* and *The Crying Game* with instantly recognizable standards excavated from a cultural treasure trove of American, British, and Irish popular music. When music assumes the form of sentimental standards like "Mona Lisa," "Danny Boy," and "When a Man Loves a Woman," it becomes a gothicizing force. Through familiar songs, the past returns again and again. Thus, music, like Jordan's ghosts, disrupts the chronological march of time and suggests temporal and spatial displacement. To gothicize time in this way, Jordan relies on a peculiar duality of popular songs: they can't help but refer to a specific place and time, while the fact that they are standards implies that they have transcended their point of origin. They embody a different kind of temporality based on repetition (when the original version is replayed) and revision (when a cover of the original is played or performed).

The content of the lyrics and the historical associations aroused by these songs contribute to a common narrative emphasis in these three films: the near-destruction of male characters who cling to traditional notions of gender, sexuality, and national identity. As the films unfold, songs become occasions for performance, and thus they reflect the notion that identity—including masculine identity—is a construct that emerges through repeated performances. Jordan's use of these familiar songs links the gothic concept of cyclical time to the postmodern understanding of identity as a series of repeated performances.

It is appropriate to focus on popular music in Jordan's films rather than their scores because the director's distinctive voice emerges through these songs. Formerly a professional musician, Jordan once proposed that filmmakers "should just take bits of music that have this incredible emotional meaning for you and stick them in the movie" (*Crying Game* commentary). Jordan has collaborated successfully on film scores with accomplished composers such as Anne Dudley (*The Miracle* and *The Crying Game*), George Fenton (*The Company of Wolves, High Spirits,* and *We're No Angels*), and Elliot Goldenthal (*Interview with the Vampire, The Butcher Boy,* and *In Dreams*). But he often chooses a popular standard to evoke the emotional center of a film and, sometimes, to serve as its title. Examples of the latter include *Mona Lisa, The Crying Game, The Butcher Boy, In Dreams,* and *Breakfast on Pluto.*

Mona Lisa is a textbook example of a Jordan film in which a popular song "disestablishes" time and space while also setting the emotional tone and theme of the story. The film opens with Nat King Cole's 1950 hit song "Mona Lisa." Images of urban London unfold as Cole's smoky voice asks a mysterious, unapproachable woman: "Are you warm, are you real Mona Lisa? / Or just a cold and lonely, lovely work of art?" Cole's voice accompanies George (Bob Hoskins), a lone figure who walks across a bridge. (The bridge is a common architectural element in Jordan's work that suggests a journey, a transition, or a leap of faith.) In the next shot, George sits for a moment on a park bench, surrounded by the morning mist, as the Cole song continues to play.

According to Jordan, George "seems a little bit outside time and definitely outside place" (*Mona Lisa* commentary). The pairing of a song whose heyday was in the 1950s with images of 1980s London is central to an understanding of George as existing outside time and place. The fact that this juxtaposition occurs in the opening scene, which is typically devoted to establishing the place and time of the action, only enhances the viewer's sense of dislocation.

One obvious way to tie the song to the images would be through its lyrics. Like Mona Lisa, George is isolated and lonely: as he moves through the city, he is surrounded by empty space, not people. Given the casting of Hoskins, however, it is a stretch for viewers to assume that he is the mysterious object of desire named in the song. Could the schmaltzy song be an expression of his sentiments? If George shares the singer's longing, then he does so without any tangible love object in sight. This conundrum becomes central to *Mona Lisa.* George's search for romantic fulfillment is a quest for his imaginative projection of the ideal woman, an ephemeral image that dwells in George's consciousness but no longer has a referent in the real world. This theme is far from apparent in these opening moments, however.

In this opening scene, Jordan plays with conventions of film music in two ways. First, he works against the idea that popular music establishes a concrete sense of time and place. He also challenges the conventional wisdom derived from the work of Christian Metz, Claudia Gorbman, and Jeff Smith—that film sound is a secondary attribute that only serves to enhance the meaning of the images. Whereas Metz lamented the fact that sound is generally considered to be an attribute, like color, rather than an object in its own right (366), Gorbman emphasizes the inaudibility of the classical film score. The same idea—that music complements the image—underlies Smith's concept of polarization, where the affective qualities of music "move [a] viewer's understanding of images to one side or the other of a semantic scale" ("Movie Music" 166).

At the opening of *Mona Lisa,* Cole's American standard does not function as a secondary attribute of the image. On the contrary, it dominates the scene, partly because the song is played almost in its entirety, and partly because so little action takes place to distract viewers. The music hardly seems to comment on the action, much less clarify the meaning of the images or move viewers along a semantic scale. The perplexing combination of sound and image remains a puzzle, making it a highly effective entrée into a film whose title refers to the art world's most famous enigma and whose narrative assumes the form of a detective story.

Jordan combines music and images in intriguing and dissonant ways in the opening scenes of *Mona Lisa, Angel,* and *The Crying Game.* Because he uses popular music to destabilize space and time rather than establishing a specific milieu for the action about to take place, an analysis of each film's opening scene offers insight into the effects of this choice on viewers. Whereas the use of music from a past era suggests that Jordan's characters are unable to fully inhabit the present, the particular songs he has chosen also contribute to the theme of each film in important ways.

In *Mona Lisa,* linking George with the Nat King Cole song confounds the story's time frame and yet also hints at George's emotional state. "Mona Lisa" conveys nostalgia for a distant past of thirty years earlier, perhaps even the period of George's teenage years. The song marks George as having lost more time than the seven years he spent in prison (a narrative detail introduced in the film's early scenes); he seems to be suspended in youthful romance and idealism.

In the film's initial sequence, "Mona Lisa" migrates from nondiegetic to source music. As George approaches a London row house, the music diminishes to silence. His attempt at a family reunion turns ugly as his wife refuses to let him inside to see her and their teenaged daughter, Jeanie (Zoe Nathenson). George's friend Thomas (Robbie Coltrane) rescues him from an altercation with the neighbors, instigated by George's public fit of retaliation against his wife during which he overturns trash cans. Thomas, an auto mechanic and dealer in novelty items, has maintained George's vintage Jaguar during his incarceration. The two take it for a drive. When George presses a tape into the dashboard player, "Mona Lisa" returns to the soundtrack as source music.

The song's repetition as nondiegetic and diegetic music calls attention to an important narrative transition from exposition to the story about to unfold. It also reveals several parallels. "Mona Lisa" accompanies George's loving reunion with his Jaguar, highlighting the contrasting silence that underscored his earlier failure to reconnect with his family. Further, the source music helps George's character to fall into place. He is a driver resuming his chosen profession. The song seems highly appropriate to the ambiance of George's luxurious cream-colored automobile, which, like him, is visibly out of step with the times. When "Mona Lisa" returns to George's world as source music, it establishes that his most stable environment is, paradoxically, a vintage car that incessantly prowls the streets of contemporary London. From this point forward, George frequently plays or hums "Mona Lisa" or Cole's "When I Fall in Love." Notes and phrases from the songs make their way into the score, a standard Hollywood practice that underlines a character's narrative importance.

Cole's songs not only emphasize the nostalgia of George's worldview; they also hint at his traditional expectations regarding gender, sexuality, and race. George makes evident his discomfort with the changing status of women and black people in the first scene, when he attacks his assertive wife, calls her a "cow," and disparages the integration of his neighborhood. After upending the trash cans, he peevishly asks Thomas about the neighbors who have gathered to watch his display. "Where did they come from?" he asks. When Thomas tells him that they are residents, George replies, "Since when?" The comments underscore George's temporal and spatial displacement ("where" and "when") and his investment in a white, "Little English" identity (Jordan's term for him on the commentary track of the *Mona Lisa* DVD). Throughout these sequences, Nat King Cole's popular music doesn't establish the historical time of the action but instead presents George's retrograde view of a world from which he has been displaced and a cultural milieu that has undergone radical changes during his absence.

Jordan's first feature film, *Angel,* also opens with an unconventional use of popular music. The film was originally conceived of as a musical entitled *Brute Music.* The story is loosely based on the Miami Showband killings of 1975, when loyalist paramilitaries, who support British rule in Northern Ireland, killed several members of a band returning to the Irish Republic after performing in Northern Ireland. (Jordan reiterates this concern about the danger musicians faced when crossing the border in *Breakfast on Pluto:* Kitten Braden travels with a bar band, and they are stopped at a checkpoint on Bloody Sunday in 1972.)

As in *Mona Lisa,* the popular music playing in the opening scenes of *Angel* serves to disestablish time and place rather than to clarify the action. In the opening scene, a tenor saxophone solo plays over the credits. At first, scales are prominent, but gradually the melody of the

Irish ballad "Danny Boy" emerges. A long static shot frames a parking lot in front of an isolated dance hall whose neon sign reads "Dreamland Ballroom." Men unload equipment from a white van parked near a billboard that advertises Coke.

After the credits roll, the camera cuts to a reverse shot. This shot reveals the interior of the van where Danny (Stephen Rea) plays the sax, using the vehicle as an echo chamber. The music, now revealed to have a source, has attracted a young woman, Annie (Veronica Quilligan), who hovers nearby. Oddly enough, Annie is deaf and mute, so the assumption that the music draws her to Danny should be questioned, though it is never resolved. Annie observes Danny throughout the evening's performance. She seeks him out at closing time and wordlessly invites him outside, where they have a sexual encounter inside a large concrete conduit. As Danny watches from inside the circular pipe, loyalist paramilitaries shoot the band's manager because he refuses to pay protection money and then turn their guns on Annie, who has witnessed the first shooting. Bombs explode, engulfing the club in flames. Shaken out of his complacency, Danny becomes the avenging angel of the film's title, tracking down and killing the men he holds responsible for the deaths.

In the opening moments of the film, Danny's tenor sax is light and melodic, defying placement within the jazz-pop fusion style consistent with the story's time frame of the 1970s. (When the band performs later, it generally plays a form of jazz-pop fusion.) In addition, the images of the musician's van, the Coke billboard, and Danny's shiny costume are icons of youth music culture, so the jazz instrument playing a traditional Irish ballad seems doubly misplaced. The symbolism embedded in the name of the Dreamland Ballroom contributes to the sense of temporal and spatial suspension that the music creates.

The solo is played by Keith Donald in a style reminiscent of the big band sound of the 1940s rather than a contemporary form such as syncopated bop or cool. The nostalgic association is confirmed later when the band manager refers to Danny as "the Stan Getz of South Armagh." A widely popular postwar American tenor saxophonist, Getz was known for his "fluffy tone and melodic approach" (Gridley 133–44), which are two characteristics of Donald's solos. Getz is best known for popularizing Brazilian Bossa Nova music. His most recognized piece is a 1964 recording of "The Girl from Ipanema," with vocals by Astrid Gilberto that became a huge international hit.

Danny's playing establishes him as a man who is slightly out of step with the times, a young upstart who warms up by playing a sentimental ballad known around the world as the quintessential song of Ireland. In fact, the film was released in the United States in 1984 as *Danny Boy*, a title change that seems to capitalize on American viewers' familiarity with the song. (Arthur Flynn reports, however, that the name was changed because a softcore porn film entitled *Angel* had been released in the United States [121]).

The automatic association of "Danny Boy" with Ireland seems to narrow the film's possible resonances by framing the story as a question of Irish essentialism. But the song's arrangement and performance style widen the context for Danny's dilemma. The music invokes Ireland, but Danny's instrument evokes jazz, an international musical style long deemed wicked by Irish Catholic priests, who associated it with African paganism and primitivity. Nationalist narrative meets international jazz—a merger that metaphorically extends the story's reach beyond the boundaries of the nation. Danny's search for the individuals responsible for Annie and the manager's deaths finally does assume those proportions. The unfolding narrative reveals that current and historical practices of British colonialism overshadow the apparently local, sectarian conflict in Northern Ireland.

In a similar vein, popular music played in the opening scene of Jordan's celebrated political thriller *The Crying Game* confounds time, space, and national identities. The film opens with a slow tracking shot of a carnival, which is visible in the distance beneath a bridge that spans a body of water. By sandwiching a rotating Ferris wheel between the heavy horizontal line of the bridge and the horizon itself, Jordan and the cinematographer Ian Wilson create a spatial metaphor for stalemate. The image reflects a tension between linearity and rotation, between forward progress and cyclicality. Percy Sledge's 1966 hit "When a Man Loves a Woman" plays over the opening credits. The camera's distance from the carnival grounds implies that the music is nondiegetic.

At the end of the credits sequence, a distinct aural shift can be heard on the soundtrack. The screams of people on carnival rides infiltrate the Sledge music, which shrinks noticeably in color and volume, acquiring a

The Crying Game. Cycles contained within a linear frame. Courtesy of Photofest.

flat, tinny timbre. A cut to a close-up of a Tannoy loudspeaker mounted on a wooden pole completes the physical transition to the fairground, where the action begins. The camera tracks down the pole and moves forward in space, entering the tent where Jody (Forest Whitaker) wins a huge pink bear for his female companion, Jude (Miranda Richardson).

As in *Mona Lisa* and *Angel,* the opening song makes it difficult to establish the place and time of the images. Sledge's song was released in 1966, the year in which the Troubles began, but it accompanies action taking place more than a decade later. The song can be recognized as a "golden oldie" only after another song displaces it from the soundtrack: a pop song from the 1980s entitled "Baby Jump," recorded by Mungo Jerry.

The music assumes prominence in this opening scene because the images are somewhat vague. Like the London bridge of *Mona Lisa* and the Dreamland Ballroom in *Angel,* the carnival in *The Crying Game* is a place where time has been suspended. Sledge's lyrics tell of a romantic obsession, but they are of little use in interpreting the relationship between the two individuals at hand. The audience quickly learns that the characters barely know one another: Jody asks Jude to tell him her name and then sings it back to her in a parody of the Beatles' "Hey Jude" (another late 1960s song). Viewer expectations about these characters deriving from cultural connections are thwarted as well: any attempt to link Sledge's southern R&B song directly to the African American actor Forest Whitaker would be frustrated by the actor's British accent.

Minor business during the opening scene contributes to the sense of temporal dislocation: a baleful glare directed at the interracial couple seems to come straight out of the 1960s. That disapproving look temporarily masks the surveillance of the couple by the film's main character, Fergus (Stephen Rea). When Jude pulls Jody away from the fair with the promise of sex, the plot emerges: Jody, a British soldier, is taken hostage by the IRA in retaliation for the British government's detention of IRA operatives.

Here the film ostensibly turns from a romance to a tale of political intrigue. But the songs—"When a Man Loves a Woman," "The Crying Game," and "Stand by Your Man"—act as set pieces to underscore a double narrative that explores the linkages between ideologies of nationalism and masculinity. In the love-story and the political-thriller subplots, Jordan first exposes and then destroys romantic mythologies.

Jordan's use of popular songs in the opening scenes of *Mona Lisa, Angel,* and *The Crying Game* does more than simply unsettle viewer expectations about place and time. In each case, the songs are initially understood as nondiegetic, existing outside the world of the story. But later they are shown to emanate from sources within the story world. Marking the disjunction between nondiegetic and source music as Jordan does draws attention to the process of entering the narrative.

Jordan asks viewers to hear these songs first as well-known popular songs that exist independently of the film's context. By inserting the songs into stories, he invites viewers to carry their associations into the diegesis. The migration of the music blurs the boundary between the shared social space of the popular song and a character's emotional interiority. By highlighting the role of the music as it ushers the viewer into the narrative, Jordan honors the gothic concern with subjective, interior states as well as the genre's self-consciousness regarding narrative form.

The way Jordan uses popular music blurs yet another boundary, one more properly associated with postmodern aesthetics. Viewers gain access to the subjective states of characters like George precisely because they recognize the music, which, as a mass form of art, is profoundly unoriginal. The songs simultaneously offer listeners universal recognition and personal significance. Songs like "Mona Lisa," "Danny Boy," and "When a Man Loves a Woman" define eras, locations, and cultural aspirations and thus "bring the immediate threat of history" (Kassabian, *Hearing* 3). Yet each song leads a double life, transcending those origins to become ahistorical and generic. What seems to be a form of personal expression inevitably reveals itself to be something that is reproduced and reproducible—a contemporary and commodified version of the uncanny double.

Moving beyond the formal aspects of Jordan's use of popular music, it is important to consider why these particular songs haunt these films. Jordan selects music that speaks to the cultural milieus in which the characters live. The films focus on the breakdown of traditional markers of stability, including race, gender, and national identity. They depict male characters whose experiences assault their ideas about who they are. George sees himself as a knight in shining armor; Danny assumes the role of an avenging angel; and Fergus paints himself as a proud Volunteer engaged in the righteous Republican cause. Jordan selects these songs because they express the nameless terrors that plague these characters as their identities undergo irrevocable rupture.

Jordan's films portray men in crisis, and the songs in these films speak to their dilemmas. In this regard, Jordan participated in a wider trend in cinema the 1980s and 1990s, including Hollywood films, in which popular music was used to articulate "the changing pressures of identity formation such as race, ethnicity, sexuality, and gender" (Kassabian, *Hearing* 4). George, Danny, and Fergus—all would-be defenders of imperiled women—have difficulty understanding the changing world around them. They are oblivious to the fact that both men and women may be agents of phallic power in addition to, or instead of, being its victims. They seem completely unaware that they are vulnerable. The fact that these films focus on the potential vulnerability of white male characters may partially explain the objections of critics who have denounced their sexual and racial politics. For example, Aspasia Kotsoupolos and Josephine Mills write that *The Crying Game* "espoused a reactionary position with respect to women, blacks and queers, and displaced concrete political concerns onto a transhistorical notion of human nature" (15). Jordan explores the personal implications of political matters, looking in particular at the intimate terrors that these male characters encounter as their nostalgic image of traditional masculinity disintegrates.

The songs provide thematic significance, but the full extent of that significance depends upon viewers' awareness of ideas and events that exist independently of the film, a dynamic process that Anahid Kassabian has termed "affiliating identifications" (*Hearing* 3). Drawing upon viewers' affiliating identifications, the songs allude to a dominative brand of masculinity that George ascribes to, that Danny unwittingly adopts, and that Fergus enacts and then rejects. In each film, this white British masculinity stages an uncanny return, but not always in a form these characters recognize.

By the conclusion of *Mona Lisa,* George comes to terms with the fact that the persona of chivalrous knight to which he aspires encompasses the very brutality against women that he wants to reject. In *Angel,* Danny learns that his desire for revenge mirrors British colonial violence as he becomes a tool of those in power. In *The Crying Game,* Fergus learns that the nationalist rhetoric of us and them—which has no capacity for conceiving of "us" or "them" as diverse and ever-shifting categories—is a thin veneer used to justify the victimization of others. These ideas about gender and nationality are embedded in the popular music Jordan has selected for these films.

Mona Lisa's title song expresses a man's feeling of inadequacy when contemplating an ideal woman who can be visually, but not emotionally, possessed. Firmly linked with George in the scene where he reclaims his Jaguar, the song suggests that his central conflict involves his relationship with women. As he adjusts the rearview mirror, looking forward and backward at the same time, an extreme close-up emphasizes his eyes. The shot provides a metaphor for the film's quest narrative and for George's tendency to misconstrue what he is seeing, since he is looking backward. George puts the tape in and smiles. Before Cole begins to sing, George asks Thomas, "Why does she hate me?"—a question about his estranged wife. Thomas's answer hints at the troubling way that he, George, and Cole (as the song's narrator) consider femininity to be an unsolvable mystery. He tells George, "You can never tell with women,

George; they're different." Over the course of the film, George's literal and figurative rearview vision, which can only see gender differences through a nostalgic lens, fuels his misperceptions about Simone (Cathy Tyson), the woman who comes to dominate his romantic fantasies.

Simone is the beautiful black prostitute he has been assigned to drive around London for his underworld crony, the repulsive Dinny Mortwell (Michael Caine). Initially, George tells Thomas that Simone is a "tall thin black tart," but he later modifies his assessment as he begins to fall in love with her, calling her a Sister of Mercy (a nun), a princess, and then, simply, a lady. The rules of courtly love apply. George dubs his Jaguar her chariot. Like St. George, he battles various dragons, ranging from her former pimp, Anderson (Clarke Peters), to Mortwell himself. Simone's wish is George's command: she asks him to help her locate Cathy (Kate Hardie), a younger prostitute whom Simone has lost touch with. Their joint quest exposes the neogothic victimization of young women by powerful businessmen who exploit men's desires for the ideal woman (another echo of Hitchcock's *Vertigo*).

As Simone comes to rely on George to help her find Cathy, her eyes replace George's in the rearview mirror. Her quest for Cathy absorbs George's attention, subsuming and redirecting his gaze. The image of her eyes in the mirror and the fact that she looks ahead at the road while George looks back at her suggest Simone's increasing control of the narrative. The soundtrack repeats the Nat King Cole songs again and again, hinting at George's acquiescence. While the music underlines George's romantic nostalgia, these repetitions also manifest the process whereby his sexual desire for Simone becomes a full-blown obsession.

The song lyrics hint at the way adulation becomes a fixation and leads to exploitation. The words evoke a male overinvestment in women as images. Cole's songs idealize women the singer does not know; in the case of "When I Fall in Love," the relationship is explicitly hypothetical. When appropriated for a film that explores the cost of human trafficking, the music's darker connotations emerge. In the context of a high-class prostitution ring, the songs imply that men's control over women's bodies, which they exploit as profitable commodities, is based on the same ability to objectify them that innocuous popular songs convey.

As a title song, "Mona Lisa" provides instant name recognition (Smith, "Popular Music" 415) and may "predispose spectators toward certain affective meanings" (Smith, "Movie Music" 166). The song invokes a complex, even contradictory, set of references. In cinema, jazz music connotes "'lower-class' people involved in sleazy drams of sex, drugs, and/or crime" (Brown, *Overtones* 183) and "loose sexuality and drug abuse" (Gabbard 248). Although the corny style of Cole's songs and his wholesome persona may mitigate those associations, they are nevertheless appropriate here. Heard in the context of George's chaste obsession, Cole's ballad sounds worshipful; when linked to the sordid prostitution underworld, its implications become horrific.

The music's ambiguity finds a counterpart in the film's visual style. Whereas the film opens with George returning to London at daybreak, its most memorable scenes take place in George's Jaguar at night, a fact that elicited numerous comparisons between *Mona Lisa* and Martin Scorsese's *Taxi Driver* (1976). In the dark, the city of London becomes a carnival of women's bodies, readily procured at peep shows and at the nightmarish King's Cross, amidst bonfires and lurid shadows. Repeatedly, women are framed in ways that convey their entrapment, evoking the female gothic. Women are visible through the windshield of George's Jaguar and through the mirrors at Dinny Mortwell's mansion. They appear boxed in at peep shows and on porn videos.

Like many of Jordan's characters, George constantly looks through transparent layers of glass, but he isn't able to see clearly. Mirrors, windows, and windshields appear to provide a clear line of sight; but in fact they cannot guarantee that George's view of the world will be accurate or even adequate. *Mona Lisa* draws upon a British gangster-film tradition in which apparently savvy main characters have difficulty seeing the web of crime and deceit in which they become embroiled. That legacy includes *Get Carter* (dir. Mike Hodges; 1971) and *The Long Good Friday* (dir. John MacKenzie; 1980), which feature Caine and Hoskins, respectively, in lead roles. Although *Mona Lisa* was based on a true story reported in the British press and possesses the visual trappings of an urban crime thriller, the film moves beyond its realist precursors to embrace surrealism. With its fairy-tale references to St. George, the frog prince, and *Alice's Adventures through the Looking Glass, Mona Lisa* takes a decided turn away from realism toward the gothic lyricism apparent in other 1970s gangster films, including *Performance* (dir. Nicolas Roeg; 1970) and *Chinatown* (dir. Roman Polanski; 1974).

Mona Lisa. George (Bob Hoskins) and Dinny (Michael Caine), surrounded by women who perform. Courtesy of Photofest.

The key to the film's dark secrets, and the explanation for George's utter inability to see these depraved dynamics, lies in the idealized figure of the Mona Lisa, a beloved and reviled work of high art and kitsch that pervades the film through the title song. The painting, and what it represents, helps to explain the ways in which George is hopelessly out of his element. "La Gioconda," Leonardo's widely recognized icon of Western beauty, is a portrait of a woman painted by a man. Mona Lisa is a man-made image of a mysterious woman, an untouchable portrait of perfection. By definition, her feminine image can be worshiped, reviled, and reproduced but never understood. As it turns out, George shares this view of the feminine not only with Thomas but also with Mortwell and his cronies, who use it to exploit men as well as women.

Mortwell uses the notion of the ideal woman to entrap powerful men. It is no coincidence that he refers to the man he intends to use Simone to blackmail as "the Arab." The dynamics of male power have changed with globalization, and Mortwell must branch out beyond aging English government ministers to the new, racially diverse elite. By working for Mortwell, George participates in a corrupt patriarchal economy that

Mona Lisa. A gothic sense of disproportion.
Courtesy of Photofest.

assimilates women, immigrants, and black people and yet leaves racial and sexual hierarchies intact. Anderson, who is black, has risen in the underworld ranks from porn star to pimp, but Mortwell remains in charge, working through his upper-class connections.

George rescues Simone's friend Cathy from one such upper-class British man, literally reaching from behind a looking glass at Mortwell's mansion to snatch her out of a scene of depravity that is, oddly enough, accompanied by opera music. After reuniting Cathy and Simone, George feels betrayed when he learns that Simone is in love with Cathy. Even worse for George, Simone is capable of wielding the same kind of phallic power that makes Anderson and Mortwell so dangerous. She treats others as objects, shooting and killing Anderson and Mortwell and threatening George with the same gun.

Until this moment, George cannot see that his desire for Simone, expressed by the Cole songs, is inextricable from the practices of power that Mortwell and Anderson, and even Simone, have adopted to control others. The sentimentality of the music belies its ante- and antifeminist vision—a vision that enforces the sexual politics that sustain Mortwell's empire and resonates with Thomas's admonition. In this view, women are different from men; they can never be understood and therefore are dangerous. But George learns that such a static view of gender cannot be trusted: women can be dangerous in the same ways that men are.

Jordan has said that *Mona Lisa* is "really about very vulgar things that are only elevated by a certain sense of romanticism" (qtd. in Finney 125). George's romanticism must be radically revised when he discovers that he has fallen victim to the dynamics of objectification expressed in the song. George finally rejects the phallic domination implicit in his dream of becoming a knight in shining armor. To do so, he rejects romance altogether, a somewhat radical solution that entirely eliminates the threatening figure of the woman. When "Mona Lisa" plays over the final scenes of George, Thomas, and George's daughter Jeanie together, the parallel with the film's opening scene suggests an entirely new chapter in George's narrative. This notion is reinforced by George's verbal summary and analysis of the entire affair in the third person, a narrative process that turns his experiences into a mystery story, akin to those he and Thomas swap throughout the film (a reference to Hitchcock's *Shadow of a Doubt* [1943]). In this context, the song acquires a different resonance. The threesome promises to become a family whose relationships are based on bonds of friendship and which, notably, excludes the figure of the adult woman. In short, George joins Thomas in a retreat from heterosexual romance.

Like George, *Angel's* saxophone-playing protagonist is disabled by practices of white male power. Danny unwittingly colludes with police authorities to investigate the Dreamland Ballroom murders. These authorities work within a political power vacuum that reflects the province's return to colonial status. During the height of the Troubles in 1972, Britain suspended the Irish government of Northern Ireland and imposed direct rule, stationing British troops in the province with the ostensible goal of protecting the Catholic population. Many Irish Republicans treated it as an occupation, and the troops were viewed as exacerbating the oppression of the Catholic minority. Given an oppositional context pitting Ireland against Britain, the apolitical Danny is completely unaware that the paternalistic authority figures within Northern Ireland—Bloom (Ray McAnally) and Bonner (Donal McCann)—might have an interest in perpetuating, rather than eradicating, sectarian violence of the sort he has witnessed.

Like *Mona Lisa, Angel* emphasizes the surreal and uncanny aspects of Danny's quest, moving between a raw documentary style in violent scenes and fantastic moments during the band's gigs. In this way, Jordan's visual style highlights the absurd task that Danny has set for himself, as he oscillates between murders and musical performances. Danny kills the men he believes are responsible for Annie's death while wearing his pink satin stage costume. In one scene, Danny's band plays in a mental institution as searchlights from a nearby prison sweep the room. The metaphor becomes increasingly apt: like Danny, the ghostly inmates have lost touch with reality. They wander dreamily around the room, illuminated by the beams of light, as if they were the performers. Near the film's conclusion, Danny stumbles upon a sideshow tent. The attraction is a boy whose father touts him as a prophet because he's the seventh son of a seventh son. The boy, like Danny, seems more paralyzed than functional: another charismatic performer controlled by a powerful father figure.

Assisting Danny in his revenge spree is the gothic duo of Bloom and Bonner. They show Danny mug shots and give him the names of suspects, ostensibly to jog his memory. These photographs signify a profound and widespread destabilization of masculine identity. The images seem to erase identities rather than recording them: the photographs transform the entire male population of Northern Ireland into uncanny doubles. By virtue of having been photographed, they are all implicated in the violence. Bloom gives voice to this fact, saying, "Nowadays around here, everybody's guilty." Danny studies the photographs, finds the men he believes are responsible, and kills them. With each murder, he takes on aspects of the identities of the men he kills. He converses with his victims and asks them questions before shooting them; in the process he is slowly emptied of his own identity. Danny comes to resemble his victims and the police: everyone except himself. The band's singer, Deirdre (Honor Heffernan), notices the change: "Them [the police], like you, only in uniform," she says to Danny.

Like the men in the mug shots, Danny grows increasingly distant, strange, and anonymous. The shift is reflected in Danny's changing relationship to the song he plays in the film's opening scene. Before a gig late in the film, Deirdre tells Danny they'll be playing his tune: "Danny Boy." He replies, "That's not my tune, that's everyone's." The

Angel. Danny (Stephen Rea) as his own gothic double. Courtesy of Photofest.

line implies that Danny's relationship to a collective identity is troubled. He fails to acknowledge that if the song is everyone's song, then surely it is his as well.

The troubles associated with asserting a collective Irish identity are an inherent part of the song's history. Generally referred to as "Londonderry Air" or "the Air from County Derry," "Danny Boy" probably originated in the city of Derry, the site of an important battle of the Williamite war. The Siege of Derry (1689) helped turn the tide in favor of the Protestant King William of Orange and against his father-in-law, the Catholic James II. The song thus involves long-standing historical divisions: British versus Irish nationality, Protestant versus Catholic religious traditions, and loyalist versus republican politics.

The song may be synonymous with Irishness, but it also reflects the danger of relying on essentialist ideas about national identity. Properly speaking, the song is not Irish; it is a complex hybrid. The Derry composer Jane Ross annotated the song in 1851 after she heard an itinerant blind musician, possibly the fiddler Jimmy McCurry, playing the music. But the melody has been linked to a tune from the Scottish lowlands, and it also resembles a traditional Irish air documented in the 1790s called "The Young Man's Vision" (McCourt 31; Robinson; Hunter). The music was first published in *The Ancient Music of Ireland* (1855), but the now-familiar lyrics weren't added until 1912, penned by an English lawyer and professional songwriter, Frederic Weatherly. Malachy McCourt reports that more than ninety poets and writers have written lyrics for the tune (45–46).

"Danny Boy" is not "essentially" Irish. The song is understood to be Irish because of a collective agreement forged over the course of many performances. Reiterating the Irishness of the song in various contexts reestablishes its claim to an Irish identity, and recent public performances have continued to renew that claim. In 1985, the boxer Barry McGuigan, known as the "Clones Cyclone," became the World Boxing Association champion. McGuigan's father famously sang "Danny Boy" before his son's matches to confirm that McGuigan, a Catholic man married to a Protestant woman, represented all of Ireland.

Danny's estrangement from "Danny Boy" reflects the profound transformation he undergoes as he abandons music for murder. Playing music allows Danny to establish an individual identity as a soloist and to participate in a collective identity within the band. Music also provides an opportunity to modify existing frameworks of identity—for example, through his jazz version of "Danny Boy." By contrast, the violence he practices destroys individuals in the name of collective sectarian and/or national identities. Becoming an assassin destroys identities and meanings rather than allowing them to proliferate, which can occur when songs like "Danny Boy" are performed again and again in different contexts. Or, as Bonner tells Danny in the final scene of the film, the gun is "a lot easier to play than the saxophone; you only have the one tune." Ironically, Danny's ability to move from artist to assassin emphasizes a fluidity of identity that undermines the essentialist notions that sectarianism is based upon.

Two other well-known pieces of music also contribute to the film's themes. Lewis Allen and Billie Holiday's "Strange Fruit," a song that Danny and Deirdre's band performs, expresses the view that the Troubles are rooted in same deep-seated racism associated with lynching in the United States. Giuseppe Verdi's "Requiem," a piece that is heard several times nondiegetically, is a musical form played at the mass seeking repose for the souls of the dead. These three pieces of music also provide a formal structure to the film: that of the gothic cycle. Richard Kearney has emphasized that the film's "deep-structure unfolds 'synchronically' by repeating key visual and sound motifs" (*Transitions* 179).

During the final confrontation between Danny and Bonner, the police officer who has been orchestrating the paramilitary violence, the film returns full circle. "Here we are again," Bonner remarks, dragging Danny into the ruins of the Dreamland Ballroom as the requiem plays. Danny's efforts have served the government authorities who are manipulating the Troubles for their own ends. Poised to kill Danny, Bonner is instead killed by Bloom, who has been using Danny to confirm his suspicions about Bonner. Danny assumes the role of witness again, this time watching power-mad authority figures engage in violent retribution. In the closing image, a shot of the rotating blades of Bloom's helicopter reiterates the threat of being drawn into the proverbial vicious cycle.

The film's musical repetitions and cyclical structure emphasize the "radical deromanticization of the cult of heroic violence which has fueled sentimental nationalism" (Kearney, *Transitions* 183) by creating a sense that events are preordained and by shaping a dead-end narrative. The contrast between Danny's musical performances, which have the potential to produce new meanings and identities, and his murderous acts, which destroy meaning and identities, reappears as a theme of *The Crying Game.*

The Crying Game deromanticizes violence and nationalism but proceeds in a dramatically different direction than *Angel.* In early notes for the film, Jordan wrote that "the whole movement of the film is the reverse of *Angel,* showing the gradual process whereby a man sheds the world of violence" (NLI Accessions 4761, box 1). This film poses its challenge to romantic mythologies of all kinds through its protagonist, Fergus. Like George and Danny, his name suggests an alter ego: George becomes St. George, Danny initially identifies with Danny Boy, and Fergus refers to a mythical Celtic king who preferred poetry and chariot riding to the exercise of power. Like George and Danny, Fergus doesn't see things clearly at first. He doesn't recognize the way that IRA nationalism depends on the brutal suppression of other racial and sexual identities. Despite the widespread attention the film has garnered among popular and academic critics alike, the fact that its popular songs contribute to the central theme of identity destabilization has escaped notice.

Jordan's emphasis on the performance and repetition of popular music dramatically underscores the film's challenge to fixed identities. In the course of developing the project, Jordan changed the title of the screenplay from "The Soldier's Wife" to "The Crying Game," a move that shifts the focus from the feminine object of desire (the wife) to the social and psychological process through which desire is enacted (the game). Musical performances were an element of the screenplay from the beginning, but the details of the music underwent profound changes. In Jordan's earliest treatments, the soldier's wife was a "beautiful throaty soprano": a famous, white opera singer who performs Verdi (NLI Accessions 4761, box 1). By the time the screenplay reached its final version, the soldier's wife had become a black transvestite who lip-syncs at a local gay bar, indicating Jordan's growing interest in unsettling Fergus's reality through an engagement with multiple modes of difference.

The shift to "The Crying Game" also brings forward the notion that ritualized games define romance. The title and lyrics echoe those of an Irish song that is never heard in the film but that also deals with ritual, performance, and sacrifice. "The Patriot Game" was a hit for the Kingston Trio in 1964, the same year that Dave Berry's "The Crying Game" was released and became a huge success. In both songs, narrators lament the way romantic illusions cause them to lose themselves, literally and figuratively. In "The Crying Game" those illusions surround romantic love, whereas in "The Patriot Game" they involve the love of one's country. The connection between the two songs is not as arcane as the simple comparison of titles might make it appear. Dominic Behan wrote "The Patriot Game" in 1957 after the death of a sixteen-year-old IRA Volunteer. Dominic was the brother of Brendan Behan, whose play *The Hostage* was a source for *The Crying Game*'s opening sequence (Hawkins 194).

On the DVD commentary track, Jordan acknowledges the brutality with which he shatters Fergus's romantic illusions about love and war. The film "punish[es] this little Irish man with every possible compromise to what he imagined his reality was, his identity was." Those compromises play out through the film's music.

The Percy Sledge, Dave Berry, and Lyle Lovett songs support dramatic reconfigurations of sexuality and gender. The opening Sledge song expresses male vulnerability, departing from the kind of phallic assertion contained in rock music of the same period (e.g., the Rolling Stones' "Play with Fire" or the Who's "Legal Matter," both recorded in 1965). Its lyrics tell of a man who gives everything to the woman he loves. Its narrative function is to cast Jody (and, later, Fergus) as a gentle lover rather than a cruel warrior; the fact that Jody does not wear a military uniform reinforces that image. He is vulnerable to love and war: he is captured during Jude's seduction, and he gives his life for the British nation. His final wish is for Fergus to take care of his lover, Dil.

All three of the film's popular songs comment on the sacrifices entailed in the game of love, although "The Crying Game" ultimately assumes center stage. "The Crying Game" functions as a thematic and formal motif, heard three times and in three different versions, always as source music and always in connection with a performance of some kind. Peter Lehman argues that the song can be viewed within the framework of music that indicates masculine vulnerability. He places "The Crying Game" within a tradition of male melodrama that includes Johnnie Ray's "Cry" (1952) and Roy Orbison's "Crying" (1962). To Lehman, Jordan's musical selection challenges the polarization of masculinity as either phallic dominance or comic collapse (26). The music's refusal to embrace a polarized masculinity migrates to the main character, as Fergus himself becomes part of the challenge to the narrow definitions of gender, race, and sexuality that inform the politics of the IRA and the British government. By the end of the film, Fergus steps into Jody's shoes as Dil's lover and as a hostage. Like Jody, Fergus is a vulnerable man; he rejects his role as a gun-wielding patriot and hints at his potential to move beyond normative heterosexual masculinity by remaining open to a relationship with Dil and continuing to reconsider his emotional connection to Jody.

The repetition of the title song links practices of identity to the dynamics of performance and spectatorship. The first time "The Crying Game" is heard, Dil lip-syncs a version of the song recorded for the film by Kate Robbins. The latter two performances are repetitions with a variation. During the second one, the Dave Berry original serves as background music for another of Dil's performances. She plays the song alone in her apartment after Fergus has rejected her; he waits outside and watches her through the window. Finally, the Boy George version, also recorded for the film, plays when Dil holds Fergus captive, having learned that he was responsible for Jody's death.

Dave Berry's original performance is a spectral presence that informs all three versions of the song. Jordan describes his memories of Berry's 1964 television appearance: it was the "first music video" and it was notable in part because of the singer's distinctive hand gestures. He "traced moonbeams" (*Crying Game* commentary)—a gesture that Dil re-creates in her first performance at the Metro. The song's "image" is thus multilayered: Dil lip-syncs to a remake recorded by a woman vocalist while re-creating the hand gestures of the original male singer. The obviousness of the lip-syncing calls attention to the performance, violating realist conventions that dictate that characters should not acknowledge themselves as performers. (The fact that Dil's performance may have been obvious to some but not all viewers as a drag act provides another challenge to realist vision and its implication that there is a single, objective, and universally visible truth.)

The Crying Game. Performances stop time: Dil (Jaye Davidson) lip-syncs a hit song from 1964.

Each time the song is heard, it is marked explicitly as a performance, which enhances the gender blurring already associated with it: Dil's transgender stage show, Dil's "secret" penis, and Boy George's ambiguous persona inform each of the three iterations. Calling attention to these interludes as performances questions the notion that any of the singers and performers "are" men or women.

The Crying Game deconstructs romantic fantasies of love and honor: its primary target is the nationalist fantasy of phallic, heterosexual masculinity. Arguably, the film remains ambiguous when it comes to practical realities, which may account for criticism of it on the grounds that it pays insufficient attention to concrete politics. Jordan's film, like much of postmodern art, is subversive mainly to the extent that it exposes identities as fictions. The film refuses to endorse an oppositional political rubric, a refusal that suggests that positions defined in opposition to the status quo are all too often based on the same dangerous adherence to essentialist notions of "us and them" that characterizes the status quo.

The critical importance of fluid identities is particularly evident during the third reiteration of "The Crying Game," when Dil drops the needle on the Boy George version of the song as she holds Fergus hostage. By now, Dil has turned the song into her theme music: it is not a reflection of her "authentic" identity but an accompaniment to yet another drag performance. This time she plays a terrorist with a gun; her most scandalous role yet. Dressed as Jody because Fergus wants to throw the IRA off her trail, she assumes the role of a cricket-playing black British soldier. The scene replays the film's opening hostage scenario as farce (a term Jody pointedly used to describe his incarceration). Although Dil has become her former lover Jody's uncanny double, it is less obvious that she also becomes Fergus's double: Dil's performance mirrors Fergus's position in the opening of the film and exposes it as a performance. Unlike Fergus, however, Dil is able to kill. She avenges Jody's death and punishes Jude for enticing Jody as a "real" woman by killing her.

In the film's closing moments, Fergus serves his time in a high-tech glass cell in a British prison, taking the rap for Dil and possibly assuaging his guilt for Jody's death in the process. The film closes with another nostalgic return gone awry: just as Kate Robbins and Boy George's renditions of "The Crying Game" bring it into new contexts, Lyle Lovett's cover of Tammy Wynette's "Stand by Your Man" acts as a campy rejoinder to the opening Sledge song.

Mona Lisa, Angel, and *The Crying Game* portray characters who have difficulty conforming to the time and space of their own narratives. The songs they listen to and perform speak to their temporal and spatial dislocation. Jordan's use of popular standards to invoke nostalgia, and the way subtle repetitions inform these cyclical narratives, suggest the director's interest in a gothic sense of time in which the past persists and influences the present.

Jordan also emphasizes the way music mediates identities, highlighting the significance of repeated performances to plots, themes, and character development. The musical numbers evoke a comforting sense of the past, with connotations of a more stable reality, yet they also point to the ephemera of popular culture as a source of identity. In highlighting the ubiquitous popular song, Jordan's films also explore questions related to postmodern aesthetics.

Jordan's use of popular music alludes to an important attribute of postmodern culture: the leveling of distinctions between high art and low culture. In *Mona Lisa,* the title song captures the film's central dilemma: the confusion between the lover's projection and the actual object of his desire. This confusion produces real, even deadly, effects. According to the historian Donald Sassoon, "The theme of falling in love with an image had become so common that many found the idea of Mona Lisa enchanting Leonardo almost irresistible" (113–14). Much speculation has centered on the possibility that Leonardo's painting is a self-portrait, which resonates with the idea that, in Jordan's film, George's representation of Simone simply reflects his desire, not Simone herself.

A "Mona Lisa" refrigerator magnet briefly glimpsed on Thomas's refrigerator serves as an emblem of the mass culture whose techniques of mechanical reproduction made the painting a superstar. The magnet is associated with Thomas, an illegal trafficker in dubious goods, including garish simulations of spaghetti and glowing madonnas. Like Thomas's bizarre sculptures and the popular detective novels he and George love—all of which are multiples—popular songs may be a degraded form, but they are the "raw materials" that global capitalism provides with which to build an identity, replacing older constructs such as nationalism. These newer identities are based on a shared aptitude for the creation and consumption of images of all kinds.

Thus, the film critic John Simon and art historian Donald Sassoon miss the point when they scoff at any resemblance between Jordan's film and Da Vinci's painting. "The sordidness of the story, its improbability the only high thing about it, is in direct, jarring clash with its high-flown aspirations" (59), writes Simon. Sassoon demurs, "This harsh gritty film has nothing to do with Leonardo's picture, even indirectly" (224). In their desire to preserve the painting's exalted status, they fail to acknowledge that no one controls the myriad uses to which art can be put.

By contrast, Jordan seems well aware that representations—whether visual, musical, or cinematic—can be modified, copied, and reproduced and that their meanings cannot ultimately be controlled by their authors. Instead, they are vulnerable to reappropriation, which is one basis for creativity. As proof of this fact, Jordan orchestrates stunningly sordid moments in each of these films and accompanies them with grand musical forms. When George rescues Cathy from Mortwell's mansion, opera music issues forth amidst a scene of grim exploitation. The Anne Dudley orchestral score that plays when Fergus chases Jody to his accidental death at the hands of his own army is entitled "Dies Irae," or "Day of Wrath," a title that refers to the Latin hymn, often played at funeral masses, that describes Judgment Day. And when Danny returns to the scene of the crime only to find he has become an uncanny double of himself, Verdi's "Requiem" wishes his soul repose.

In each case, Jordan repurposes the high-art forms of opera and religious music. He implies that music's capacity for spiritual uplift is not an inherent property but rather is contingent upon the context of performance. In these scenes, Jordan engages in the postmodern practice of recycling to engineer sublime juxtapositions, using the height of human creativity to underscore humanity's horrors.

Jordan's predilection for the gothic cycle and the sublime juxtaposition manifests itself not only through nostalgic popular songs but also in his frequent depictions of memories, dreams, and visions. In four films that address the childhood traumas that torment young male protagonists, reality and fantasy become indistinguishable as Jordan's characters grapple with the destabilizing effects of leaving, and losing, home. These films are curious coming-of-age tales in which young men assert their masculinity while at the same time they explore their similarities to, rather than their differences from, their mothers.

Dream Lovers, Dream Mothers: *The Miracle, The Butcher Boy, In Dreams,* and *Breakfast on Pluto*

> I think it's about time we took our nightmares seriously.
> —Neil Jordan

Neil Jordan employs popular songs to "disestablish" time and place and to convey the notion of time as a cyclical process. In so doing, he suggests that identities are not fixed essences but are continually redefined through repetition within new contexts, like musical standards that are replayed and rerecorded. In Jordan's oeuvre, the popular song is not the only medium capable of removing an individual from the linear stream of time to redefine his or her identity. In four films that deal with young boys who come of age in the midst of difficult circumstances, Jordan emphasizes the way that dreams, visions, memories, and hallucinations, which are standard fare in gothic literature and film, can become more compelling and credible than reality. In *The Miracle, The Butcher Boy, In Dreams,* and *Breakfast on Pluto,* a focus on characters' dreams and visions reveals the fragility of identity while underscoring the awesome creative power of the imagination.

In these four films, the surreal visions of young male protagonists assume tremendous significance in their coming-of-age experiences. Their dreams depict a familiar world that has become distorted, strange, and terrifying. Visions include a body erupting into flames (*The Miracle*); a nuclear apocalypse and alien invasion, comic-book style (*The Butcher Boy*); an underwater chamber of horrors (*In Dreams*); and a "primal scene" of conception involving a Catholic priest, his housemaid, and a plate of rashers (*Breakfast on Pluto*). In these bizarre scenarios, expressionist devices such as extreme angles and distorted perspective convey a sense of unreality. Although the images are outlandish, they are wholly in keeping with the worlds that the films depict. In other words, Jordan's visionary sequences defamiliarize an already unstable reality. This is an intentional choice on the director's part. For example, Jordan stated that he wanted to turn *Breakfast on Pluto* into "a fairy tale, the fairy tale that [the main character] Patrick manages to create out of his own harsh life" (*Breakfast on Pluto* Home Page).

In all of his films, Jordan uses mise-en-scène to externalize characters' emotional states, a technique borrowed from German Expressionism. Fidelma Farley describes the visual texture of all of Jordan's films in terms of dreams: "[E]motions are conveyed through facial expression and atmospheric locations, resulting in a dream-like feel" (187). Jordan's dreamy expressionism can make it difficult to distinguish between characters' subjective states and objective reality, a conundrum that lies at the heart of the gothic mode.

In *The Miracle, The Butcher Boy, In Dreams,* and *Breakfast on Pluto,* dreaming provokes the uncanny dread inspired by an eerie combination of familiarity and strangeness. More specifically, the uncanny "articulates the presence of a secret at the core of the familiar" (Bronfen 23). Sigmund Freud wrote that the uncanny arises when one reencounters infantile complexes that have been repressed or primitive beliefs that have been surmounted. Freud also observed that the meaning of the word *Unheimlich* (uncanny or unhomelike) coincides with that of its opposite, the *Heimlich,* which denotes something familiar or something secret. Thus, one important aspect of the uncanny is the way that apparent opposites merge into the same thing.

In Jordan's dream films, boys attempt the transition to manhood through rites of passage that involve violence and sexual exploration. Their practices of extraordinary vision, including hallucinations, daydreams, nightmares, and bouts of madness, uncover disturbingly familiar secrets about themselves, their families, and their cultures.

The dreams and visions of Jimmy (Niall Byrne), Francie (Eamonn Owens), Vivian (Robert Downey Jr.), and Patrick (Cillian Murphy) are associated with their sexual awakening, with home and family, and, most important, with their mothers. This is not especially surprising, since the uncanny is "bound up with generative, creative uncertainties about sexual identity" (Royle 42). The uncanny often is linked to the maternal body, whose womb represents the original space of home, a location that is both familiar and strange.

Kaja Silverman writes, "[A]t the heart of the woman's otherness there remains something strangely familiar, something which impinges dangerously upon male subjectivity" (17). The "something" that impinges upon the young dreamers in these films is the fact that they are like their mothers; their gender and sexual identities do not conform to the oppositional categories of masculine and feminine, male and female. Their daily lives are nightmarishly violent, yet their most scandalous secret seems to be that their mothers are more closely intertwined with their psychic and sexual desires than they can safely acknowledge.

Jordan's engagement with the mother as a source of social and psychic disturbance parallels a number of contemporary Irish films that deal with disruptive maternal figures. These films, which include *Hush-a-Bye Baby* (dir. Margo Harkin; 1990), *December Bride* (dir. Thaddeus O'Sullivan; 1990), and *The Snapper* (dir. Stephen Frears; 1993), have been described as "charged 'family romances' [that] operate politically, as alternative national narratives to the official discourses of faith and fatherland" (Gibbons, "On the Beach" 13). They tend to treat paternity as incidental, as they depict young women who must come to terms with the cultural expectations that surround maternity. Jordan's films similarly connect sexual awakening to home and to mother figures, although his films differ from this group because they focus on young male protagonists.

The dreams in these films express secret terrors that emanate not only from maternal figures but also from home, the idealized cultural institution with which mothers are associated. *The Miracle, The Butcher Boy,* and *Breakfast on Pluto* deal with boys growing up in Ireland in the 1960s and 1970s, the era in which Eamon de Valera's strict Catholic ideal of home and family began to dissipate, due in part to the internationalization of Irish culture through radio and television. These boys experience what can only be described as a schizophrenic surrealism produced when Old Ireland collides with postwar geopolitics and popular culture. These seemingly external changes are felt at the intimate level of the family unit, which seems to break apart with the emotional force of a nuclear explosion. *In Dreams* is set in the United States during a similar period, from the 1960s to the 1990s. The film examines changing family and social dynamics and especially the overreach of American postwar social engineering. In the film's prologue, set in the 1960s, the fictional town of Northfield, Massachusetts, is flooded to make way for a recreational lake in a parody of the American agrarian ideal. The fact that social engineering affects physical geography and psychic landscapes becomes evident through the character of Vivian Thompson, an abandoned boy who is rescued from his Northfield home after it has been submerged and who endures unspeakable horrors during his treatment at Stapleton psychiatric hospital.

In these films, Jordan's visual style draws on influences as disparate as fairy tales, the *aisling* (dream vision) poem of the Irish bards, Catholic iconography, Classical Hollywood cinema, and glitter rock. His images possess a heightened degree of theatricality reminiscent of the work of the British director Michael Powell. Jordan moves away from the stagy Technicolor dreamscapes on display in Powell's *Black Narcissus* (1947) and *The Red Shoes* (1948), as well as in Jordan's own *The Company of Wolves,* and toward a style that blends realism and expressionism and evokes Powell's later work.

Powell's classic psychological horror film *Peeping Tom* epitomizes the delicate balance between realism and expressionism that Jordan adopts in his dream films. *Peeping Tom* confounds the distinction between fantasy and reality by showing that dreams and visions migrate from the imagination to the film medium and into reality. In Powell's film, the serial killer Mark Lewis's childhood traumas are documented on film: his repressed memories exist as cinema. Grainy, black-and-white home movies shot with a handheld camera reveal that Mark's father, Dr. Lewis, tortured his young son and recorded it under the auspices of scientific research. Events such as the death of Mark's mother are presented in this visual language of documentary realism, but they signify the nightmares that haunt Mark in his adult life.

Peeping Tom is important to Jordan's dream films for several reasons. First, like Jordan's films, it features a young male protagonist whose troubled family dynamics underlie antisocial and violent behavior. Second, Powell's approach merges the gothic interest in depicting a character's distorted perspective with an ironic self-consciousness that regards the cinema as the medium ideally suited to presenting distorted perspectives *as* reality. Powell's film has exerted a tremendous influence over thrillers and horror films throughout the late twentieth century. As J. P. Telotte notes, the subgenre of the reflexive horror film that was produced in the wake of Powell's *Peeping Tom* forces the audience to see "how consistently our perceptions and our understanding of the world around us fall short of their potential, most often because we are conditioned by our experience and culture to see less and less, to dismiss from our image contents those visions for which we might not be able to account" (122).

Many horror films, mysteries, and psychological thrillers since the 1960s have used dream states of one kind or another to call reality into question, including *Altered States* (dir. Ken Russell; 1980), *Jacob's Ladder* (dir. Adrian Lyne; 1990); *Living in Oblivion* (dir. Tom DiCillo; 1994); *Twelve Monkeys* (dir. Terry Gilliam; 1995); *The Cell* (dir. Tarsem Singh; 2000), *Vanilla Sky* (dir. Cameron Crowe; 2001), and *Waking Life* (dir. Richard Linklater; 2001). Perhaps the most influential horror film to do so is Wes Craven's *A Nightmare on Elm Street* (1984), in which a serial killer stalks his victims in their dreams. "In the world of *Nightmare*," writes Mark Edmundson, "it's only when you fall asleep that you see life for what it is" (55). Because the most egregious acts of failed vision are attributed to adults, Craven's critique delivers a "ferocious . . . indictment of the society that parents are leaving to their children" (Edmundson 56).

Like *Peeping Tom* and *Nightmare on Elm Street,* Jordan's dream films explore children's experiences of horror and indict the families and cultures that are responsible for those terrors. Unlike these two directors, Jordan places his dreamers at the center of stories that borrow from several genres, including the picaresque, the thriller, the fairy tale, and the horror film. Like most Jordan films, the dream films explore the desire to bury a troubling past that refuses to stay dead and imply, as gothic novels and films always do, that it is impossible to escape from the nightmare of history. In these films, however, Jordan relocates the gothic fascination with repressed trauma to the surreal visual landscape of postmodern culture, where images readily assume the status of reality.

The Miracle, based on Jordan's original screenplay, opens with a saxophone rendition of "Stardust" playing over the credits. The song's "purple dusk of twilight time" introduces themes of returning to the past and of rediscovering lost love. Its lyrics suggest a suspension in time and a return to an earlier era, two ideas that pervade the look and feel of the film.

The film expresses the nostalgia associated with returning home on several levels. Foremost among them is Jordan's return to Ireland after

High Spirits and *We're No Angels*, which critics considered "Hollywood-financed setbacks" (Schruers). At the time of its release, Irish film critics in particular hailed *The Miracle* as Jordan's homecoming. They referred to the film as a home movie because of its setting in Bray, where Jordan lived at the time; its intimate scale; and its source material in Jordan's short stories (Dwyer; O'Dea; O'Donnell; Staunton).

Although he touts the film's Irish origins, the *Irish Times* critic Michael Dwyer aptly notes that Jordan and Philippe Rousselot, the director of photography, worked hard to establish a sense of the location's foreignness. With Rousselot's "shimmering images," Dwyer writes, Bray "takes on an exotic Mediterranean atmosphere" ("Summertime" 10). The town was completely made over for the shoot, underscoring the way the film blends strangeness and familiarity. "The film-makers transformed Bray's seafront with pink railings along the [promenade], fairy lights, and new facades for cafes, hotels and amusement arcades. The tourist season commenced early with a protracted stay by Fossetts Circus and a carnival" (Flynn 144).

The film's beach setting, presented through Rousselot's filmy images, emphasizes the suspension of normal social rules in pursuit of pleasure. At the beach, everyone seems to be on vacation. Jordan has described the location as a place where reality can easily be eclipsed by fantasy: the seaside town is "that shifting sandy place where the logic of dreams invades the logic of the everyday" (qtd. in O'Dea).

This coming-of-age story focuses on Jimmy, a bored young upstart who combs the beach on a daily basis with his equally precocious friend Rose (Lorraine Pilkington). Together, they make up elaborate stories about the people they encounter. At night, the motherless Jimmy plays the saxophone with his father's middle-aged dance band, but he soon tires of this activity and gets a job with the circus, accompanying the muscular female contortionist. In keeping with Jimmy's snarky and sometimes snarly adolescent rebelliousness, even the contortionist's choice of music reflects the fact that Jimmy is desperately waiting for something exciting to happen. He plays "Quando Quando?" for her, a title that translates as "when when?"

Jimmy's interest is piqued by a beautiful and intriguing stranger who strolls along the beach. When Jimmy follows her by train to Dublin, he learns that she is Renee Baker (Beverly D'Angelo), an American actress performing in a stage revival of the film *Destry Rides Again* at the Olympia Theatre. Jimmy watches her perform again and again, visits her in her dressing room, and falls in love with her, despite the fact that she deflects his advances as often as she invites them. His father Sam forbids him from seeing her.

Visual clues might unlock the mystery of Renee's behavior, but Jimmy ignores them. Playing the doomed Frenchy, Renee's white costume becomes streaked with fake blood across her abdomen during her death scene, suggesting mature sexuality and maternity. Only later, when Jimmy invites Renee home and rummages through her handbag, does he acquire information that explains the obstacles to their romance. He finds a photograph of Sam and Renee and realizes that Renee is his mother. In a gender reversal that casts Penelope as the wanderer instead of her husband Odysseus, Renee has returned to a son who thought she was dead. Sam has fabricated the story of her death, probably to keep her from ever coming back.

The film's dream sequences focus on Jimmy's incestuous desire for Renee. They offer only slightly distorted versions of his everyday reality, borrowing elements from Jimmy's life, such as the circus animals, to create a sense of parallelism and uncanny duplication similar to that in *The Company of Wolves*. To Jordan, *The Miracle* is concerned with "making things unreal, other than they are. . . . The whole thing is very dreamlike and I've added to that by photographing the dreams more really than the reality" (qtd. in O'Dea).

Jimmy's dreams defamiliarize his routine experiences and introduce oedipal dynamics. After Sam forbids Jimmy from seeing Renee, Jimmy dreams of his father's photograph burning, then of his father's body in flames. Jimmy sees himself as the circus ringmaster, spinning Renee wildly on the rope. Later, he dreams that Sam and Renee are elephant trainers. These vignettes blend seamlessly with scenes of Jimmy's waking life; they are short, and they depict the same colorful carnival setting, complete with costumes, characters, and animals. The only difference is that, in Jimmy's dreams, the oedipal struggle over Renee is conveyed through the slightly sinister and absurd visual rhetoric of performance. In his waking life, Jimmy and Sam eventually come to blows.

Dreams are not the only form of alternative vision depicted in *The Miracle*. Other modes of seeing are manifested in the fictions Jimmy and

Rose concoct as they prowl the promenade; in musical performances by Jimmy, Sam, and Renee; and in Renee's theatrical production.

One crucial scene offers a powerful example of the practices of vision that Jimmy's postmodern society of the spectacle demands. In this scene, normal optics become so distorted as to be useless; in their place, cinematic vision supplies meaning. After a stroll on the promenade, Jimmy and Renee enter a fun-house hall of mirrors. Jimmy approaches Renee romantically, and she rejects him; at that moment, Sam looms at the edge of the frame. The scene re-creates iconic moments from Orson Welles's *The Lady from Shanghai* (1948) and *Citizen Kane,* drawing on the codes of film noir and film history to articulate Jimmy's emotional turbulence and to hint at the existence of a duplicitous femme fatale.

Equally important, the visual distortion of the mirrors is precisely attuned to the narrative conflict. The way the mirrors multiply Jimmy's and Renee's images offers a metaphor for their relationship. Jimmy is a replica of Renee, a mirror image that reflects similarities as well as differences (notably, age and gender). The hall of mirrors suggests the

The Miracle. A hall of mirrors distorts and reveals the relationship between mother and son. Courtesy of Photofest.

way that Jimmy's sexual desire is confounded; his desire for difference is combined with his equally powerful yearning for someone who is just like him.

The hall of mirrors scene enacts the slippage between images and reality. To Jimmy, Renee is his American Lady from Shanghai, a mysterious, powerful woman from an exotic place. The same idea is presented during a performance where Jimmy and Renee act out a romance but uncover real sexual tension between them. Jimmy accompanies Renee on the piano after she is called upon to sing "Stardust" at a post-*Destry* party. He assumes the posture of the adoring lover as Renee slowly makes her way across the stage to his piano bench. To highlight the physical intimacy between Jimmy and Renee, Rousselot uses a circling camera, two-shots, and close-ups.

As the film progresses, performances, like dreams, become more and more difficult to distinguish from reality. At the Olympia Theatre where Renee performs, Jordan's compositions evoke a layered reality in which every character plays roles. In one scene, Renee seamlessly moves from a whispered discussion backstage with her son and would-be lover to a rousing performance of the song "Tell the Boys in the Backroom" for her theater audience. In another, Jimmy watches his father, who is seated in the audience at the Olympia. Believing Sam to be his rival for Renee's affection, Jimmy monitors interactions between Sam and Renee more closely than he watches the stage performance.

In another motif that connects performances and dreams as alternative forms of vision, Jimmy falls asleep in two theatrical spaces: the Olympia Theatre (where he has the elephant-trainer dream) and the church in Bray. In the latter scene, he seeks solace in the church after a night spent on the beach with Renee. The critic Michael Dwyer praises Jordan's somewhat ambiguous or "delicate approach" to the beach scene ("Summertime" 10). However, by cutting away from the beach to shots of intertwined legs dancing to Sam's music and then to a scene where Rose seduces the lion tamer, Jordan metonymically suggests a sexual encounter between Jimmy and Renee. In the church the next morning, Jimmy falls asleep, but he does not dream. At this point, his waking existence has become the dream or, possibly, a nightmare. When he awakens, his dreams have invaded reality. The elephant from the circus, and from his dreams, stands in the doorway of the church.

Jimmy's secret desire has assumed the status of reality, unloosed like the elephant that Rose has freed. Renee, as a mother, is the "invisible or secret or absent center of forbidden desire to which [gothic] terror always, ultimately, returns" (Morris 305). Absence and secrecy define Renee from the outset: she wears sunglasses, prompting Jimmy and Rose to describe her as a woman who "wants to hide." Before Jimmy knows Renee's name, he discovers the poster for *Destry* and exclaims, without any irony at all, "That's her secret: she's famous!"

The most dreadful secret involving Renee is that she may be desirable to Jimmy because they are alike. During his courtship of her, Jimmy notices certain similarities but interprets them as grounds for pursuing romance rather than seeing them as family resemblances. Like Jimmy, Renee is a performer; like him, her favorite color is blue; and, as Jimmy has done, she tells Sam off with the American saying "it's a free country." As the hall of mirrors suggests, Jimmy and Renee are doubles, a troubling prospect for either a romantic or a filial relationship.

Ultimately, Jimmy does not retreat in the face of these socially unauthorized desires, just as Rose does not retreat from her carefully planned adventure. At the film's conclusion, Rose stages "The Circus Animals' Desertion" (a well-known W. B. Yeats poem) by opening the cages and freeing the animals. Although this only temporarily unleashes libidinal energies, Jimmy takes advantage of this suspension of social rules. He introduces the elderly man and woman who have passed by one another for years on the boardwalk without acknowledging one another. At the end of the film, Jimmy returns "home" to the promenade with Rose, where they recapitulate their recent experiences in thinly disguised third-person narratives. Having temporarily lost his equilibrium, Jimmy reclaims himself in the process of generating a new story.

The Miracle reveals Jimmy's inability to see the "homey" attractions of Bray, including a potential romance with Rose. His desire for Renee is a craving for the exotic, foreign other. That yearning for a mysterious other is partly motivated by his dissatisfaction with an Irish culture mired in the past, as represented by Sam, with his musty band's derivative Aloha shirts and soggy sentimentality. Ironically, however, while Jimmy's desire seems to propel him outward, he ultimately returns to his origins, to someone as uncannily close as his own mother.

In *The Butcher Boy*, adapted from Patrick McCabe's 1993 novel,

Neil Jordan gives voice to the disturbed imagination of a boy growing up in Ireland in the early 1960s, at the intersection of Irish modernization and cold-war catastrophe. Whereas *The Miracle*'s Jimmy and Rose are inveterate storytellers who swap fables, Francie Brady addresses the audience directly. His jaunty first-person narration is delivered by an adult Francie some "twenty or thirty or forty years" after the events depicted. This fact, along with Francie's intermittent mention of his alter ego, Algernon Carruthers, emphasizes this character's split psyche and the self-conscious irony with which he represents himself.

Francie's everyday reality is gothically dark. Although he grows up in a small, parochial, Irish town, he is a product of the global atomic age, a fact made clear through constant references to radio and television broadcasts, to Communism, to nuclear weapons, and to the Cuban Missile Crisis. His alcoholic father Benny (Stephen Rea) and his mentally ill mother Annie (Aisling O'Sullivan) fight constantly, so he immerses himself in role-playing games with his best friend, Joe Purcell (Alan Boyle). In their games, they assume the identities of Geronimo, Sitting Bull, Al Capone, and the Fugitive. Together, he and Joe terrorize the bookish Philip Nugent (Andrew Fullerton), son of the town's high-minded and high-handed Mrs. Nugent (Fiona Shaw). The middle-class Nugents are recently returned from England, and they represent everything the poor, back-alley Bradys are not. For one thing, the Bradys are never quite at home in their homeland.

Early on, the film establishes a pattern of exile and return that suggests Francie's homelessness and, more specifically, his inability to establish any place for himself. During a vicious parental argument, Francie runs away to Dublin, returning a few days later to find that his mother has killed herself. Blaming Francie, Benny sends his son to a Catholic boys' home. Francie's institutionalization represents a vicious family cycle, because Benny and Francie's Uncle Alo were raised in just such a "home." The fact that Benny blames his problems on being raised in an abusive institution has no bearing on his willingness to send Francie away. These events introduce a cyclical pattern that dominates the film's structure: Francie leaves his small town, attempts to return home, and finds that conditions there have deteriorated. Like Rosaleen in *The Company of Wolves,* Francie learns that no place is home.

On the surface, the talkative and exuberant Francie seems to feel at home everywhere. As his creative reenactment of comic-book, film, and television scenarios suggests, the highly impressionable boy absorbs everything he sees and hears. In Dublin, he hunkers down in the front row of a movie theater to take in *The Brain from Planet Arous* (dir. Nathan Juran; 1957). Significantly, the images of space aliens he sees there will later appear in a dream about the destruction of his hometown. There, Francie merges the cinema's aliens with his culture's fear of Communist aliens.

Not only does he absorb every image he sees, he is also a consummate performer. Francie seems to inhabit the stories he sees and hears. After Father Sullivan (Milo O'Shea) delivers a sermon about the children who witnessed the visitation of the Blessed Virgin Mary at Fatima, Francie experiences his own visions of the Virgin (Sinead O'Connor) as a glowing two-dimensional picture superimposed on the bog. His visions bring him to the attention of the same Father Sullivan, a pedophile whom Francie dubs "Father Tiddly."

Blowing the whistle on Tiddly secures Francie's release from the Catholic home, and he is sent home to Benny. But, inevitably, things

The Butcher Boy. Francie's movie vision.
Courtesy of Photofest.

are not the same. Joe has become friends with Philip, and Francie must assume the roles of father and mother to take care of his ailing father. He dons an apron as an apprentice to Leddy the butcher and wears his mother's apron to do housework. After Benny dies and his decomposing corpse is discovered, the town authorities institutionalize Francie yet again, this time committing him to the mental hospital that at one time housed his mother, instigating another family cycle involving institutionalization.

Francie escapes from the hospital and once again returns home, where two events push him beyond the breaking point. On a visit to the seaside resort of Bundoran, where his parents had honeymooned, he learns that the oft repeated stories of the Bradys' happy times there are nothing but lies. He visits Joe at boarding school, breaking into the dormitory in the middle of the night, but Joe publicly repudiates him. Having lost all emotional grounding, Francie retraces his steps. He returns to the village and brutally murders Mrs. Nugent, the woman he blames for all his troubles. The murder scene at the Nugent home becomes a tableaux condensing Irish images of home that includes Mrs. Nugent (the "good mother"), a statue of the Virgin Mary, and a comfortably appointed middle-class living room. The confluence of maternal figures and domestic space underscores Francie's lack of access to the comforts of home.

Francie's murder of Mrs. Nugent is carried out against a backdrop of mass hysteria, which suggests that social as well as psychological factors have contributed to Francie's madness. His act of violence takes place at the culmination of the tense standoff between the United States and the Soviet Union over nuclear missiles in Cuba. As Francie dispatches Mrs. Nugent by shooting her and butchering her corpse, the townspeople await a visitation from the Blessed Virgin, who has announced that she will appear on the dot of six. In a scene that presents the Sublime as rapturous terror, the townspeople mistake the horrified screams of the first witness to Francie's handiwork for someone's ecstatic response to the Virgin. The entire town's population converges on the Nugent home, which Francie has desecrated. The hysterical search for Francie circles back to the Brady home, which Francie, in keeping with the apocalyptic tone of the entire sequence, has set on fire. Rescued, and once again institutionalized, Francie's voiceover moves the viewer decades forward in time as he narrates the film's epilogue. He is released from the mental institution as a middle-aged man and indulges in one last conversation with the Blessed Virgin.

To convey Francie's subjective reality, Jordan relies on subtle and blatant expressionist techniques: strange as Francie's dreams and visions are, his reality is sometimes equally surreal. The film alternates among the Dickensian gray exteriors of the town center, the desolate bog of the Catholic boys' home, and the Technicolor fantasy world of the Lone Ranger, Al Capone, and Geronimo, that latter of which is associated with the lush green Irish countryside. Exterior scenes emphasize the cool tones of the small town's forbidding gray structures, which are echoed in Francie's omnipresent gray tweed suit. Using canted angles and deep shadows, Jordan and the director of photography, Adrian Biddle, call attention to traditional gothic settings, such as the dank alley where the Bradys live, the stony buildings of the town square, and the imposing grandeur of the orphanage. By contrast, when Francie and Joe roam the countryside, meeting at their home away from home near the river, saturated reds and greens infuse the color palette, along with the pristine blue of a beautiful lake nearby.

Jordan's visual balancing act subtly suggests the distorted character of Francie's reality, which juxtaposes comic-book images, television shows, and larger-than-life villains such as Geronimo and the Communists. That delicacy extends to the actors' performances as well, as Ryan Deussing has noted: "Jordan's direction allows his actors a moderate degree of realism so they don't all come across as mere puppets of Francie's dementia. It's a layered effect: what Francie perceives and doesn't perceive are both visible to us. We live within his insanity without being deluded by it" (118).

The one exception to this subtlety occurs during Francie's drug-induced dream, which takes place when he is hospitalized after his father's death. In this dream, Francie's hopes and fears collide in an eerie re-creation of a world that is slightly out of proportion and seriously out of whack. As Francie awakens in the woods near the lake, Joe's head abruptly appears in the foreground as the strains of Frank Sinatra's "Where Are You?" play on the soundtrack. The boys' reunion is interrupted when a mushroom cloud obliterates the sylvan mountainside and lays waste to the town. The boys pick through the smoking rubble, which is strewn with the corpses of pigs instead of people. (The pig, a national symbol of Ireland, provides an additional layer of significance throughout the film: Mrs. Nugent calls the Brady family pigs, and Francie works as a butcher, which, in turn, links him to his mother's favorite song and the film's title. The Bay of Pigs debacle in Cuba is also relevant to the nuclear standoff depicted in the film.) An alien priest on horseback—a figure that represents a collage of television and film images Francie has seen—seems to be responsible for the destruction.

This instant apocalypse depicts the end of history, leaving Francie and Joe to begin the world anew. Francie's dream obliterates the world of his small town and takes realist representation—including stereotyped images of Irish pastoralism—with it. Francie imagines a "postmodern nuclear sublime" that "gestures toward a world [whose] symbolic forms are exhausted: reality becomes a dream, realist representations a nightmare" (Mishra 157). The destruction Francie envisions is tangibly linked to patriarchal power. In an early scene, Benny beats Francie in front of a television set that depicts a mushroom cloud. But Francie's visions

The Butcher Boy. Another kind of vision: Francie's apocalyptic dream reunites him with Joe (Alan Boyle). Courtesy of Photofest.

of phallo-nuclear power pale in comparison to the destructive forces unleashed when he confronts the maternal principle within Irish culture and within his own psyche.

Francie's fantasies are often linked to maternal figures, including Annie Brady, Mrs. Nugent, the Blessed Virgin Mary, and the women of the town who gossip at the grocery store. These women seem to offer a respite from the overt and sadistic violence associated with male figures on the local scene and the global stage. But women's violence proves to be equally destructive. Offering a sharp contrast to the outward orientation of male violence, women's violence is directed inward, as exemplified by Annie Brady's suicide.

Annie's madness is the direct result of her victimization by her husband and her culture. Her manic moments are vicious parodies of the social roles that Irish women were accorded in the mid-twentieth century: homemakers and mothers. The Irish constitution of 1937 designated the woman's place as the home, and legal restrictions prohibited married women from holding civil-service jobs (these remained on the books into the 1970s). In a darkly hilarious scene, Annie returns home from the mental institution and goes on a baking frenzy for Uncle Alo's visit, filling the tiny Brady house with cakes and buns, desperate but unable to fill the emotional black hole that gnaws at her.

Food, kitchens, aprons, and music connect Francie and his mother. Francie's signature tune is the Bobby Darin recording of "Mack the Knife," a song about a charismatic killer. Annie's is "The Butcher Boy," a song whose title resonates with the weapon-wielding "Mack the Knife" but whose sensibility is completely different. Annie's is a lament for a woman's lost maidenhood. She listens to it repeatedly, and Francie begins to identify her with the song. When Francie hears the song, he and Joe twirl each other around joyfully, mimicking dancers in a pub. Francie inherits his mother's penchant for romance and nostalgia, investing those feelings in his relationship with Joe and attempting to re-create their youthful antics every time he returns home. But Annie's maternal legacy is an emotional version of Baudrillard's hyperreality: she imbues in Francie a misplaced nostalgia for a romance that never existed, as the boy learns on his trip to Bundoran.

Mrs. Nugent's aggressiveness presents a sharp contrast to Annie's distracted gentility. Sharing the name of a heroine from a nationalist song (Gracie Nugent), Mrs. Nugent invariably dresses in green. Yet she uses the Irish national symbol of the pig to disparage the Bradys; her assertive Irishness is synonymous with a British colonialist view of the Irish as backward and uncultured.

Francie internalizes Mrs. Nugent's vision of the Bradys and transforms her disdain into intense self-hatred. He refers to himself as a pig, snorts like a pig, and tries to collect a pig toll tax. But he also externalizes his anger, accusing the Nugents of being pigs in the scene where he breaks into their house and destroys the elegant cakes Mrs. Nugent has made in a bright, modern kitchen. The sumptuous baked goods and gleaming counters of the Nugent home—not to mention their working television—represent the polar opposite of the Brady home, with Annie's cramped kitchen and precariously balanced stacks of butterfly buns. Francie attacks the Nugent home itself, defecating in the living room and scrawling "pig" in lipstick across photographs, the television, and the walls (which seems to reference the killing frenzies of Charles Manson's "family" in 1969). In his ultimate act of violence in the film's climax, Francie destroys the "good mother" and besmirches the middle-class home; the two are inseparable in his mind and in the Irish national imaginary.

Francie's visions of the Blessed Virgin, the revered maternal symbol of Catholicism, offer an alternative to the images of mothering associated with Annie and Mrs. Nugent. His encounters with Our Lady represent another form of alternative vision: that of the faithful. Although the Virgin apparitions initially seem motivated by his desire for special privileges or for an early discharge from the boys' home, Francie's meetings with the Blessed Virgin are always real to him. During her second visit, he drops to his knees on the bog as an animated two-dimensional portrait of Our Lady shimmers in the sky. When he gazes upon her in awe, the composition is uncannily similar to the arrangement of the fame during Francie's visit to the movie theater in Dublin. A rabid consumer of postmodern image culture, Francie is equally moved by visions of the Virgin and *The Brain from Planet Arous*.

Despite Francie's faith, the Virgin seems as distant and mired in denial as Annie. She doesn't understand Francie's concerns over losing Joe's friendship. Later she appears inside the shattered television set that an enraged Benny has kicked to pieces, and she encourages Francie to visit Bundoran. There he discovers unpleasant truths about his parents and loses Joe once and for all. Her companionship thus brings Francie grief rather than glory: Father Tiddly uses Francie's visions as a pretext for molestation, and when Francie mentions his relationship with the Blessed Virgin to his doctors, they prescribe electroshock therapy.

Repeatedly disappointed by his mothers, Francie nevertheless attempts to return home again and again. An important prop symbolizes the impossibility of his quest: a traditional Irish cottage that he purchases for his mother when he is in Dublin. The souvenir appears many times throughout the film: when visible within the Brady home, it creates an ironic *mise en abyme,* calling attention to the un-homeyness of Francie's environment.

Like the mushroom clouds on television, the traditional cottage represents an uncanny object—familiar and strange at the same time—and one that is specific to Irish culture. It represents an ideal Ireland that never actually existed, which is highlighted by the contrast between the quaint cottage and Francie's real home, the cramped back-alley row house. He wants to give his mother something that can stand in

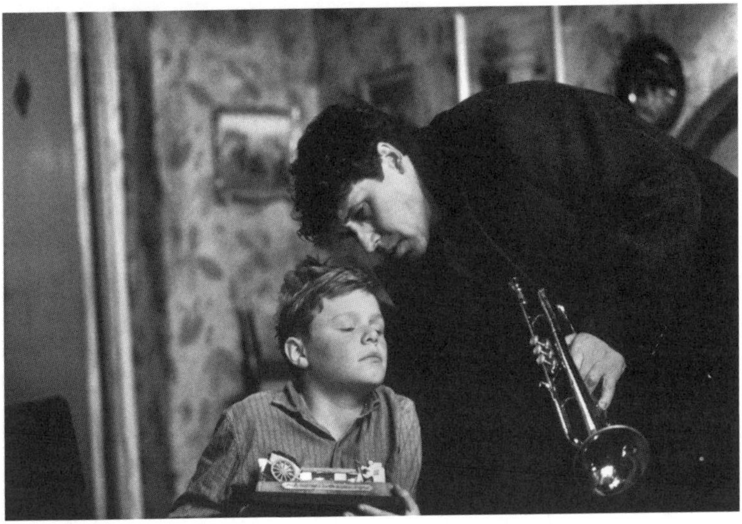

The Butcher Boy. Francie (Eamonn Owens) holds the Irish cottage, an uncanny double of home. Courtesy of Photofest.

for the unhomeyness of the dilapidated house, but Francie is unable to comprehend what home means. He acquires a kitschy image created for tourists; a manufactured object that has little to do with his, or his mother's, experiences of Ireland. Francie has become an alien—a tourist in his own culture, acquiring a manufactured simulacrum that touts the traditional values of hearth and home but bears no relationship to the Irish past that his family has lived through.

When he renews his search for home in Bundoran, he carries the cottage with him. When he discovers that his parents were never happy together, Francie must relinquish the fictional story of his origins. "He wanted to know he came out of love, so when [the innkeeper] says that to him [that Benny was drunk and mistreated Annie during the honeymoon], it really does destroy his last connection with reality" (Jordan qtd. in Sheehy, "*Butcher*" 15).

For Francie, the secret at the heart of the familiar is that his parents' union contained nothing of the romance Annie craved. Francie's cultural and personal prehistories turn out to be filled with the pain and degradation that he shared with his mother as he was growing up. No longer able to manufacture a simulacrum—an unreal nostalgic past into which he can project happiness—he gives up his search for home and severs his connection with reality.

Francie's murder and dismemberment of Mrs. Nugent at the precise moment that the town awaits the Virgin suggests a desire to violate the maternal principle itself. Francie relocates the apocalyptic destruction of the world into maternal, domestic space, a site of security and stability that Francie has never had access to. No mother figure has provided Francie with a literal or figurative home. Because the powerful feminine principle resonates within Irish nationalism, in figures such as Mother Ireland, and within Catholicism, through the Virgin Mary, destroying the mother is also an act of aggression toward Irish Catholic culture itself. That fact is made evident when Francie returns to his parents' house. When he sets the Brady house ablaze, he tosses the traditional Irish cottage on the heap to be burned.

Francie's immersion in his culture, not his alienation from it, secures his self-destruction. Francie has been likened to Mark Twain's Huckleberry Finn because Huck and Francie are precocious young boys who critique corrupt social institutions with an often unwitting sense of irony. Huck Finn is the quintessential American antihero: his humble beginnings and street smarts make him a uniquely innocent rebel. An inveterate wanderer, he finds the comforts of home traveling the Mississippi with Jim, a runaway slave.

Unlike Huck, Francie never discovers a place he can call home, despite repeated attempts to find one, to build one, or to purchase one. Huck represents the iconoclastic hero synonymous with American individualism, whereas Francie represents a tragic victim. *The Butcher Boy* draws upon a long history of representations of Ireland as a damaged child, as Richard Haslam and Martin McLoone have pointed out. From the prose of nineteenth-century British travel writers and the illustrations in *Punch* magazine to the lyrics of Sinead O'Connor's "Famine" (1994), Ireland has repeatedly been cast as the "abused child of history" (McLoone, "Abused" 32).

Despite his adulation of violent criminals and masculine cowboys, Francie cannot escape his destiny. He seems fated to play the same role that his mother played: that of the helpless victim. Denying the uncanny familiarity that links him to his powerless mother, Francie responds by "going nuclear," enacting the paternal role of the ender of worlds, killing Mrs. Nugent and burning his own house down. In his apocalyptic dream, he imagines starting anew with Joe, but it will take forty years before Francie can begin again, after his release from another unhomelike institution. His only hope is that, given the seismic shifts in Irish culture during the previous two or three or four decades, the new social landscape might offer him some place that feels like home.

In *The Butcher Boy,* popular films, comics, and television shows provide sources for Francie's visionary experiences. But in Jordan's adaptation of Bari Wood's 1993 novel, *Doll's Eyes,* he returns to the fairy-tale world of *The Company of Wolves.* In *In Dreams,* Jordan weaves narrative and visual elements from "Little Red Riding Hood" and "Sleeping Beauty" through a story that involves the disturbing dreams of Claire Cooper (Annette Bening), an illustrator of children's books (notably, Grimm's fairy tales) who becomes psychically connected to a serial killer, Vivian Thompson. As the lyrics from Roy Orbison's 1963 title song suggest, in their dreams these characters walk together. Claire envisions the coming-of-age traumas that Vivian is unable to repress: his memories invade her art, her dreams, and ultimately, her waking reality.

The release dates of the Orbison song and the Wood novel furnish a temporal frame for the story: the earliest events in Vivian's memory occur sometime in 1965, when the town of Northfield, Massachusetts, was flooded. The present-day events take place during the 1990s. Despite some obvious markers of time and place, including an intertitle card preceding the film that explains the manufactured reservoir, Jordan's fairy-tale-inflected narrative and Darius Khondji's cinematography work against the establishment of concrete time and place.

Khondji captures the relentlessly dark tone of Claire's hallucinatory dreams through images such as blood-red capes, translucent angel wings, and an apple-cider factory where Vivian stashes his prey, and also through mobile point-of-view shots. Khondji, best known for his work on another dark tale of serial killing, David Fincher's *Se7en* (1995), drapes the Massachusetts setting in rich autumn browns and reds, conveying the overripe and sinister atmosphere of the American gothic. In one scene, a mobile camera tracks Claire as she runs through the woods and stumbles upon the police chief, whose sudden appearance raises suspicions that he may have something to do with the recent spate of child abductions. The encounter could have been taken directly from Nathaniel Hawthorne's "Young Goodman Brown."

Vivian's violence always involves water, and Jordan uses drowning as a metaphor for the madness and creativity that Vivian and Claire share. Throughout the film, Claire is swamped by vivid images of Vivian's actions and experiences. The set piece is a scene in which water surges through the rose window of a clapboard house, inundating the young Vivian, who has been chained to the bed by his mother. These apocalyptic images of the deluge signify Vivian's abusive upbringing and his loss of control, yet they also represent a cultural history of denial. The reservoir's calm surface belies the brutality of Vivian's childhood, as well as the violence and denial implicit in the decision to eradicate an entire town.

Through Vivian's possession of Claire, the film examines individual and cultural repression. The concern with repressed knowledge is hinted at in the film's opening moments, which depict Claire's life with her husband Paul (Aidan Quinn), a commercial pilot, and their daughter Rebecca (Katie Sagona). Claire and Rebecca practice the girl's lines for the school production of "Snow White": Rebecca has been cast as the truth-telling mirror. As they walk along the shore, police are dredging the reservoir for the body of a missing girl. When Rebecca asks what they are doing, however, Claire replies, "Nothing." She gives the same reply to Paul when he returns from a trip and asks her about drawings of her grotesque and frightening dreams.

Claire begins to connect her fantasies to the rash of child disappearances, but she awakens to this reality too late to save her own daughter. Claire loses sight of Rebecca at the performance of "Snow White," which takes place outdoors in the woods. Rebecca seems to melt into the forest, amidst dozens of girls wearing identical angel wings. Claire stops several children in her search for Rebecca; but in their gossamer costumes, they all look alike. Another dread-evoking scene depends upon uncanny duplication, this time between mother and daughter. When Rebecca's dead body is raised from the lake—offering an ironic and tragic rejoinder to her question in the opening scene—crosscutting reveals that, at the moment Rebecca's body emerges from the water, a distraught Claire intentionally drives her car into the lake. Close-ups depict Claire and Rebecca's faces breaking the surface of the water simultaneously: Claire heads into the water, reversing the movement of Rebecca's face as it pierces the surface from below as her body is dredged up.

After her attempted suicide, Claire is incarcerated in the same mental institution in which her tormentor had been held years before, a plot point that recalls the pattern of repeated institutionalization in *The Butcher Boy.* These intergenerational parallels suggest that "individual" traumas must be situated within a larger context. Inherited mental instability (if indeed it is inherited) is at least exacerbated by the neglect, corruption, and well-meaning ignorance of social institutions such as the church and the medical-scientific establishment.

The postwar breakdown of the nuclear family and the rise of alternative social institutions are crucial elements in this film, as they are in *The Miracle, The Butcher Boy,* and *Breakfast on Pluto.* Robin Wood has described *In Dreams* as offering "a radical statement about our impossible (so-called) civilization" ("What" xviii). That radical statement assumes the form of a vigorous challenge to the totalizing narratives of family, faith, and even modern science: these institutions are shown to be corrupt, and children are the victims of their corruption. Vivian's violent psychosis has its origins not only in his mother's horrific abuse and abandonment but also in his subsequent commitment to Stapleton Hospital, where he is subjected to the miracles of modern science—water treatments and electroconvulsive therapies—that are associated with the midcentury rise of psychiatry.

Jordan hints at the midcentury locus of Vivian's trauma with popular music. Just as Annie's favorite song in *The Butcher Boy* conjures a prelapsarian Irish past, the musical motif of *In Dreams* is "Don't Sit under the Apple Tree (with Anyone Else but Me)," Glen Miller's World War II hit, recorded in 1942. The song is a wartime lover's lament that not only connects to the film's fairy-tale motif through the apple but also makes reference to the importance of returning home. For Vivian, like Francie Brady, returning home is no longer an option.

Vivian's home, with its drowned bedroom, is a space bearing family secrets of sexual violence, and it must be submerged and forgotten. The underwater bedroom parallels the moldering basement of Stapleton Hospital where the patient files are stored. Late in the film, Claire's psychiatrist visits the basement and uncovers the horrific violations that Vivian underwent as a ward of the medical establishment. It is not clear from the notes whether Vivian was a hopeless monster upon his arrival or became one as a result of his treatment. What is clear is that the damage Vivian sustains as a result of familial abuse is magnified and exacerbated by the misguided attempts of overzealous medical experts, all of whom seem to have forgotten him along with his buried files.

After Claire is hospitalized at Stapleton, she ceases to resist Vivian's mental colonization because she is determined to save Ruby, a young girl Vivian has just kidnapped. Vivian engineers Claire's escape from the hospital by turning her into his uncanny double. He sends her a dream/vision that shows her the escape route Vivian used many years earlier. In a sequence that relies on meticulous crosscutting, Claire and Vivian escape from Stapleton Hospital "together," crawling through ventilation ducts and hitching rides with police officers. They meet in the present day at an overlook near the lake. After Vivian takes her to the apple-cider plant, he reveals his plan to create a new family with Claire and Ruby. He has chosen Claire as his dream-lover (and Ruby's mother) because of her illustrations. Her images of the dark fairy tales of the Brothers Grimm lead him to believe that they share the same gothic vision of the world.

In depicting Claire's psychological breakdown, Jordan and Khondji make the most of the theme of confinement associated with the female gothic, subjecting Claire and Vivian to oppressive physical spaces. Several scenes in Claire and Paul's house are shot from the second-floor landing, an angle that emphasizes the horizontal beams of the first-floor ceiling and the spindles on the staircase. The film's compositional pattern repeatedly captures people inside frames and boxes, notably Vivian's mother and Claire, who appear in almost identical shots. Thus, while Vivian and Claire are doubles in the escape sequence, Claire is also a double of Vivian's mother (whose clothing she wears in an attempt to dominate Vivian).

The breakdown of Claire's marriage and her eventual union with Vivian also is conveyed through spatial metaphors involving confinement. When Claire and her husband Paul kiss, she bites him because she momentarily believes that he is Vivian. After Paul moves into the

In Dreams. Vivian's mother framed in a box.
Courtesy of Photofest.

In Dreams. Portrait of the artist:
Claire (Annette Bening) as the double/mother.
Courtesy of Photofest.

bathroom to nurse his wound, his reflection in a mirror on the bathroom door remains in the scene as he berates Claire. The audience thus sees a split-screen composition. The scene takes the confinement motif a step further. The frames surrounding Claire and Paul emphasize their lack of connection: they do not share the same space, nor do they move logically in relation to one another. By contrast, in the scene of the hospital escape, shots alternate between Claire and Vivian crawling through the same square ventilation duct. Claire and Vivian inhabit the same space at two different points in time.

While individual characters can be contained in boxes and frames, dreams cannot be. Conventional techniques are unable to contain the psychic power unleashed when Vivian and Claire share dreams, a fact that is suggested by the use of morphs to open or close dream sequences. Space appears to bend as the shared images distort the geometry of realism.

These distortions underscore the visions of fairy-tale horror that Claire and Vivian communicate to one another. But they also highlight the fact that both characters—one a graphic artist, the other a violent murderer—see the world differently than the people around them. They share a sense of alienation from and disappointment with the normative institutions of home and family. During his escape from Stapleton, Vivian holds a policeman at gunpoint. When he asks the officer to stop the police car at the Northfield overlook, Vivian tells him that he is home. The absurdity of Vivian's return home is apparent to the officer. Incredulous, he asks, "A lake? You live in a lake?" Vivian shrugs and says, "I used to," before shooting the policeman in the head. The gunshot shatters the glass of the car window and threatens to shatter the film frame itself. Like the calm surface of the lake, the window and the frame are static, reflective surfaces that Vivian threatens to destroy.

After Claire's flight from Stapleton, Jordan again makes use of the silvery, translucent surface of the car window—this time creating an image of merging. When Claire arrives at the overlook, driving the police car, Vivian approaches her. His reflection, slightly distorted by the curve of the window glass, is superimposed on Claire's face, which is visible through the window. The doubled image in the glass confirms Vivian's possession of Claire. This shot represents a culmination of earlier scenes where these characters had been boxed in but occupied separate spaces. The superimposition reveals two people sharing the same frame at the same time; one reflects the other. The conflation of their identities—as Vivian, Claire, and as the mother—is made evident after Claire follows Vivian to the cider plant. Vivian is unable to assume a stable position within the family: sometimes he is the mother, sometimes Claire is the mother, and sometimes Claire becomes Vivian's mother.

Eventually, Ruby escapes to safety, and Vivian chases Claire to the dam at Northfield Lake. After a struggle, Claire falls into the water and is reunited with her dead daughter Rebecca, who invites her to come home. Claire thus meets her death underwater, in Vivian's closest approximation of home. Given the intensity of their psychic connection, it is not surprising that Claire returns from her watery grave to torment Vivian. The film concludes with his entrapment in a prison cell that he shares with his psychic double. Vivian has destroyed Claire and her nuclear family—murdering everyone, including her dog—yet, like Norman Bates in *Psycho,* he cannot control the mother who has found her psychic home within him.

Although he was meant to remain submerged as one of America's dirty secrets, Vivian rises from the drowned room to disrupt a placid middle-class world of denial. Despite her peaceful exterior, Claire's imagination generates disturbing visions that she sublimates by creating artwork. The two characters share dark visions, yet neither one is able to fully understand their power. Vivian remarks upon the inadvisability of trusting dreams, telling Claire: "That's the thing about dreams; they're always right . . . and they're always wrong." Vivian and Claire cannot control their nightmarish scenarios of collective childhood traumas associated with the loss of a traditional family that likely never existed and the ruinous social institutions that have arisen to replace that nostalgic ideal.

Breakfast on Pluto reiterates this emphasis on the family as a social institution that is just as likely to damage its youngest and most vulnerable members as it is to nurture them. The film condenses the sensibilities of *The Crying Game, Mona Lisa,* and *The Butcher Boy* as it traces the brutal but sometimes beautiful coming-of-age experiences of its protagonist, Kitten Braden. Born Patrick, Kitten leaves the small border town of Tyreelin, Ireland, for London in the late 1960s. While he seems to escape from the violence of the Troubles, which has spilled over the border into the South, his primary goal is to find his long-lost but much admired mother, Eily Bergin (Eva Birthistle).

Unlike Jimmy, Francie, and Vivian, whose families implode before their eyes, Patrick's family never existed. As a young boy growing up in the Braden household, he discovers a check from the local priest, Father Bernard (Liam Neeson), and begins to piece together the story of his existence. In school, Patrick writes an essay that describes his fantasy of his origins: it depicts the semi-comical semi-rape of a young Eily by Father Bernard. While the fanciful reenactment, complete with exaggerated slapstick gestures, owes a great deal to Patrick's affection for Hollywood musicals starring Mitzi Gaynor (whom Eily is said to resemble), his narrative offers a more truthful account of the events than Patrick is likely to hear from any eyewitness. The essay—one of many irreverent acts—earns him a harangue from his teacher.

From these humble beginnings as a visionary and a storyteller, Patrick assumes his rightful identity as Kitten, a glamorous figure of indeterminate gender and infinite style, and moves forward in life and literary pursuits. Kitten leaves home, takes to the road with a grubby Irish band, and falls in love with the lead singer, Billy Hatchet (played by an Irish punk musician from the 1970s, Gavin Friday). The boys in the band don't take kindly to Kitten's attempts to glam up the act, and even Billy finally abandons him, having run afoul of the IRA. In fact, Kitten has destroyed the IRA weapons cache that Billy is responsible for: having recently witnessed the horrific accidental death of a childhood friend, Laurence, Kitten throws the guns into a lake.

Kitten moves to London and works as a magician's assistant, a streetwalker, and, eventually, a peep-show performer. With the help of Father Bernard, he eventually locates his mother and his half-brother, who is also named Patrick, but does not reveal his identity to them. When his old friends Irwin and Charlie come to visit, Kitten learns that Irwin has become involved in the IRA's bombing campaign, and Charlie is pregnant. Irwin's subsequent death at the hands of his IRA comrades and Charlie's despondence draw Kitten back to Ireland, where he and Charlie take refuge with Father Bernard. But the residents of the small town begin a campaign of harassment that mirrors the political violence of the IRA: townsfolk burn down the church and rectory, forcing Kitten and Charlie to move back to London to raise the child.

Throughout the film, Kitten creates an identity from the available materials of international youth culture, relying heavily on Hollywood imagery—lovingly parodied by Jordan in the frequent use of soft-focus close-ups of Cillian Murphy—and contemporary glam rock. Kitten depends upon his fantasy life as a means of survival: he dodges the violence of the Troubles but is not lucky enough to emerge unscathed. "Through this insane insistence on seeing the world as a beautiful place," Jordan points out, "[Kitten] never really loses, even when he loses everything" (*Breakfast on Pluto* Home Page). Two of his three closest friends from childhood are killed in inexplicably absurd moments of violence: Laurence, who has Down's Syndrome, mistakes a bomb-detonating robot for his beloved robot costume. Irwin, who is pressed into service by the IRA, is clumsily assassinated by his immature mates because he has informed to protect Charlie.

As was the case with *Michael Collins,* Jordan was aware of certain historical parallels between the events depicted in this film and events taking place at the time of its 2005 release. "The experience that the film represents is really quite instructive for anybody living in these times," he writes. "With all these nasty ideologies telling you what you should be, in a world where you can go into a bar and the bar may explode, how do you make your way in the world?" (*Breakfast on Pluto* Home Page).

As Kitten navigates the ugliness of the Troubles from Tyreelin to London, tracking the movement of the IRA bombing campaign from Northern Ireland to the Irish Republic to the British mainland, Jordan blends horror and comedy. He layers Kitten's already compromised sense of reality with surreal touches. During a romantic dance with a soldier at a bar that resembles the Metro where Fergus meets Dil in *The Crying Game,* Kitten is injured in a bomb attack. After his transvestism is discovered, he is taken in for questioning, accused of planting the bomb, and beaten nearly senseless before he offers a confession. The confession, like the schoolboy essay, is a fantasy that Kitten narrates in the first person. He conjures up an Avengers scenario where he assaults his enemies while wearing black leather and armed only with Chanel No. 5. Oddly enough, the perfume is the only real element of the scene: Kitten has used Chanel No. 5 as a weapon in an earlier scene to blind a john who tried to strangle him.

Kitten's coming-of-age experiences differ in one important way from those of Jimmy, Francie, and Vivian because he embraces femininity and, more specifically, shapes his persona around an imaginary maternal figure. As a youngster, he dons his foster mother's clothing and makeup. He later develops a uniquely ambiguous gender, sometimes wearing wigs and dresses but not always passing as a woman. Like the other young men in Jordan's dream films, Kitten's sense of identity is tied to a troubling maternal figure. Unlike the others, he manages to establish a sense of home and family even in the most dire circumstances: in a dingy trailer that doubles as an IRA weapons dump, or on the somewhat hostile streets of London. In this way, Kitten represents an optimistic deviation from the earlier Jordan narratives in which the fear of feminine engulfment drives boys mad. Kitten is a survivor. When he finally does encounter his mother in London, costuming and lighting make it clear that Kitten is a far more Hollywood-worthy blonde bombshell than his mother ever was.

More clearly than his other dream films, *Breakfast on Pluto* endorses the creative imagination that enables Kitten to survive and implies that fantasies provide him with the tools to remake the world. Kitten insists that immersion in the magic of theater, music, cinema, and television—performances of all kinds—may be a life-saving attribute, regardless of its origins as a tool for staving off emotional deprivation. Whereas Francie and Vivian are punished for their visionary tendencies and turn to murderous violence, Kitten manages the traumas of being a motherless and fatherless child without a home by borrowing, copying, and adapting the imagery of femininity from the world around him, from Ma Braden's wardrobe to Mitzi Gaynor's hairstyle. Kitten's ability to acquire new identities is one way to rise above the irrational violence and narrow sexual mores of the period in which he grows up: it is no accident that the Tyreelin townspeople express their disapproval of the unholy family composed of Father Bernard, Kitten, and Charley by firebombing the rectory.

Finally, it must be noted that Jordan grants Kitten a greater degree of narrative authority than Patrick McCabe extends to this character in the novel. In McCabe's book, Kitten narrates his memoir from a mental institution, hoping to meet with the approval of a handsome doctor. In the film, Kitten's flights of fantasy are not attributed to mental illness. On the contrary, they seem to indicate a healthy, if comically stubborn, talent for constructing desirable images, and images of desire, out of a nightmarish history.

Like *Mona Lisa, Angel,* and *The Crying Game,* Jordan's four coming-of-age films, *The Miracle, The Butcher Boy, In Dreams,* and *Breakfast on Pluto,* speak to masculine anxieties concerning the shifting roles of men and women and the changing notions of gender and sexuality in the postwar era. The American actress Renee chooses her wanderlust and her career over her son and husband. Mrs. Nugent, who presides over the Nugent household, not to mention the small Irish town they live in, becomes the target of Francie's rage. Vivian resents and adores his phallic mother, whereas Claire's art and her independence threaten her family life.

More dramatic than the challenges posed by these characters, however, is Kitten Braden's feminine masculinity, which exemplifies the desire to cast off limiting gender and sexual identities. *Breakfast on Pluto* dramatizes a transitional cultural moment when the window of opportunity for such experimentation opened, yet it tempers what could easily become an unabashed celebration of postmodern fluidity with the bizarre logic of Ireland's severe cultural proscriptions and the grotesque reality of ongoing political violence.

These dream films present the consequences of not taking our nightmares seriously. All four films point to problems within families, but they indict broader communities as well for abusing and neglecting children who are forced to take refuge in their imaginative worlds, for better and for worse. Jordan balances ominous gothic and apocalyptic undertones with an unabashed admiration for the absurdly comical aspects of characters' fabrications, fabulations, and performances. Enacting these vulgar fictions may be the only way to cope with the disintegrating institutions and schizophrenic politics of global postmodernism.

In several other films, Neil Jordan explores a slightly different manifestation of the uncanny in contemporary culture, linking the gothic double to the postmodern obsession with repetition and replication.

Doubles, Remakes, and Repetition: *We're No Angels*, *The End of the Affair*, "Not I," and *The Good Thief*

> You're cursed with remakes, now, because
> it's all they seem to make.
>
> —Neil Jordan

In Neil Jordan's films, characters frequently adopt new personas and construct alter egos, engaging in performances that transform them. In treating identity as a process of becoming someone or something else, Jordan revisits the notion of the double, one of the central preoccupations of the gothic. The gothic double, or Doppelgänger, is the mysterious "other" that inhabits and possesses an individual. The double is a frightening and dangerous evil twin. Two well-known literary works that elaborate the dynamics of this figure are Théophile Gautier's "The Double Knight" (1840) and Robert Louis Stevenson's *The Strange Case of Dr. Jekyll and Mr. Hyde* (1886). The double has a long history in cinema as well, appearing in early films such as *The Student of Prague* (dir. Stellan Rye and Paul Wegener; 1913) and in postmodern horror classics such as *Psycho* and *The Silence of the Lambs*.

Jordan frequently depicts character doubles. Rosaleen and Red, Francie Brady and Algernon Carruthers, Claire Cooper and Vivian

Thompson, and Kitten Braden and Eily Bergin are a few examples of characters who either grapple with their internal divisions or face the frightening prospect of encountering another, slightly different version of themselves in the world. Such doublings and divisions make it difficult to distinguish what is the self from what is not the self. Through these characters, Jordan highlights the instability of identities within postmodern culture.

Neil Jordan articulates the significance of the double for identities and for aesthetic practices in *We're No Angels, The End of the Affair,* "Not I," and *The Good Thief.* The narratives of these films are centrally concerned with doubles: characters assume new identities, pursue mysterious strangers, and grapple with their inner demons. But the films also force viewers to consider the dynamics of duplication on a metatextual level because they are remakes of existing texts. To varying degrees, these films extend the implications of the gothic double to postmodern identities and postmodern art.

The gothic double is thought to have originated in fairy tales. It is a staple of gothic literature and serves as "the classic genre marker of the gothic in film" (Hopkins xi). The double also assumes a prominent position in the discourse of Freudian psychoanalysis, informing not only Freud's theory of the conscious ego and unconscious id but also the concept of the uncanny, which blends the familiar (self) and strange (not self). Freud's belief that the double initially functioned as a defender of the ego but at some point became a menacing harbinger of death, "a vision of terror" (Freud, "Uncanny" 143), underscores its ambiguous character. Freud also linked the double to the repetition-compulsion, the need to repeat traumas in order to master them.

At the most basic level, the double suggests that identities are unstable. But its dynamics are more profound: the double is a division and a multiplication, a fascinating merger of same and different, a distorted mirror image that calls the integrity of the self into question. It defies the logic of sexual difference and heterosexual reproduction by asserting that new identities can be produced through splitting and mimesis. In *We're No Angels, The End of the Affair,* "Not I," and *The Good Thief,* Jordan resituates the gothic double within a postmodern framework where identity becomes a series of imitative performances, and art becomes a matter of borrowing from existing works of art.

In postmodern culture, art and identity are productions that depend upon citation, imitation, and remaking. As John McGowan writes, "[U]nlike the heroic modernist, who created works out of pure imagination, the postmodern artist works with cultural givens, trying to manipulate them in various ways (parody, pastiche, collage, juxtaposition) for various ends" (770). Jordan uses parody and pastiche to explore the way identities are constructed and art is fabricated by working with the "cultural givens" of postmodernity.

Theorists of postmodernism disagree about the political implications of repetition. Fredric Jameson argues that imitation has lost its satirical potential, devolving into pastiche, an apolitical or blank parody. But Linda Hutcheon contends that postmodern repetition can function as parody when it signals "how present representations come from past ones and what ideological consequences derive from both continuity and difference" (93). In contrast to Jameson, Hutcheon argues for the critical potential of postmodern aesthetics.

The debate regarding pastiche and parody is relevant to Jordan's four remakes. Two of the films—*We're No Angels* and *The End of the Affair*—are remakes of Hollywood films that serve as examples of Jameson's pastiche. They explore the figure of the double through characters, plot, and style, but they stop short of exploring the satirical potential of repetition. "Not I" and *The Good Thief*, however, engage in postmodern parody because they self-consciously explore the ideological consequences of imitation, citation, and duplication. "Not I" is a short film based on a Samuel Beckett play that portrays the fragmentation of the individual through a failed monologue, whereas *The Good Thief* is a remake of a French noir classic that questions the notion of the authentic original, whether that be a work of art or an identity. In *The Good Thief*, Jordan moves from the concept of the gothic double, which blurs the relationship between self/other and same/different, to engage with the postmodern simulacrum theorized by Jean Baudrillard. The simulacrum is a copy so far removed from an original that its existence confounds the very idea of an original.

Before proceeding to an analysis of these films, it is important to consider their status as remakes. By definition, a remake is an uncanny double: it is a new version of an already existing text. "Even more so than other forms of narrative," writes Andrew Horton, "the remake announces itself as negotiating . . . the familiar and the new of the familiar 'transformed'" (174). A remake does not eclipse or erase the earlier text but re-creates it *as* an original, turning it into an antecedent. The fact that a remake tends to bring the reference text into sharper focus and attract renewed attention to it helps to explain the commercial appeal of the remake in the age of the DVD, when remaking a film becomes a two-for-one proposition. A case in point is the 2000 DVD release of *The End of the Affair* as a double feature containing Edward Dmytryk's 1955 film and Neil Jordan's 1999 version.

The cultural significance of remakes might be overlooked if they are considered only in light of commercial motives, however. Remakes have been a feature of cinema since its inception but have proliferated in the post-studio Hollywood corporate environment, and they embody several postmodern aesthetic practices. First, they epitomize the practice of manipulating "cultural givens." Second, they challenge the distinction between high art and mass culture. Their very existence questions the value of uniqueness and rejects the notion that any text achieves the status of a definitive work. They also undermine definitive cultural identities. As Lucy Mazdon points out, Hollywood remakes of European films threatened not only the French art cinema but also French national identity: "Hollywood menaced French cultural identity . . . because it epitomized the mass production which was anathema to the defenders of a French tradition of 'great art'" (149).

Paradoxically, remakes secure the notion of cinema as an artistic tradition because emerging filmmakers often develop their craft and establish themselves by engaging with work that has come before. Film remakes "demonstrate that filmmakers . . . learn from, copy from, and expand upon the work of their predecessors, exploring and exploiting their own tradition" (Kolker 37).

In the films where he self-consciously explores and exploits the cinema tradition, Neil Jordan turns to the figure of the double and to the process of doubling. *We're No Angels, The End of the Affair,* "Not I," and *The Good Thief* all point to the increasing difficulty of distinguishing between inner and outer selves, and between the counterfeit and the real thing. In Jordan's postmodern gothic framework, the focus shifts from the figure of the double to doubling as a process, a performative repetition that generates unstable identities and serves as the basis for the citational bent of postmodern art. Jordan moves from postmodern pastiche in his two Hollywood remakes to critical postmodern parody in "Not I" and *The Good Thief.*

Jordan's Hollywood remakes, *We're No Angels* and *The End of the Affair,* deal with men and women who remake and redeem themselves by acknowledging the power of belief. While both films make overt reference to Catholicism, miracles occur because people act on faith in an unknowable universe, not because a specific deity's power is invoked. In *We're No Angels,* two escaped convicts are given a second chance, whereas in *The End of the Affair* a writer must come to terms with the devastating and abrupt end of a wartime love affair.

Both films are examples of postmodern pastiche. Works of pastiche dispense with critique; their retro sensibility celebrates nostalgic familiarity by citing earlier texts rather than using repetition as an opportunity for examining aesthetic, cultural, economic, and ideological shifts.

One reason why a sense of empty repetition emerges from these films may be the fact that they recycle the Hollywood tradition itself. Rather than domesticating an exotic art-cinema tradition, they re-present classical Hollywood narratives. In fact, *We're No Angels,* which was released in 1989, seems to have presaged the vibrant resurgence of the Hollywood-on-Hollywood remake during the 1990s and 2000s, examples of which include *The Nutty Professor* (dir. Tom Shadyac; 1996), *Psycho* (dir. Gus Van Sant; 1998), *Ocean's Eleven* (dir. Steven Soderbergh; 2001), *The Stepford Wives* (dir. Frank Oz; 2004), *Bewitched* (dir. Nora Ephron; 2005), *Mr. and Mrs. Smith* (dir. Doug Liman; 2005), and *Yours, Mine and Ours* (dir. Raja Gosnell; 2005). If remakes themselves are symptomatic of the international dominance of Hollywood films (Mazdon 151), then the Hollywood-on-Hollywood remake is symptomatic of the film industry's increasing corporatization, risk aversion, and self-cannibalization. One consequence of the increasingly corporate nature of the industry has been the devaluation of original screenwriting (a trend brilliantly satirized in Michael Tolkin and Robert Altman's *The Player* [1992]). A reinforcing cycle has taken hold in which Hollywood films and television shows—whose copyrights are owned by studios—are seen as sure bets for a profitable box-office as well as lucrative merchandising receipts.

Jordan's Hollywood-on-Hollywood remakes share a theme of mistaken identity, but the films differ greatly in terms of genre, tone, and style. *We're No Angels* is an absurdist comedy, whereas *The End of the Affair* is a gloomy romantic mystery. Jordan's involvement and investment in the two projects also differed greatly. He served as a director-for-hire on *We're No Angels,* whereas he cowrote and directed *The End of the Affair* because of his admiration for Graham Greene's novel. In fact, his painstaking faithfulness on *The End of the Affair* resulted in a film that can claim to be "truer" to the novel than Dmytryk's film.

The original Hollywood version of *We're No Angels* was based on the French playwright Albert Husson's *La Cuisine des Angles* (renamed *My Three Angels*). Directed by Michael Curtiz, the film starred Peter Ustinov and Humphrey Bogart, in one of his last screen performances. One of only a few Bogart comedies, the offbeat and sentimental *We're No Angels* follows the antics of three convicts who have escaped from the Devil's Island penal colony off the coast of French Guiana. They decide against robbing a naïve middle-class French family that owns a general store. Instead, they put their skills to use saving the family from itself. In an unlikely role, Bogart plays a once-wayward accountant who helps the family preserve their failing business.

Just as the Curtiz film relied on Bogart's star power and yet cast him against type, the remake was tied to a star persona. The project represents an early attempt on the part of Robert De Niro, one of the film's coproducers, to explore comedy, a genre in which he found success a decade later with *Analyze This* (dir. Harold Ramis; 1999) and *Meet the Parents* (dir. Jay Roach; 2000). Paramount hired David Mamet to write the screenplay, and rumors circulated that he refused to allow one word of his script to be changed. The studio asked Neil Jordan to direct the film after the screenplay had been written and after De Niro (Ned) and Sean Penn (Jim) had been cast in the lead roles.

Departing somewhat from the play and the Curtiz film, Mamet and Jordan's film emphasizes the comedy of mistaken identities. Set in the 1930s in the American Northeast, the film depicts two petty criminals, Ned and Jim, who escape from a workhouse-prison in the company of their evil alter ego, Bobby (James Russo). Bobby is a hardened murderer slated for execution; he takes Ned and Jim as near-hostages, improvising a violent escape from the prison just as he is about to die in the electric chair. After leaving the injured Bobby for dead, Jim and Ned wander into a small town near the U.S.–Canada border where they are mistaken for two celebrity priests, Fathers Brown and Reilly, who are expected at the local monastery, which houses the shrine of the Weeping Madonna.

For the duration of the film, the resourceful convicts impersonate the missing priests while planning their getaway, but they are repeatedly thwarted in their attempts to make it across the bridge that separates the two countries. They must elude the warden, outwit the local deputy, and remain convincing to a community of silent monks. A worshipful acolyte (John C. Reilly) hounds Jim for words of wisdom, while Ned becomes involved in a trying romance with Molly (Demi Moore), an embittered prostitute whose young daughter is mute. As Jim becomes more and more enamored of monastery life, Ned finds himself oddly compelled by both the (Weeping) Madonna and the whore.

We're No Angels functions as a palimpsest: it reflects numerous diverse influences. The understated irony of the Curtiz film, the linguistic focus of the Mamet screenplay, De Niro's attempt to develop his comic talents, and Jordan's interest in a narrative of change and redemption are visibly conflicting elements in the film. My characterization of the project as a collection of undigested elements draws upon another definition of pastiche as a hodgepodge of incongruous parts, a meaning that predates Jameson's recruitment of this term to signify postmodernism's tendency toward empty repetition.

Derek Malcolm contends that Jordan's *We're No Angels* is "a terrifying example of what can happen when a talented director goes to Hollywood, is accorded the honor of two major stars, a decent budget and a screenplay from a well-known name, and ends up making a film that simply does not work" (26). Malcolm overstates the case when he uses the term "terrifying," but he correctly diagnoses the film's overall incoherence, which seems to be related to the disparate elements he names. Jordan was aware of the problem, and he felt his status as a hired hand acutely, writing in his production notes: "Directing someone else's script with two actors already in place and a crew . . . leaves the question open of what there is for *moi* to do . . . the thing being how to make the whole thing personal" (NLI Accessions 4761, box 6). One element that Jordan does manage to tease out both narratively and visually is the figure of the gothic double.

We're No Angels develops the theme of the double in a number of ways. The concept of bifurcated identity informs the film's main characters: they are always themselves and someone else at the same time. Throughout the film, Ned and Jim impersonate the missing priests; moments when their own words and ideas threaten to break through the façade and expose them are defused because onlookers cannot see past their priestly personas: the difference between their "true selves" and their performances are repeatedly minimized. Moving beyond this comic device, Jordan intended the characters to evoke a sense of internal division: in production notes, he suggests that De Niro play the role "alternatively mercurial and dark. Get a sense of being possessed by another" (NLI Accessions 4761, box 6). Eventually, even these duplicitous sinners attain states of grace. Ned and Jim's role playing—their embrace of their own doubleness—changes them. Jim chooses to remain behind with the monks, whereas Ned risks his life to save Molly's daughter and finally escapes to Canada with her.

The film externalizes a central question raised by the double—How should we define sameness and difference?—by establishing strict dualisms and then undermining them. The opposition between good and evil is established as the central conflict, since convicted criminals masquerade as cloistered monks. But Jordan debunks that opposition by establishing parallels between the two communities of men. Their similarities are manifested in the film's spatial organization. The prison and the monastery environments are uncannily similar: each one depends on a contrast between height and depth. The prison contains a working mine, yielding a vision of hell that recalls Fritz Lang's *Metropolis* (1926). The space of the monastery also breaks down into high and low spaces, with a steep pulpit overlooking the main hall. Its spiral staircase rhymes with the prison's labyrinthine stairway into the pit. These parallels suggest the similarities between these two environments, paving the way for Jim's ultimate decision to remain at the monastery.

In many ways, the film's focus on character and spatial doubling is overshadowed by the omnipresent theme of the duplicity of language. This might be thought of as another form of doubling, wherein all speech acts carry hidden meanings. Language fails to stabilize identities or meaning. A familiar Mamet motif emerges, where language is understood as an obfuscating medium rather than as a transparent mode of communication. The visiting dignitary Bishop Nogalich and his cynical interpreter (Wallace Shawn) remind viewers of this fact; the bishop's words must be spoken twice, and it soon becomes apparent that not all of them are translated. More generally, Mamet's script underscores the fact that words cannot guarantee meaning. The lines Ned and Jim deliver to the monks are always capable of several interpretations. Jim offers humble platitudes, yet he is taken for a prophet. When he is called upon to deliver a sermon, he pulls a brochure advertising a Colt .32 out of his pocket and reads its message about a fearful encounter with a bear in the woods. To conclude, he offers the ecumenical message that people should believe in whatever comforts them.

In Mamet's screenplay, meaning does not reside in words themselves but emerges in the context of utterances. This point is made abundantly clear just after the film's climax. A shootout takes place on the bridge after Bobby returns and takes Molly's child hostage, using the ceremony during which the Weeping Madonna is carried across the border to make his escape. Molly's daughter falls off the bridge into the river. Ned saves the child by using the Madonna statue, which also has tumbled into the water, as a flotation device—the entire sequence might have come directly from a Fellini film. This trauma yields a miracle: the formerly mute child speaks. With her first words, she identifies Jim and Ned as "convicts." But Father Levesque (Hoyt Axton), the monk who presides over the shrine, hears the word differently. He glares at, then finally forgives, the two "converts." This language game is linked to the concept of the character double. Beyond the comic business of Father Levesque's deliberation over Jim and Ned's status, it becomes clear that language is both out of control and incredibly precise; at this point in the story, the men are both convicts and converts.

In classic instances of Jameson's notion of pastiche as empty repetition, Jordan's film draws upon cinematic references in its setting and plot. As critics have noted, the snowy, rough-and-tumble border town—built from the ground up by the production designer Wolf Kroeger—is reminiscent of Robert Altman's ramshackle outpost of the Presbyterian church in *McCabe and Mrs. Miller* (1971). When Ned and Jim try to catch a ride into town after their escape, a woman drives by and hits a deer, killing it. This piece of business offers a comedic homage to De Niro's role in Michael Cimino's *The Deer Hunter* (1978). These references invoke the American cinema of the 1970s, but they are far too fleeting to offer much in the way of critical commentary and thus seem

We're No Angels. The Weeping Madonna in her element: a waterfall propels her downstream. Courtesy of Photofest.

to operate primarily as inside jokes. These citations cannot function as Hutcheon's postmodern parody because they fail to provide any broader occasion for comparing the remake to the original version of *We're No Angels* or to consider the ideological consequences of continuity and difference within American cinema.

We're No Angels embodies Jameson's concept of pastiche as uncritical repetition as well as the more traditional understanding of pastiche as a collection of incongruous elements. The story is loosely based on the play and the Curtiz film; its style and plot events contain references to other Hollywood films; and the centrality of De Niro's character reflects his particular career goals. The commentary on the insufficiency of language is pure Mamet, whereas Jordan's interests can be gleaned from the focus on characters who are continually remaking themselves. Beyond its narrative emphasis on redemption, the film offers little insight into the implications of repetition or on the relationship between originals and copies. The film vaguely suggests that copies can function as adequate substitutes for the real thing, as Jim and Ned's impersonation of the missing priests has a salubrious effect on the monks and the town in general.

Jordan's second Hollywood remake offers another example of Jameson's pastiche. *The End of the Affair* embodies the notion of repetition without critique—possibly because Jordan was not acquainted with the first film version when he embarked on the project. Like *We're No Angels,* the film explores doubles and mistaken identity. Unlike the convict comedy, however, repetition is structurally embedded in the narrative, which is organized according to two characters' diary entries, as well as the film's time structure, which seamlessly moves between the past and the present.

The End of the Affair is based upon Graham Greene's novel about a love affair that ends abruptly during the London Blitz. It opens with the first-person voiceover account of Maurice Bendrix (Ralph Fiennes), a self-involved writer who wallows in memories of his relationship with Sarah Miles (Julianne Moore), the wife of a British civil servant. Bendrix questions their inexplicable separation and remains obsessed with her years after the affair ends.

The film is among Jordan's most visually evocative works; its gloomy visual style is inextricable from the story of doomed love. Jordan describes the characters as "haunted by emotions they don't fully understand" (*End of the Affair* commentary), and the film critic Hugh Linehan notes trademark Jordan elements of "eroticism, death, and an equivocal sense of the sacred" ("Greene" 15). When the film opens, two years after the affair has ended, Sarah and Bendrix remain in thrall to the feelings they experienced during the war. In this sense, they are doubles of their earlier selves. The cinematography alludes to their fractured identities; rain and fog frequently obscure the sky, lending density to the atmosphere and capturing the actors in silhouette, echoing the dominant visual effect of *Michael Collins.* In *The End of the Affair,* this effect causes the characters to appear as hollowed-out replicas of themselves.

The film has a complex double structure. Sarah and Bendrix each narrate a version of the events from a first-person perspective. The two versions are conveyed through different camera styles: within Bendrix's memories, the camera assumes a distanced posture, whereas Sarah's narration features Steadicam and close-up shots that translate her emotions

The End of the Affair. Ghostly silhouettes are replicas that can't bring the past back to life. Courtesy of Photofest.

with greater immediacy. The value of gaining access to both perspectives, however, is tempered by the fact that the accounts are retrospective, or mediated by time. They are also written accounts, and thus mediated by language. The reality of the past and, perhaps, the present cannot be fixed or made tangible, just as the London cityscape cannot be ascertained through the rain and fog.

The film's fractured time frame includes another form of doubling: the repetition of plot events. Jordan presents the bombing of Bendrix's apartment building during the London Blitz, which marked the end of their affair, two times. The first time, the scene is presented from Bendrix's perspective; much later, it is shown from Sarah's point of view. During the reiteration of the scene from Sarah's point of view, Bendrix reads her diary and learns that Sarah believed him to be dead after the bomb blast. She left his body at the foot of the stairs and went upstairs to pray to God to save his life. After recovering from the shock of the blast, Bendrix climbed the stairs to join her. Believing that her prayers had been answered, Sarah left him and committed herself to a practice of spiritual love that excluded him.

Jordan presents the transparent prose of Sarah's diary as duplicitous rather than straightforward; she writes to God, but Bendrix reads it as though she is writing to him or to a new lover. She addresses her diary to "you," so the voiceover sounds as though she is speaking directly to Bendrix. This blasphemous confusion resonates with a moment when Bendrix writes, "I hate you"; the audience assumes he is addressing the remark to Sarah, but he also is referring to God. Sarah's secretive and intense devotion to God is the reason her husband Henry (Stephen Rea) suspects she is having an affair. He confides in Bendrix. More than two years after his affair with Sarah has ended, and against Henry's wishes, Bendrix hires a private detective, as if he were the cuckolded husband. He wants to know the identity of her current lover, the mysterious double he believes has replaced him. When he discovers that Sarah has not found a mortal replacement, he seeks to rekindle their affair. But Sarah is dying of cancer. In the final scenes of the film, Bendrix and Henry care for her in her last months of life, explicitly manifesting their status as doubles.

Beyond the narrative and cinematography, an important architectural motif furthers the film's emphasis on repetition. Staircases underscore Sarah's spiritual ascent but also reflect the earthly passion she must overcome to achieve a state of grace. The staircase in the Miles home is the location of an erotic encounter that Bendrix remembers in a flashback; that memory converges with the present-day, postwar storyline. The staircase in the Miles home is also a double of the staircase at Bendrix's apartment building, the site of his loss of Sarah.

Repetitions are essential to Jordan's version of *The End of the Affair*. They also pervade the history of both film adaptations of Greene's novel. When Edward Dmytryk worked with Greene on the 1955 film, he planned to re-create precisely the novel's nonchronological structure, weaving together past and present. Against the protestations of Greene and Dmytryk, however, producers at Columbia reorganized the film, believing that temporal slippages would make the film too opaque for the average viewer. The film was released with the events in chronological order (Adamson 87).

Dmytryk himself changed an important element of Greene's story during the process of adaptation. The director eliminated several miracles that are attributed to Sarah as she enters a state of grace after renouncing her passion for Bendrix. (Her touch removes a birthmark from a boy's face, for example.) Shortly after the film's release, Greene put out a new version of the novel in an edited collection from which he, too, had excised the miracles. Greene wrote: "I had been cheating—cheating myself, cheating the reader . . . in a later edition I tried to return to my original intention" (qtd. in Adamson 87).

In attempting to produce a faithful screen version of Greene's novel, Jordan uses the nonchronological structure and incorporates the miracles that appear in Greene's first edition. Oddly enough, Jordan's film exhibits a fidelity to an "original" text that the author himself later repudiated. Jordan's *The End of the Affair* remains faithful to a literary text that might be described as being plagued by its own doubleness: Greene's novel had not, apparently, revealed its true self until after Dmytryk's film was released and Greene rewrote it.

Jordan's modifications were in no way intended to be a self-conscious commentary on the process of remaking. Jordan did not see the Dmytryk film until after he had written the screenplay and had embarked upon the project, nor was he aware of Greene's reissue of the novel until our discussion about it in 2005. Nevertheless, Jordan's film ultimately confounds the differences among original, adaptation, and remake, even though it does not self-consciously consider the implications of continuity and repetition.

In contrast to Jordan's Hollywood remakes, "Not I" and *The Good Thief* self-consciously explore remaking; the issue of repetition appears at the level of plot and style but also informs Jordan's approach to remaking as perhaps the most privileged and perilous form of creativity in postmodern culture. Jordan moves from films that engage in the neutral practice of pastiche to a critical engagement with repetition as a cultural and aesthetic practice.

Perhaps the most unusual film in Jordan's oeuvre, "Not I" is a fourteen-minute stream-of-consciousness monologue written by Samuel Beckett. Jordan's film is part of a larger Beckett project developed by Michael Colgan, the director of Dublin's Gate Theatre. In 1991, Colgan staged all nineteen Beckett plays at the Gate and then matched each play with a director to produce film adaptations. The result was *Beckett on Film.* The Beckett estate, which has licensed Beckett's works since his death in 1989, remains committed to Beckett's stringent requirements that his work be performed exactly as written. So Colgan sought out writer-directors who understood the significance of the plays and the best ways to exploit their cinematic possibilities.

Given Samuel Beckett's love-hate relationship with the film medium, it may be surprising to learn that he committed "Not I" to film. In 1977, he recorded a Royal Court Theater performance of the piece for BBC television that featured his frequent collaborator, the British actress Billie Whitelaw. Beckett modified his own staging of the piece for this filmed version. In the original stage directions, an Auditor and a Mouth share the stage: the Auditor stands without speaking, while the Mouth delivers a monologue. The Mouth is illuminated by a spotlight as it spouts a rapid-fire rant. For the BBC film, Beckett eliminated the Auditor, and the film became a single shot: the Mouth in an extreme close-up.

Beckett's elimination of the Auditor changed the dynamics of the piece in important ways. When the Mouth speaks alone, the staging emphasizes the play's theme of internal division. The Mouth speaks for a fragmented being, someone who "can only speak about themselves as something other than what they are" (Jordan in Lehane, "Check"). The Mouth is so utterly alienated as to be unable to use the first-person pronoun—hence the title, "Not I." The Mouth also fails to produce a complete sentence.

In his remake, Jordan intensifies Beckett's focus on the Mouth. "I decided to do just what Beckett had specified," Jordan states in "Check the Gate: Putting Beckett on Film," "just to photograph nothing but Julianne Moore's mouth from as many possible angles as I could" (Lehane). Jordan begins from a position of mimicry, reiterating Beckett's concept, yet he introduces several elements that call attention to the discrepancy between Beckett's play and his own cinematic rendering of divided identity. At the beginning of Jordan's film, Moore walks in front of the camera and sits down before she begins to speak. This gesture introduces the body that is associated with the Mouth, something Beckett did not do. Jordan also filmed the Mouth using six cameras placed at different locations and edited the footage into a single reel.

Jordan's modifications amplify the psychic fragmentation that underlies the stuttering monologue. First, he establishes the woman's physical wholeness. The contrast between this bodily integrity and Beckett's shattered sentences highlights the fact that the woman's dividedness is internal; it is a condition of her existence.

The woman, who tells the audience she was "practically speechless all her days" (Beckett 18), is unable to tell her own story because she has internalized prohibitions against speaking. She fails to speak coherently not because someone else prevents her from doing so but because she stops herself. Her double or evil twin admonishes her that she is not to broach certain topics: "What? Not that? Nothing she could tell? . . . What? Nothing she could think?" (Beckett 22). In Beckett's text, her split subjectivity is rendered grammatically. The Mouth interrupts itself with "what?" and answers unspoken questions twenty-two times as it haltingly summarizes a life of seventy years' duration. Jordan's staging and editing of the six simultaneous takes render this verbal disintegration in visual terms. The cuts punctuate certain moments, but they also disrupt what little continuity is achieved by the Mouth through its utterances.

The use of multiple cameras represents a significant departure from Beckett's version, in which the disembodied Mouth is captured frontally by one fixed-position camera. With this decision, Jordan moves from the blank repetition of Fredric Jameson's pastiche to the politics of Linda Hutcheon's postmodern parody. His editing translates the linguistic fragmentation of Beckett's script into visual terms, marking this film as a meditation on film form as well as a commentary on postmodern identity. Jordan's film reconsiders continuity and difference with specific reference to the Irish oral and theatrical tradition of which Beckett is an important part. Brilliant as he was, Beckett lacked an understanding of the twentieth century's most powerful medium, film. Jordan rejects the venerated Irish oral tradition as insufficient to the task of elaborating the dividedness of postmodern subjects. Jordan's "Not I" powerfully engages with the tension between original and remake by self-consciously exploiting the visual possibilities inherent in film.

In a supremely postmodern instance of recycling, Jordan has produced yet a third version of the project, or, perhaps, a second remake. Expanding the aesthetic possibilities of the piece through recycling, Jordan returned to the six unedited takes of the performance and used them to construct a video installation. On permanent exhibit at the Irish Museum of Modern Art in Dublin since 2001, the installation traveled to the Wexner Art Gallery at Ohio State University in 2003 as part of Image Stream, a show that focused on narrative in contemporary video art.

The installation is composed of six monitors arranged in a circle, presenting the same performance simultaneously from six different angles. "Neither cinema nor theatre, but something quite different," the work was intended to convey the "multiplicity with which cinema presents the world" (Jordan qtd. in Horrigan 74). Jordan's installation also emphasizes the multiplicity and dividedness of postmodern identity and the capacity of cinema to represent and to exacerbate that fragmentation. The individual cannot resolve herself into a single image or a valid sentence because the forces of entropy are too great.

Jordan's two remakes of "Not I" honor Beckett's notion of a divided self, a condition made manifest in a Mouth unable to narrate its own story. But Jordan literally divides and multiplies Beckett's inarticulate double through editing in the film and through the multiple points of view in the video installation. In doing so, he emphasizes the importance of the image to the experience of fragmentation in postmodern culture, something Beckett's linguistic emphasis does not address. Jordan not only engages in the critical work of parody by drawing attention to the postmodern investment in images that is absent from Beckett's text, he also implicates the image-making apparatus of cinema as one source of fragmentation.

In a similar vein, Jordan engages in critical postmodern parody in *The Good Thief*, his remake of Jean-Pierre Melville's beloved *Bob le Flambeur* (1955). This film explicitly connects Jordan's gothic sensibility with postmodern and transnational culture. In *The Good Thief*, the gothic double serves as merely a starting point for an exploration of duplication, repetition, and postmodern imitation. The double serves as a motif that winds through the film's narrative, characters, plot, and locations, but it also functions at a metatextual level, where Jordan self-consciously links doubling to postmodern identities and to art.

Given the proliferation and popularity of heist films, possibly inspired by Steven Soderbergh's remake of *Ocean's Eleven*, *The Good Thief* was something of a box-office disappointment, bringing in only $3.5 million in the United States. Critical opinion ranges from highly complimentary to overtly disparaging. Charles Taylor pronounced it one of Jordan's best films, whereas Stanley Kauffman scorned it as a remake that did not do justice to the original. The *Hollywood Reporter* called the film the "dark underbelly of *Ocean's Eleven* made with a scruffy international cast all playing deformed versions of their sleek American counterparts" (Honeycutt, "Good Thief").

The characterization of the film as a knockoff of a contemporary film with a seedy (and, implicitly, second-rate) multicultural cast effectively captures the overarching postmodern trope of the film: the problem of distinguishing between the original and the copy and, ultimately, the question of whether such distinctions remain important. On the narrative level, Jordan imitates and reuses Melville's film (not Soderbergh's); in the process of exploring the difficulty of distinguishing real from fake and original from copy, he engages in postmodern parody.

Melville's *Bob le Flambeur* concerns a gambler named Bob (Roger Duchesne) who has hit rock bottom. When he bets his last franc on a losing horse, Bob agrees to helm a casino heist with his former cronies. Despite the fact that his plan is betrayed by a young woman whom he has taken under his wing, Bob emerges from the fiasco unscathed. During the doomed heist, his luck changes: he cleans out the casino's safe legally by running the *chemin de fer* table. He is arrested on the charge of criminal intent, but Bob and the sympathetic police detective who arrests him agree that his winnings will allow him to hire the best lawyers and beat the rap.

Jordan's film borrows from, imitates, and complicates Melville's. It is more than an uncanny double; it explicitly questions concepts of the original work of art and the authentic self. In *The Good Thief,* Jordan uses doubling in myriad ways: he re-creates and complicates Melville's plot; he explores the notion of individual possession; and he questions the meaning of authenticity in relation to postmodern art and culture.

Jordan re-creates the gambling scenario at the center of Melville's film but reframes Bob's desire as an addiction that resides at the physical level. Jordan's Bob (Nick Nolte) has a gambling problem and a heroin habit, manifesting the gambler's appetite in the junkie's bodily cravings. Addictions reveal the instability of the individual; they imply a state of possession by another aspect of the self. This metaphorical possession may ultimately lead to a more literal form of possession by others, including drug dealers and loan sharks. Addictions have an additional element that invokes the gothic mode: addicts experience time in cycles rather than through the measured regularity of Enlightenment chronology. To the junkie and the gambler, the critically important span of time is the distance between fixes; life is a cycle of sublime excess and punishing deprivation. To even consider participating in the heist plot, Bob must remake himself by kicking his heroin habit. Throughout the film, he continues to remake himself by telling stories to his newfound sidekick, Anne (Nutsa Kukhianidze).

Jordan doubles Melville's film on the level of the plot as well, where Bob engineers a real heist and also fabricates a decoy. Unlike Melville's protagonist, Jordan's Bob expects someone to betray him and builds the predictable double cross into the plan. He concocts a plan to rob a casino safe merely to distract the police. His actual target is a collection of valuable original paintings that hangs in an underground vault near the casino. The paintings are owned by a Japanese corporation that also owns the casino. The irony is that the corporate managers, who seek to attract a better clientele through a high-art ambience, have chosen to hang well-made fakes in the casino while they store the originals in the nearby villa. The storage vault where the originals hang resembles a contemporary art museum. (One implication may be that art museums are akin to burial vaults.)

Bob's plan falters when he is betrayed by Anne, the young Bosnian refugee he has rescued from the street. Matters are complicated by the fact that Bob isn't sure whether she has disclosed the real or the decoy plot. Anne divulges the information when she is high in drugs, one habit that makes her a double of Bob (another is the ability to fabricate stories about herself). Although the heist of the paintings fails miserably, Bob and Anne, who are dressed to the nines in purloined evening wear, fulfill their appointed duty by gambling all night long. They run the poker tables and claim their winnings, at which point the casino manager discovers that the safe is empty. In a final reversal, Bob's decoy heist has been carried out successfully by a pair of Irish twins, assisted by Bob's former associate, Paolo. (One measure of Jordan's winking self-referentiality is the casting of American directors and twins, Mike and Mark Polish, as the Irish twins and the Serbian director Emir Kusturica as the mastermind behind the technological aspects of the heist.)

In an important reversal of genre conventions, Jordan ironically deflates the expectations associated with heist films, where the intricate details of the plot provide pleasure and build suspense. Here, the successful heist takes place entirely offscreen and is only reported after the fact. Furthermore, viewers expecting an action-packed payoff in the film's conclusion might be somewhat disappointed, since the closing sequence focuses on the way Anne has absorbed Bob's views on life. As they trade stories of their youth, Anne makes it clear that she has mastered the art of self-fashioning by concocting a blatantly false tale that Bob takes as the truth.

Jordan's doublings, complications, and divergences from the heist plot may have proved too much for Stanley Kauffman, who asserted that Jordan's film is "Melville wrenched out of context" (24). But the shift of context is precisely the point. Jordan's remake invites the inevitable comparisons viewers will make to the original. By emphasizing acts of duplication, the film encourages viewers to reassess the original, to consider its relation to the copy, and, most importantly, to consider the notion of creativity as a process of recycling tradition. With *The Good Thief,* Jordan proposes that art is always a process of remaking. This

The Good Thief. That's life: lessons learned and stories told. Courtesy of Photofest.

proposal defies the modernist aesthetic that privileges radical departures from previous forms. It also reiterates the gothic critique of modernity because it refuses to endorse the notion that progress is defined by repudiating the past.

In keeping with the film's celebration of postmodern practices of borrowing, citation, and recycling, Jordan repeatedly undermines the distinction between original and copy. Several scenes duplicate the dialogue of the Melville film exactly, although the visual style and settings are completely different. Jordan conflates characters and actors: for Bob's police file, he inserts an actual mug shot of Nick Nolte as a young man alongside more recent shots taken for the film. (Nolte's infamous skirmishes with the law and notorious substance-abuse problems around the time of the film's release also contribute to the blurring of actor and role.) To visually convey the problem of distinguishing between real and fake production, Jordan had the designer, Anthony Pratt, create two sets of identical paintings to hang in the casino and the vault as the originals and the copies. (Only Bob and the police detective Roger are able to distinguish between them. Even so, Bob praises counterfeit paintings *as* counterfeits throughout the film.)

The film's geographical setting offers another opportunity for Jordan to pursue the implications of repetition and to establish a critical perspective on tradition. He relocates the Deauville location of Melville's film to the gambling underworld in the south of France. Here, he cites a number of films, not only Melville's. Re-presenting the familiar scenery of the French Riviera as a landscape of lurid, neon-lit club interiors in Nice and the blinding, sun-bleached exteriors of Monte Carlo, Jordan intentionally works against the expectations of glamour arising from the location's association with films like Hitchcock's *To Catch a Thief* (1955), made the same year as Melville's original (*Good Thief* commentary). Jordan reframes generic conventions to suggest that an exploitive economy of international drug traffickers and pimps is the mirror image—or, perhaps, the uncanny double—of characters like John Robie, Cary Grant's sexy cat burglar in the Hitchcock film. In references like this one, Jordan moves beyond the inside jokes of *We're No Angels* to comment on film history as well as cultural history.

Jordan's visual style contributes a great deal to the film's sense of doubling, layering, and inversion. Chris Menges's cinematography rejects

Melville's black-and-white poetic realism, along with its lucidity. Jordan's production design moves toward murky abstraction, taking into account the peach and blue hues that are prominent in the modern paintings at the center of the plot and working those tones into the environment. Furthermore, Menges often presents the larger environment of Nice as a glowing and flattened backdrop for the action. The velvety textures and the emphasis on the two-dimensional frame are reminiscent of the painterly compositions of Robert Altman, a director whose interests in gambling are well documented.

At certain moments, Jordan's flattened images become doubles for the cubist paintings of Pablo Picasso, an artist whose canvases and working practices assume a prominent role in the story. To bankroll the heist, Bob sells a fake Picasso painting to an art fence, Tony Angel (Ralph Fiennes, relishing the opportunity to play a lowlife aesthete). Picasso is a heroic figure for Bob and Tony because he blatantly stole from other artists (including Jean-Auguste-Dominique Ingres, Amedeo Modigliani, and Diego Rodriguez de Silva Velasquez) and yet succeeded in making something all his own.

The use of freeze frames as scene transitions throughout the film underscores the film's affinity for cubist fragmentation. More generally, however, Jordan and Menges's images resemble the pastel surfaces of fragmented and two-dimensional cubist paintings. This link between the three-dimensional world of the film and the two-dimensional existence of art objects is made explicit when Tony, angered at having discovered Bob's duplicity, has one of his minions slice up the canvas face of the fake Picasso and threatens to do the same to Anne's face if he doesn't get his money back.

If *The Good Thief*'s references to art history suggest that imitation is the sincerest form of flattery, a glance at its own lineage provides evidence for the view that, in cinema, originality is overrated. In a 1970 interview, Jean-Pierre Melville claimed that at least seven films plagiarized his *Bob*, including Lewis Milestone's original *Ocean's Eleven* (1960) (Melville, "Jean-Pierre Melville"). Yet Melville's film is a remake of John Huston's *Asphalt Jungle* (1950). And Huston's film, adopted from a W. R. Burnett novel, has been remade across several decades and genres, reappearing as a western (*Badlanders* [1958]) and as a black action film (*Cool Breeze* [1972]). This somewhat tangled pedigree underscores the idea that the cinematic past is never completely buried and also suggests that copying is an inescapable element of creativity.

Not surprisingly, given this lineage, Jordan's film participates in the postmodern collapse of high and low art. His film is a version of a French film that itself was a remake of an American film, so its convoluted ancestry defies the notion that films migrate from art cinema to Hollywood and challenges the distinction between the two. The identification of France as the locus of high art cannot be guaranteed when all filmmakers, including French and Irish directors like Melville and Jordan, are shown to be good thieves like Picasso.

The collapse of these aesthetic boundaries resonates at the level of setting and story as well, contributing to the film's commentary on transnational identities. Melville set this American story in Deauville, and Jordan further displaces the action, moving it from Deauville to a French border zone that he calls a "nowheresville" (*Good Thief* commentary). Jordan's film not only blurs geographical locations but also confounds national identities. Bob is a cultural hybrid in several ways. His mother was French, and his father was an American marine. Bob seems to have avoided the American curse of monolingualism; he speaks English, French, and Arabic, a useful skill in the diverse underworld through which he moves. Beyond the central character of Bob, Jordan populates the film with a mélange of characters from across Europe and North Africa, including France, Algeria, Bosnia, Russia, the United States, and Italy.

The Good Thief uses questions of citation and repetition to address the complex relationship between cultural boundaries, art, and violence; in this regard, it returns to the territory of Jordan's first film, *Angel.* In the "nowheresville" setting of *The Good Thief,* a border zone ruled by the laws of probability, cultural convergence occurs in two ways. The first is through war, and the second is through creative exchange, including aesthetic theft. Wars bring together combatants, civilians, victims, and refugees: in a fairly innocuous instance, Bob's paratrooper father landed in France and married his mother (or so his story goes). Wars force individuals to enter new cultural contexts; they create new people and social institutions. But they also displace and destroy individuals and cultures. At one point, someone asks Anne if she is from Bosnia, her presumed homeland. She responds by saying, "Is that what they are calling it these days?"

In perhaps its strongest assertion of postmodern parody—where acts of repetition acquire a critical edge—*The Good Thief* contrasts the brutal forms of remaking that are accomplished by armies with more prosaic acts of aesthetic theft, which potentially lead to rich cultural expression. One form of cultural exchange is music. Jordan pokes fun at the French pop star Johnny Hallyday, who is notorious for his cheesy adaptations of American rock music. Bob disparages Hallyday's musical remakes not because he has stolen the music but because his cover songs are *bad* thefts of the classic rock music of Jimi Hendrix and the Rolling Stones (a band often accused of stealing from American blues music). In another nod to cultural borrowing, the film's soundtrack features a form of musical remaking that is not subjected to ridicule. Jordan incorporates Rai, a musical style from northwest Algeria that blends electronic music, African American hip-hop, and jazz with traditional North African music.

In emphasizing these cultural thefts, *The Good Thief* not only undermines the hierarchical relation between Hollywood and art cinema, and between original paintings and fakes, but also questions the national and cultural identities that such aesthetic distinctions are supposed to endorse and enforce. The seemingly self-perpetuating dynamics of borrowing that Jordan's film endorses are a fitting tribute to the director of *Bob le Flambeur,* who engaged in some cultural borrowings himself, and not only in terms of his film. Melville was born with the surname Grumbach and changed his name because of his admiration for the American writer Herman Melville.

In *The Good Thief,* another of Jordan's tales of faith and redemption, the director moves beyond the pastiche of *We're No Angels* and *The End of the Affair* and presents a remake that critically engages with repetition as an unavoidable aspect of postmodern identity and an inevitable element of postmodern art. Stopping short of a wholesale celebration of the postmodern culture of imitation, Jordan challenges artists and non-artists alike to be good thieves, to create and re-create themselves using cultural givens, and to eschew the modernist valorization of the new.

One critic called *The Good Thief* "an ode to the joy of thievery" (Taylor, "*Good Thief*"). But the film is more than that—it alludes to practices of destructive and creative remaking and heavily favors the latter.

By posing war and aesthetic creation as alternative modes of cultural convergence, Jordan's film underscores the ways that postmodernity and globalism enact gothic transgressions of boundaries, for better and for worse. The extent to which an individual can shape or control these transgressions remains an open question, especially in a film in which luck, chance, and probability feature so prominently. Yet Jordan strongly emphasizes the narrative of Bob's redemption; he is quick to point out that he was less interested in the mechanics of the heist film and more invested in Bob's transformation (*Good Thief* commentary).

The film's title refers not only to Picasso and to Bob but also to a religious parable, the story of the thief who was crucified next to Jesus and who experienced a last-minute conversion. By focusing on Bob as a good thief, Jordan suggests that it is never too late to remake oneself and that the manner in which boundaries collapse does matter: active engagement with creative approaches to remaking rather than violence can make all the difference in the world.

Throughout this book, I have argued that, despite the fact that Neil Jordan's projects and production contexts are extremely diverse, a postmodern gothic sensibility pervades his films. The paradox that Jordan highlights to varying degrees in these last four films is the difficult matter of whether an original vision can exist within a mass culture of imitation and simulation. Jordan's work in *The Good Thief* explores this conjunction, using the gothic double and the process of doubling to suggest that filmmakers and their characters might be invigorated by the postmodern challenge to authenticity, originality, and uniqueness.

Notes

1. In 1969–71, the Provisional IRA split from the Official IRA. The goal of the former was to "render the existing State inoperable so that the [British] army would have to withdraw" (Coogan, *IRA* 285). The Official IRA maintained a goal of a socialist, thirty-two-county Ireland. The INLA was formed in 1974 and the Real IRA in 1997.

2. The Blair government has promised a historical inquiry and a reassessment of the Widgery Commission report, which exonerated British paratroopers who fired on unarmed, peaceful civil-rights marchers. Just as *Michael Collins* intervened in history, Paul Greengrass's docudrama *Bloody Sunday* (2002) contributed to the equally painful process of revisiting that official historical record.

Interview with Neil Jordan

June 7, 2005

MARIA PRAMAGGIORE: Because of your background as a writer and your involvement on most of your film projects as a writer, do you see yourself in the mode of the European auteur? There are very few directors whose reach extends from the writing through the entire process.

NEIL JORDAN: Do I consider myself belonging to the auteurist tradition, you mean? I don't think that applies to contemporary cinema anymore. I don't think the contexts are there for it to be a private, confessional kind of medium, you know? That definition of cinema isn't helpful anymore, really. I started as a writer, a novelist. I began to make films, almost accidentally. And I've kept making films. In many ways, I've substituted the procedure of writing novels with the act of making films. I've made very independent movies that very few people have seen, and I've made big Hollywood movies that an enormous number of people have seen. I've made independent movies that a lot of people have seen.

I definitely don't belong to, let's say, the European auteur definition of things. I make films in many different genres, in many different styles. I generally tend to make things about the same concerns, but in many different shapes. When I think of an auteur, nowadays, I think of somebody like Wim Wenders.

I think it's just the way people have to work nowadays. I don't have that much in common with directors like Mike Leigh or Jim Jarmusch or Atom Egoyan, not really. I kind of regard that as a cinema that nobody sees. I came into making films because it seemed like a big country that I'd never explored before. Anytime I make a film, I want to do something different from what I've done before. Often that means an entirely new genre. The films are similar in their concerns and their ways of seeing, but they're very different in the kinds of films they are.

MP: Do you make a distinction between your literary voice and your cinematic vision? Your writing voice has a fluid, poetic, even confessional quality to it, whereas your films are much more expansive in their expression.

NJ: The way I began to write prose is the way I've continued writing prose. I suppose most of the exploration or the exciting changes that I've done have been in cinema. Most of the wild, about turns and looking at different territories and experimentation, all that sort of stuff has been in the cinema, really. Because I always thought not a lot of people ever read what I wrote, I regard it as the more private affair, more self-exploratory, more an investigation of myself, rather than an investigation of the world in general.

MP: Your films have a melodramatic, almost an operatic quality to them . . .

NJ: . . . that the writing never had; yeah, I know. The [film] medium allows you to use theatricality and melodrama and far more bold forms of storytelling. For whatever reason, I've never tended to do that in the prose. Part of the reason I have kept making films and was so excited about them was that it gave me the opportunity to do all that kind of stuff. To be much more aware of something that is being seen, that is being viewed by people as well.

MP: Can you comment on the sense you had of Irish cinema when you were growing up?

NJ: The "Irish" films I was aware of were those of John Ford, who's not really Irish, and there was a handful of films like, say, *Odd Man Out* [dir. Carol Reed; 1947], *Shake Hands with the Devil* [dir. Michael Anderson; 1959], and *Mise Éire* [I am Ireland; dir. George Morrison; 1959] and *Saorise?* [Freedom?; dir. George Morrison; 1961], which were glorified documentaries. I know there were films being made in Ardmore that mainly came out of the Abbey Players in the 1950s. [Ardmore Studios opened in 1958. Initially government-run and later a private facility, Ardmore often was used by foreign filmmakers shooting in Ireland.] I was aware of growing up in a country that had a huge literary tradition and no cinema tradition whatsoever. I suppose it's one of the reasons I found it so refreshing to make films in the first place: there didn't seem to be any precedents here for that kind of thing. There wasn't the overwhelming weight you get if you write.

The figures like Wilde, Shaw, Yeats, O'Casey, Joyce, and Beckett—they're quite large. In cinematic terms, it's like you had Akira Kurosawa, Ingmar Bergman, Luis Buñuel, and John Ford working in the same country at the same time. From my point of view, in film you had none of that. Making films in a way was an escape from the weight of literature for me.

MP: Some critics make a distinction between your "Irish films"—which would include *Angel, High Spirits, The Miracle, The Crying Game, Michael Collins, The Butcher Boy,* and *Breakfast on Pluto*—and your "non-Irish" films. Do you see your work in this way, that there's a return to Ireland in certain films? Or do you see yourself as bringing an Irish perspective to bear on all the films you make?

NJ: There could be an Irish perspective brought to bear on all the films I've made, definitely, because of the elements of folktales and fairy tales and the elements of the fantastic and what you call the gothic. That comes directly from something that is in this country. Actually, one of the reasons I wrote *Shade* [Jordan's 2004 novel] was because it was the first time I told a gothic story—there's a secret, there's a house, there's people that are haunted by the past, a crime that explains stuff. It is a gothic story, but I suppose it's not like a Sheridan Le Fanu ghost tale. It has all the elements, doesn't it? The elements obviously come from here, and they come from the things that influenced me in Irish literature, the theater, the poetry, the folktales.

MP: Do you perceive that there is an emphasis on, or bias toward, literature and drama as the primary or exclusive forms of aesthetic expression in Irish culture?

NJ: There is, yes. I think there's a profound lack of a visual sense here—in everything. It's an inheritance of a sense of cultural inferiority, of the colonial experience. Most beautiful things in Ireland were made in the eighteenth century, by the British, basically. And most of the energy since independence has been devoted to tearing these beautiful things down.

And I think it's almost an exclusively verbal culture. It's like they find it very hard to get to grips with things that are nonverbal. Even the television. The radio is kind of unique; the television is absolutely dreadful. It's imitative of the modes of soap operas in England and America. There has been some really good cutting-edge visual comedy that has come out of Ireland, like "Father Ted," to take a silly example. But that was made by Channel Four. It seems that we don't belong to a culture that actually looks at things. We belong to a culture that hears things. It was evident when I grew up, and it's still that way.

There's some very, very good [visual art] coming out now. There's Dorothy Cross, Alice Maher; many women, actually. My sister is a painter, too [as is their mother, Angela Jordan].

MP: One of your recent works is a video installation at the Irish Museum of Modern Art based on "Not I" [Jordan's fourteen-minute film of the Samuel Beckett play, filmed in 2000 as part of the *Beckett on Film* project. The installation consists of six video monitors arranged in a circle, each giving a different perspective on Julianne Moore's mouth as she delivers a monologue.] Do you see yourself pursuing more of this kind of work?

NJ: That came about just because of the way I had shot the Beckett thing. We had these enormous two-thousand-foot film rolls, and we photographed her from different perspectives. And they all were a different record of the same event. It just struck me as being interesting to show it in that way. But I wouldn't do more of that.

It's a different world. What do you call it now—video art? The work of Bill Viola, Matthew Barney. I've seen their work: I like a lot of it. It's entirely free of any sense of, say, an audience as a mass group of people watching. It's freed of a lot of constraints from that point of view. But it's not my world.

MP: Do you think of an audience—even a different audience—with each project your work on?

NJ: Yeah, absolutely. It's always the same. It's always an audience that may happen to be there that you're trying to stimulate into some kind of awareness or trying to meddle with their brains.

MP: In terms of visual style, you draw from a broad range of world cinema.

NJ: I was tremendously influenced by horror movies, by any films that were from an unrealistic tradition and perspective. Sergio Leone, Luis Buñuel. The kind of kitchen-sink realism that you get in the British cinema in the sixties didn't influence me at all. The improvisational thing—the John Cassavetes exploration of situation—didn't influence me one bit. The things that have influenced me in movies have been the more fantastic elements. Buster Keaton I love, for example.

I suppose it's the more starkly visual aspects of movies that have affected me. Everything from film noir is very pictorial, very graphic. Certain aspects of Orson Welles are very graphic, and everything in Buñuel is terribly graphic. Ingmar Bergman has not influenced me. It's directors like Nicholas Ray that interest me.

I love Robert Altman. I like cinema with brains. I like movies that are thinking—that make me think and that are thinking on their feet. I love the extravagant visual sense that Steven Spielberg exhibits in the way that certain movies he's made could only exist as movies.

MP: You are a musician, and it seems that music occupies an important place in your films—particularly popular music. Many of your films have popular songs as their titles, including *Mona Lisa, The Crying Game, In Dreams, The Butcher Boy,* and *Breakfast on Pluto.*

NJ: I've just made *Breakfast on Pluto.* That was fascinating because, in many ways, it's my memories of the seventies. I was kind of a musical snob when I was in my twenties. I didn't listen to popular music at all, just classical music. So I had to go back to these swathes of David Bowie and of Harry Nilsson. I had to kind of plow through everything—to construct the soundtrack out of that music. I stopped listening to the rock-and-roll genre in the seventies when it became self-referential. When I was doing the editing of *Breakfast on Pluto,* I listened to almost everything from the seventies, and of course I realized I knew it all along, but I had not been thinking about it. And you miss an enormous amount if you ignore what's happening in popular music, even now. I thought it was kind of dead through that period, and it wasn't.

MP: You use contemporary music from the nineties in *The Good Thief*.

NJ: *The Good Thief* is rai, really. It's basically Arabic French music, where they've taken the hip-hop mode and done extraordinary things with it, with a lot of folk North African elements. That's a beautiful form of music. I used rai because several of the characters were North African. Hip-hop has segued into world music in some of these ways.

MP: Your films are very interested in performance. Characters are actors or musicians or circus performers; your plots involve role playing, pretense, and duplicity. And you have worked with actors in quite diverse ways: casting untrained actors, casting celebrities, repeatedly working with actors such as Stephen Rea, Tom Hickey, Liam Neeson, and Ian Hart. How do you see the relationship between the actor and the role?

NJ: The casting of the actor is always a way for me to explore the role, and to develop it more fully. Often I cast the actor because there's something in the role I want myself to explore. That's one thing.

With regard to casting, of, say, Brad Pitt and Tom Cruise in *Interview with the Vampire,* often when you do these big movies, they're kind of cast for you in a way. If Tom Cruise wants to do it, and you don't want him, you've got a real problem. It's a delicate thing when casting big stars. To be frank about it, they're paid much more than any director is paid. I've never been in a situation when I've been with an ungenerous star, but I wouldn't like to be, because they would probably have far more influence over the production mechanism than any director would.

It always struck me with Anne Rice's novels that her description of vampires is very much like the description of what one wants of a Hollywood star: they're inaccessible, they're eternally young, and they live in a world that obeys different rules to the rest of humanity. So that's what the casting was about, if you understand what I mean. I thought vampires were like movie stars. In the subsequent novel, Lestat becomes a rock star. He behaves like a star, sitting in darkened palaces up in the Hollywood Hills, only coming out at night.

I always thought Tom was a really, really good actor, with a very direct and very simple kind of energy. In a way I got lucky, because he allowed himself to be far more theatrical than he ever had been before. He allowed himself to play with an enormous about of irony and a self-mocking thing, which he hadn't done before himself.

With regard to *We're No Angels,* Robert De Niro wanted to do a comedy. He had done one in *Midnight Run* [dir. Martin Brest; 1988]. It's quite a good film. Sean Penn and Robert had been cast, they sent me the script and asked me did I want to do it, and it was David Mamet, whom I admired a lot, and I kind of loved the little allegory of the story. It became all of us three serious people grappling with a comedy.

MP: So, you don't consciously bring in the idea of celebrity as adding another layer of meaning.

NJ: I've worked with stars at different times and I always try to work with stars as actors. I've cast Robert De Niro, Sean Penn, Peter O'Toole, Julia Roberts, Tom Cruise, Brad Pitt, Nick Nolte. About *Michael Collins,* Julia called me up about the part; I hadn't thought of her for that. She had read the script, and she really was interested in it. I met her, and, I mean, Kitty Kiernan was in a strange way not unlike Julia Roberts. Often when somebody like that comes to you, you have to be careful; you can do them a disservice. American audiences just love her in romantic comedy—I think she's a master of it. I think she's not given enough credit for that beautiful touch she has in those films. But American audiences don't forgive her for appearing in a more serious piece of work. When *Michael Collins* played in Ireland and Britain, people actually accepted Julia in the role perfectly. Her accent was good and her acting was good and she fitted it in a way. When they saw it in the United States, they said, "What is Julia Roberts doing in this movie?" Stars do want to do good work, and you have to be very careful when you cast them. They often work with people like me because they want to do more independent-style work, work that they would think of as having more integrity than the normal run of stuff they do.

I've written several films that have required the casting of people who have not acted before. In *Angel,* I needed to cast a singer, so I cast Honor [Heffernan], who had never acted before. *The Miracle* was about two kids, two adolescents, and I cast two people who hadn't acted before, but that was because the parts were of that nature. When it came to *The Crying Game* and I had to find somebody who could play a black guy who was a transvestite, I couldn't cast Wesley Snipes, or Prince—I had to cast an unknown for that role, really. With regard to *The Butcher Boy,* again, I had to cast an unknown. Kirsten Dunst in *Interview with the Vampire*—I think that was her first acting role.

I often find there's tremendous energy that comes out of somebody who is acting for the first time because they have no barriers whatsoever, and they have nowhere to hide. And practiced actors are often shocked by that, they're often discomfited by that, and often they're kept on their toes by that. It's not something I do as a matter of procedure, but because the parts I've written have demanded that I find somebody to play those roles.

The one thing I've never done is improvisational stuff—come up with a rough sketch of a story and got a group of actors, well, what Ken Loach does, for example; what a lot of people seem to do.

MP: And you don't necessarily want to do that.

NJ: I don't think what comes out of people's mouths when they improvise is very good. I don't think actors, generally, are writers, or they would be writers. Maybe the dialogue I write is so specific that it doesn't fit well with the kind of invention, the kind of rhythms that come out of improvisation.

MP: In the evolution of your screenplays, your early drafts seem to include more language and more directness, so that your writing process seems almost to be one of subtraction.

NJ: They are more laconic, they're more stark. Yeah, there's less of them, generally. In *Mona Lisa,* the speech that Bob Hoskins gives on the promenade about how men and women are meant to fall in love and the songs that he relates to, that wasn't in the draft when I began to rehearse with Bob and Cathy Tyson and Michael Caine. We're rehearsing the scenes, and I feel there's something missing here, an emotional thing that needs more expression. So I write that scene after the rehearsal, then the next day we rehearse it again and use that scene. That's the way I use rehearsal. I use it as a kind of writing template. I suppose that's my version of the improvisatory thing that other directors use. But I have to write it. I try to expand the parts, make the parts make sense for different actors.

MP: You work in so many different genres, but you seem to have a continuing interest in the relationship between what we call the real and what we see as the dream world, the vision, or the fairy tale.

NJ: Well, I just don't think people are rational, really, in the way they behave with one another. The American electorate isn't rational; it keeps voting for Republicans even though they're going to raise taxes on blue-collar people and take all health benefits away. Still they vote Republican.

I don't think the world behaves in a rational manner, but we all write about it and talk about it as if it does. I think that's what a lot of stories I've told have been about. How people try and make sense of their own lives with the tools available like logic and a sense of consequence, and these forces erupt into lives that make no sense. That's what *The Company of Wolves* is about. That's what *The Crying Game* is about.

MP: *In Dreams.*

NJ: *In Dreams,* definitely.

MP: And *The Butcher Boy.*

NJ: That does come from growing up in a peasant culture here. The country's changed beyond recognition from the place it was in the 1950s and 1960s. It was a most irrational place when I was a kid. Very much like *The Butcher Boy.* That's the most accurate portrait I can give of the Ireland I grew up in. People talked about Khrushchev as if he were the corner boy around the next town. They localize everything, don't they? Or they used to. Peasant culture is the wrong word, but it was a very specific culture here. Probably because the whole Second World War thing hadn't happened, and then the kind of thing that happened in Britain in the sixties had no effect here at that stage.

Growing up in Ireland was probably like growing up in Cuba now. Very much like growing up in an Eastern European country—there was a very rigid social system that seemed to have been there forever, that seemed to be unquestioned. People just try to make shape of their lives underneath it. It was a Catholic state, anti-British, in many serious ways, that had no concern whatsoever for its inhabitants. It obeyed various ideological templates that bore no relationship to the reality that was around.

I suppose a lot of these postrevolutionary countries are similar. Ireland was one of the early ones. Salman Rushdie writes in *Midnight's Children* about being born on the same day as Indian Independence in 1947. The comparable event here happened thirty years before. There's always a hangover after these nationalistic struggles. I've no idea what it was like growing up in Algeria after they threw the French out, but I imagine it was pretty grim.

That's the Ireland I grew up in. It only gradually began to change. Most writers had to go away. They were banned—actually, you couldn't make a living here. I'm talking not only about Joyce and Beckett but John McGahern and Patrick Kavanaugh, and various lesser names. But it was an interesting place.

MP: Returning to that question of tradition, I'd like to ask you about remakes, about your sense of your dialogue with tradition.

NJ: You're cursed with remakes, now, because it's all they seem to make. I don't know why. It just seems they're terribly happy doing something that existed before. They're very concerned about making something that never has been.

It's almost become irrelevant, in a way. Steven Spielberg's just making this enormous movie, *The War of the Worlds* [2005]. Everybody's talking about Orson Welles's radio broadcast. When I was a kid, I saw a wonderful film; it was called *The War of the Worlds* [dir. Byron Haskin; 1953]. I don't know who directed it. It was a very huge production. So I think we're not even aware that things are remakes anymore, which is, I suppose, maybe it's fine. They endlessly rechurned bits of Ovid in Greek and Roman culture, and nobody seemed concerned about it, did they?

If you read Shakespeare and Marlowe—is Shakespeare's "Troilus and Cressida" a remake? It's a retelling of a piece of classical storytelling. I suppose it's basically the same impulse. When I did *The End of the Affair*, I didn't think it was a remake. Because I loved the book, and the Edward Dmytryk film wasn't really very good, I'm sorry to say.

MP: Dmytryk originally planned to use a nonchronological structure [which is the structure used in Greene's novel and Jordan's film], but that didn't fly with studio executives, and ultimately the events were presented in chronological order. He also eliminated the miracles, except for the fact that the main character, the writer Bendrix, survives the initial bomb attack during the Battle of Britain. After the film was made, Greene rereleased the novel without the miracles. So your remake is actually a return to the original source material.

NJ: I just related to the novel, basically. I didn't see the Dmytryk film until people at Sony provided me with it.

We're No Angels was a French play called "Us Three." Basically the way these things happen is the producer Art Linton is sitting in Paramount, and they look through the Paramount library, and they see what have we got, and they call up David Mamet and say we've got this little property. Do you want to make a movie about a bunch of criminals escaping? He takes it and does something different with it. And I take it and see what he's done, and I don't relate it to either of the precedents, really. That's the way it seems to happen.

Except for *The Good Thief,* where the original, *Bob le Flambeur,* is a really good movie, and obviously Jean-Pierre Melville is one of the great directors. He's actually one of those great, peculiar figures who related specifically to American genres and reduced them to a little bit more truth than the American versions. *Le Samurai* [1967] and films like that. *Bob le Flambeur,* the film, is almost tiny. It's small—it's also quite beautiful. The essential metaphor of it is kind of gorgeous, so that's what I was relating to really. I thought long and hard about that. That's why I came up with that structure where the original film in some way remained in the movie I was making. It was like really making a film about remakes, and about fakes, and about the value of the original and the version, and it became an exploration of that, really. Which was fun.

MP: With *The Good Thief,* for some reason, I thought of Robert Altman—the look of the frame. I detected a sense of his style, perhaps, also because of his gambling film, *California Split* [1974].

NJ: Do you know what I related to that? That's interesting you say that, because there's a Robert Altman film with Elliot Gould called *The Long Goodbye* [1974]—that's what I kept thinking of, I don't know why, really. Probably because it was a garish color version of a black-and-white classic, and he had no reverence whatsoever for the original material, other then to ring a series of jokes around it. Altman's great. There's real intelligence there.

MP: You were acquainted with Stanley Kubrick, who lived in England, and who also made a film in Ireland.

NJ: Kubrick had done *Barry Lyndon* [1975]; the novel, by Thackeray, began here in Ireland. I used to know Stanley very well. He used to have these relationships with directors. He kept up these dialogues that went on for years with people. A wonderful man; he made too few movies. He was a really generous figure. He called me up one day after he'd seen *Angel.* We kept talking over the years. I didn't realize he knew many different directors in that way, with phone conversations.

MP: And you discussed *The Crying Game* with him.

NJ: Stanley being Stanley, he was interested by the apparently impossible task of having a man play a woman and carry the illusion that they are a woman for the first half of the film. That intrigued him, and the fact that it would have to be the lover of a Caribbean soldier, the fact that there was a race issue there. The whole impossibility of it intrigued him. If he had done that, he would have been searching for four years. He made more expensive films than I did at the time.

MP: The somewhat clichéd view of Kubrick is that he was less interested in the actors, because his stories always involved the depersonalization of his characters.

NJ: I think he was more than anything interested in the story. You see that if you look at *Full Metal Jacket* [1987], which is what he was working on at the time when I used to see him a lot. He hired the designer that I'd used on *The Company of Wolves,* Anton Furst, to design the film. There's a fascinating narrative structure in that movie—imitated many times since. That's the kind of mind he had, a very mathematical mind devoted to issues of narrative, almost like a scientific examination of what is this thing that is a story, this thing that is a movie. And he'd examine it from the ground upwards. That's why I think his films are so interesting. Perhaps because he thought so long about them.

If you look at *Barry Lyndon,* now there's magnificent use of voiceover in that film. There's a wonderful description just before the duel. There's a wonderfully ironic distance between the voice and the film itself.

MP: You've used voiceover in *The Butcher Boy* . . .

NJ:. . . in a similar way.

MP: And is there also a voiceover in *Breakfast on Pluto* [a novel by the same author, Patrick McCabe, with a first-person narrator]?

NJ: No, there's not. I was going to initially use it, but it couldn't be at all. . . . Actually, the entire inspiration for the voiceover in *The Butcher Boy* came from *Barry Lyndon* and from *A Clockwork Orange* [1971]. The idea that the voice would be doing one thing, and the story would be doing something entirely different—he's the only example of that.

MP: Would Terrence Malick's *Badlands* [1974] be another?

NJ: But in *Badlands,* she was talking straight out of a character—that was what was intriguing and hypnotic. The irony was in her lack of articulation, in a way. She was talking straight from within the character, whereas in *Barry Lyndon* and *Clockwork Orange,* Kubrick had wild explorations of language and perspective.

MP: In terms of narrative structure, you experienced the difficulties associated with exploring dream states when you made *In Dreams.*

NJ: Steven Spielberg had commissioned Bruce Robinson to write the first draft of a screenplay about a psychic and her relationship to a serial killer. Initially, I think he was thinking about the fact that police officers use psychics to solve crimes. Steven sent me the script, and he got very excited about my rewrite. It was absolutely fascinating, but it didn't have an ending. It didn't know how to end, because it's very difficult if you go into these dreamlike zones at the end—you don't know what's real or not. Has it ended or has it not ended?

The film never had a proper ending. And I shot it, and we all watched it, and it still didn't have an ending. Steven looked at me and said, "I always thought it should end this way"—and I could imagine how he would have made it work with the flamboyant technique he has. And I shot it like that, and it didn't work. The basic problem was that we had a housewife who has survived, and her entire family had been killed: her daughter, her husband, even her dog had been killed. So in the end I just said, look, even if she lives, there's going to be no sense of a release for the audience, because they know she's got nothing. So she may as well die. At least meet her daughter in this heaven that everyone in America seems to believe in, you know, that kind of thing? That's what we shot in the end. It was quite satisfactory in the end. It was the only possible one, anyway.

MP: It seemed entirely appropriate that the character only "comes home" by returning to haunt the mind of the serial killer. But the film was not well received.

NJ: There was something repellant about the subject matter, deeply repellant about child molestation and killing. There was something slightly exploitive about the subject matter. Dreamworks had finished the movie and had some quite good previews. They showed it to some critics and got an overwhelming nauseous response from the entire critical community in the United States, and they knew that, and so they put it out in January. They didn't want to deal with it that much. I had just made *The Butcher Boy,* which was a very critically acclaimed film. And all the people who had loved that movie saw this movie and they just hated it—it was extraordinary. Ah well, that's Hollywood.

MP: Now that you've completed *Breakfast on Pluto,* what is your next project?

NJ: I don't know what I'm doing. *Breakfast on Pluto* will be out in the fall of 2005. I have a few particular things I want to do. I want to do something big. Something Hollywood-financed.

MP: And so you are comfortable working within Hollywood?

NJ: Believe me, Hollywood's no more nasty than the Cannes festival or the critical community in Britain. Neither is it more or less aesthetically unpleasing. I was on the jury of several film festivals for a while. And if you have had to sit through twenty-five of the cream of European auteurist productions, believe me, it can be a mind-numbingly, soul-destroying experience. If I was watching the same equivalents from the Hollywood machine, would I have the same feeling of grayness in my soul, of utter boredom? Perhaps not—because at least they'd be trying to assault me in some way.

MP: What do you see as the important issues facing contemporary filmmakers?

NJ: The cinema that we grew up with, that European cinema, doesn't exist anymore, not in that transcendent form. The kind of merging of what you'd call high-art concerns and pure cinema—that we all love—it was specific to a certain time. European cinema is definitely in a state of awful crisis. Except for figures like Pedro Almodóvar, it doesn't know how to relate to any audience at all. All forms of cinema are in some form of crisis.

The great films to me at the moment are out of Asia, action-based, generic pictures; cop dramas. There still are some great filmmakers around. David Lynch is always doing something interesting. Robert Altman is great. Clint Eastwood is marvelous. Mike Leigh does great work.

The awful truth of movies at the moment is that big huge formal changes are happening at the higher end of those enormously expensive movies where they use digital technologies. *Lord of the Rings* [dir. Peter Jackson; 2001–3] was a different kind of event than any that had gone before. So filmmakers working in an independent mode are a bit overwhelmed by the fact that the formal exploration is going on in these huge event things, many of which are totally empty.

The new visual constructs are being made there. Independent cinema hasn't really managed to create an aesthetic out of the digital possibilities available, apart from the fact that stuff is handheld and grainy and seems to be better photographed, you know? Whereas Hollywood cinema has managed to make some visually splendid stuff out of the digital possibilities.

Filmography

Miracles and Miss Langan (1979)
Ireland
Production: Radio Telefis Éirann (RTÉ)
Director: Pat O'Connor
Screenplay: Neil Jordan, adapting his 1972 radio play for television
Cast: Deirdre Donnelly (Susan Langan), Malcolm Douglas (Ben D'Arcy), Godfrey Quigley (Headmaster)
Color
58 min.

Sean (1980)
Ireland
Production: RTÉ
Screenplay: Neil Jordan (four episodes), adapting Sean O'Casey's *Autobiographies*

Excalibur (1981)
USA
Production: Orion Pictures
Producer: John Boorman
Distribution: Orion Pictures, Warner Brothers, and Warner Home Video (DVD)
Director: John Boorman
Screenplay: John Boorman and Rospo Pallenberg, based on Thomas Malory's *Le Morte d'Arthur*
Script Consultant: Neil Jordan
Cinematography: Alex Thomson
Editors: John Merritt and Donn Cambern
Production Designer: Anthony Pratt
Music: Trevor Jones
Cast: Nigel Terry (King Arthur), Helen Mirren (Morgana), Nicholas Clay

(Lancelot), Cherie Lunghe (Guinevere), Paul Geoffrey (Percival), Nicol Williamson (Merlin), Robert Addie (Mordred), Gabriel Byrne (Uther Pendragon), Katrine Boorman (Igrayne), Liam Neeson (Gawain)
Color
140 min.

The Making of Excalibur: Myth into Film (1981)
USA
Producer: Neil Jordan
Director: Neil Jordan
Cinematography: Seamus Deasy
Editor: Rory O'Farrell
Cast: John Boorman, Tony Pratt, Alex Thomson, Paul Gregory, Nicol Williamson, Cherie Lunghi, Nicholas Clay, Helen Mirren
16mm
Color
46 min.

Traveller (1981)
Ireland
Production: British Film Institute, An Chomhairle Ealaíon (Irish Arts Council), and RTÉ
Producers: Joe Comerford and Margaret Williams
Director: Joe Comerford
Screenplay: Neil Jordan
Cinematography: Thaddeus O'Sullivan
Editor: Joe Comerford
Music: Davy Spillane
Cast: Judy Donovan (Angela Devine), Davy Spillane (Michael Connors), Alan Devlin (Clicky), Johnny Choil Mhadhc (Devine), Paddy Donovan (Connors)
Color
80 min.

Angel (1982)
Ireland
Production: Motion Picture Company of Ireland, Bord Scannán na hÉireann (Irish Film Board), and Channel Four Films
Producers: John Boorman and Barry Blackmore
Distribution: British Film Institute (UK) and Triumph Films (USA)
Director: Neil Jordan
Screenplay: Neil Jordan

Cinematography: Chris Menges
Editor: J. Patrick Duffner
Production Designer: John Lucas
Music: Keith Donald (saxophone) and Paddy Meegan (songs)
Cast: Veronica Quilligan (Annie), Stephen Rea (Danny), Alan Devlin (Bill), Peter Caffrey (Ray), Honor Heffernan (Deirdre), Ray McAnally (Bloom), Donal McCann (Bonner), Marie Kean (Aunt Mae)
Color
92 min.

Night in Tunisia (1983)
Ireland
Production: RTÉ and Channel Four
Producer: Pat O'Connor
Director: Pat O'Connor
Screenplay: Neil Jordan, based on his short story
Cinematography: Peter Dorney
Editor: Myles Merriman
Cast: Michael Lally (Bill), Ciaran Burns (Luke), Jill Boyle (Rene), Jim Culleton (Nick), Grainne O'Reilly (Rita), Rodney Chichignoud (Jamie)
Color
53 min.

The Company of Wolves (1984)
UK
Production: ITC Entertainment, Cannon Films, and Palace Pictures
Distribution: Cannon Film Distributors (USA), Carlton International Media (worldwide), and Hen's Tooth Video (DVD)
Producers: Chris Brown, Stephen Woolley, and Nik Powell
Director: Neil Jordan
Screenplay: Neil Jordan and Angela Carter
Cinematography: Brian Loftus
Editor: Rodney Holland
Production Designer: Anton Furst
Costumes: Elizabeth Waller
Music: George Fenton
Cast: Angela Lansbury (Granny), Sarah Patterson (Rosaleen), David Warner (Father), Tusse Silberg (Mother), Georgia Slowe (Alice), Micha Bergese (Huntsman), Kathryn Pogson (Bride), Stephen Rea (Bridegroom), Terence Stamp (Prince of Darkness), Dawn Archibald (Witch Woman)
Color
95 min.

Mona Lisa (1986)
UK
Production: Production Company of Ireland, Handmade Films, and Palace Pictures
Producers: Patrick Cassavetti, Steven Woolley, Chris Brown, Ray Cooper, Nik Powell, and George Harrison
Distribution: Island Pictures and Criterion Film Corporation (DVD)
Director: Neil Jordan
Screenplay: Neil Jordan and David Leland
Cinematography: Roger Pratt
Editor: Lesley Walker
Production Designer: Jamie Leonard
Music: Michael Kamen
Cast: Bob Hoskins (George), Cathy Tyson (Simone), Michael Caine (Mortwell), Robbie Coltrane (Thomas), Clarke Peters (Anderson), Kate Hardie (Cathy), Zoe Nathenson (Jeannie), Pauline Melville (George's wife), Sammi Davis (May)
Color
104 min.

The Courier (1988)
UK
Production: Eustace Films, Palace Pictures, City Vision, and Irish Film Board
Producers: Neil Jordan, Nik Powell, Stephen Woolley, Hilary McLoughlin, and John Hambley
Distribution: Vestron Pictures
Directors: Joe Lee and Frank Deasy
Screenplay: Frank Deasy
Cinematography: Gabriel Beristain
Editor: Annette D'Alton
Music: Elvis Costello (as Declan McManus)
Cast: Ian Bannen (McGuigan), Patrick Bergin (Christy), Gabriel Byrne (Val), Andrew Connolly (Danny), Michelle Houlden (Sharon), Padraig O'Loinsigh (Mark), Cait O'Riordan (Colette), Joe Savino (VJ)
Color
85 min.

High Spirits (1988)
USA
Production: Palace Pictures and Vision PDG
Producers: Stephen Woolley, David Saunders, Nik Powell, Selwyn Roberts, Mark Damon, Moshe Diamont, Eduard Sarlui, and Jon Turtle
Distribution: TriStar Pictures and MGM/UA Home Entertainment (DVD)

Director: Neil Jordan
Screenplay: Neil Jordan
Cinematography: Alex Thomson
Editor: Michael Bradsell
Production Designer: Anton Furst
Music: George Fenton
Cast: Peter O'Toole (Peter Plunkett), Steve Guttenberg (Jack), Beverly D'Angelo (Sharon), Jennifer Tilly (Miranda), Peter Gallagher (Brother Tony), Darryl Hannah (Mary Plunkett), Liam Neeson (Martin Brogan), Ray McAnally (Plunkett Senior), Liz Smith (Mrs. Plunkett), Donal McCann (Eamon), Mary Coughlan (Katie)
Color
96 min.

We're No Angels (1989)
USA
Production: Paramount Pictures
Producer: Art Linson
Distribution: Paramount (USA) and United International Pictures (UK)
Director: Neil Jordan
Screenplay: David Mamet
Cinematography: Philippe Rousselot
Editors: Mick Audsley and Joke van Wijk
Production Designer: Wolf Kroeger
Costume Designer: Theoni Aldredge
Music: George Fenton
Cast: Robert De Niro (Ned), Sean Penn (Jim), James Russo (Bobby), Ray McAnally (Warden), Demi Moore (Molly), Hoyt Axton (Father Levesque), John C. Reilly (Monk), Wallace Shawn (Translator), Bruno Kirby (Deputy)
Color
106 min.

The Miracle (1991)
UK
Production: Palace Productions, Promenade, Film Four International, and British Screen
Producers: Stephen Woolley, Redmond Morris, Nik Powell, Bob Weinstein, and Harvey Weinstein
Distribution: Miramax Films
Director: Neil Jordan
Screenplay: Neil Jordan
Cinematography: Philippe Rousselot
Editing: Joke van Wijk

Production Designer: Gemma Jackson
Music: Anne Dudley
Cast: Niall Byrne (Jimmy Coleman), Lorraine Pilkington (Rose), Donal McCann (Sam Coleman), Beverly D'Angelo (Renee Baker), Mikkel Gaup (Jonner), Tom Hickey (Tommy)
Color
97 min.

The Crying Game (1992)
UK
Production: Channel Four, Palace Productions, Nippon Film Development and Finance, Eurotrustees, and British Screen
Producers: Nik Powell, Stephen Woolley, Paul Cowan, Elizabeth Karlsen, and Diana Dill
Distribution: Miramax Films and Live Home Video (DVD)
Director: Neil Jordan
Screenplay: Neil Jordan
Cinematography: Ian Wilson
Editor: Kant Pan
Production Designer: Victoria Boydell
Costume Designer: Sandy Powell
Music: Anne Dudley
Cast: Stephen Rea (Fergus), Forest Whitaker (Jody), Miranda Richardson (Jude), Adrian Dunbar (Peter Maguire), Jaye Davidson (Dil), Jim Broadbent (Col), Ralph Brown (Dave)
Color
111 min.

Interview with the Vampire: The Vampire Chronicles (1994)
USA
Production: Geffen Company
Producers: Stephen Woolley, David Geffen, and Redmond Morris
Distribution: Geffen Pictures and Warner Home Video (DVD)
Director: Neil Jordan
Screenplay: Anne Rice, based upon her novel
Cinematography: Philippe Rousselot
Visual Effects: Rob Legato
Editors: Mick Audsley and Joke van Wijk
Production Designer: Dante Ferretti
Costumes: Sandy Powell
Music: Elliot Goldenthal
Cast: Tom Cruise (Lestat), Brad Pitt (Louis), Antonio Banderas (Armand),

Christian Slater (Molloy), Kirsten Dunst (Claudia), Stephen Rea (Santiago), Thandie Newton (Yvette), Domiziana Giordano (Madeleine)
Color
122 min.

Michael Collins (1996)
USA
Production: Geffen Pictures and Warner Brothers
Producer: Stephen Woolley
Distribution: Geffen Pictures (USA) and Warner Brothers (UK and USA)
Director: Neil Jordan
Screenplay: Neil Jordan
Cinematography: Chris Menges
Editors: J. Patrick Duffner and Tony Lawson
Production Designer: Anthony Pratt
Costume Designer: Sandy Powell
Music: Elliot Goldenthal
Cast: Liam Neeson (Michael Collins), Aidan Quinn (Harry Boland), Alan Rickman (Eamon de Valera), Julia Roberts (Kitty Kiernan), Stephen Rea (Ned Broy), Ian Hart (Joe O'Reilly), Gerard McSorley (Cathal Brugha), Charles Dance (Soames), Brendan Gleeson (Tobin)
Color
132 min.

The Butcher Boy (1997)
USA
Production: Geffen Pictures, Warner Brothers, and Butcher Boy Films
Producers: Redmond Morris and Stephen Woolley
Distribution: Geffen Pictures and Warner Brothers
Director: Neil Jordan
Screenplay: Neil Jordan and Patrick McCabe
Cinematography: Adrian Biddle
Editor: Tony Lawson
Music: Elliot Goldenthal
Costumes: Sandy Powell
Cast: Eamonn Owens (Francie Brady), Stephen Rea (Benny Brady), Aisling O'Sullivan (Annie Brady), Alan Boyle (Joe Purcell), Fiona Shaw (Mrs. Nugent), Andrew Fullerton (Philip Nugent), Ian Hart (Uncle Alo), Brendan Gleeson (Father Bubbles), Milo O'Shea (Father Sullivan), Sinead O'Connor (Our Lady)
Color
110 min.

In Dreams (1999)
USA
Production: DreamWorks SKG and Amblin Entertainment
Producers: Stephen Woolley, Redmond Morris, and Charles Burke
Distribution: DreamWorks and DreamWorks Home Entertainment (DVD)
Director: Neil Jordan
Screenplay: Bruce Robinson and Neil Jordan, based upon *Doll's Eyes*, by Bari Wood
Cinematography: Darius Khondji
Editor: Tony Lawson
Production Designer: Nigel Phelps
Music: Elliot Goldenthal and Elizabeth Fraser
Costume Designer: Jeffrey Kurland
Cast: Robert Downey Jr. (Vivian Thompson), Annette Bening (Claire Cooper), Katie Sagona (Rebecca Cooper), Aidan Quinn (Paul Cooper), Paul Gilfoyle (Jack Kay), Stephen Rea (Dr. Silverman), Krystal Benn (Ruby), Dossy Peabody (Vivian's Mother)
Color
98 min.

The End of the Affair (1999)
USA/Germany
Production: Columbia Pictures
Producers: Stephen Woolley, Neil Jordan, and Kathy Sykes
Distribution: Columbia Pictures
Director: Neil Jordan
Screenplay: Neil Jordan, based upon the Graham Greene novel
Cinematography: Roger Pratt
Editor: Tony Lawson
Production Designer: Anthony Pratt
Costume Designer: Sandy Powell
Music: Michael Nyman
Cast: Ralph Fiennes (Maurice Bendrix), Julianne Moore (Sarah Miles), Stephen Rea (Henry Miles), Ian Hart (Mr. Parkis), Samuel Bould (Lance Parkis), Jason Isaacs (Father Richard Smythe)
Color
102 min.

The Last September (1999)
Ireland/UK/France
Production: Matrix Films, Scala Thunder, Irish Film Board, RTÉ, BSkyB, British Screen, IMA, Canal+

Producers: Sara Giles, Neil Jordan, Rod Stoneman, Joe Mulholland, Nik Powell, and Steven Woolley
Distribution: Trimark Pictures (USA) and UGC DA International (worldwide)
Director: Deborah Warner
Screenplay: John Banville, based on the Elizabeth Bowen novel
Cinematography: Slawomir Idziak
Editor: Kate Evans
Production Designer: Caroline Amies
Music: Zbigniew Preisner
Cast: Michael Gambon (Sir Richard Naylor), Tom Hickey (O'Brien), Keely Hawes (Lois Farquar), David Tennant (Gerald Colthurst), Richard Roxburgh (Captain Daventry), Gary Lydon (Peter Connolly), Maggie Smith (Lady Myra Naylor), Lambert Wilson (Hugo Montmorency), Jane Birkin (Francie Montmorency)
Color
103 min.

"Not I" (2000)
Ireland
Production: Blue Angel Films, Tyrone Productions, RTÉ, Channel Four, and Irish Film Board
Producer: Stephen Woolley
Director: Neil Jordan
Screenplay: Samuel Beckett
Cinematography: Roger Pratt
Editor: Tony Lawson
Cast: Julianne Moore
Color
14 min.

The Good Thief (2002)
Canada
Production: Alliance Atlantis, Double Down Productions, TNVO, and Metropolitan Films
Producers: Stephen Woolley, John Wells, Seaton McLean, Kristin Harms, Tracey Seaward, Thierry de Navacelle, and Neil Jordan
Distribution: Fox Searchlight Pictures (USA)
Director: Neil Jordan
Screenplay: Neil Jordan, based on the film *Bob le Flambeur,* written by Jean-Pierre Melville and August Le Breton and directed by Jean-Pierre Melville
Cinematography: Chris Menges
Editor: Tony Lawson

Music: Elliot Goldenthal and Leonard Cohen
Production Designer: Anthony Pratt
Costume Designer: Penny Rose
Cast: Nick Nolte (Bob Montagnet), Tchéky Karyo (Roger), Nutsa Kukhianidze (Anne), Saïd Taghmaoui (Paolo), Marc Lavoine (Remi), Ouassini Embarek (Said), Emir Kusturica (Vladimir), Ralph Fiennes (Tony Angel), Mark Polish (Albert), Michael Polish (Bertram)
Color
108 min.

The Actors (2003)
Ireland
Production: Company of Wolves, Miramax, Film Four International, and Irish Film Board
Producers: Stephen Woolley, Redmond Morris, and Neil Jordan
Director: Conor McPherson
Screenplay: Conor McPherson, based upon Neil Jordan's short story
Cinematography: Seamus McGarvey
Editor: Emer Reynolds
Music: Michael Nyman
Cast: Michael Caine (O'Malley), Michael Gambon (Barreller), Dylan Moran (Tom), Miranda Richardson (Mrs. Magnani), Lena Headey (Dolores), Michael McElhattan (Jock), Aisling O'Sullivan (Rita)
Color
92 min.

Breakfast on Pluto (2005)
Production: Pathé Pictures, Irish Film Board, Northern Ireland Film and Television Commission, Number 9 Films, and Parallel Films
Producers: Stephen Woolley, Alan Moloney, and Neil Jordan
Distribution: Sony Pictures Classics (USA)
Director: Neil Jordan
Screenplay: Neil Jordan and Patrick McCabe, based on Patrick McCabe's novel
Editor: Tony Lawson
Cinematography: Declan Quinn
Production Designer: Tom Conroy
Music: Anna Jordan
Cast: Cillian Murphy (Patrick "Kitten" Braden), Liam Neeson (Father Bernard), Ruth Negga (Charlie), Laurence Kinlan (Irwin), Ruth McCabe (Ma Braden), Stephen Rea (Bertie), Eva Birthistle (Eily Bergin), Brendan Gleeson (John-Joe), Gavin Friday (Billy Hatchet), Brian Ferry (Mr. Silky String)

Color
135 min.

The Brave One (2007)
Production: Redemption Pictures, Silver Pictures, Village Roadshow Pictures
Producers: Bruce Berman, Susan Downey, Jodie Foster, Herb Gains, Dana Goldberg, Joel Silver
Distribution: Warner Brothers
Director: Neil Jordan
Screenplay: Roderick Taylor, Bruce A. Taylor, and Cynthia Mort
Editor: Tony Lawson
Cinematography: Philippe Rousselot
Production Designer: Kristi Zea
Music: Dario Marianelli
Plot: In this psychological thriller, Erica (Jodie Foster) avenges the brutal murder of her lover, David (Naveen Andrews), by taking justice into her own hands. The film's visual style recalls the gritty depiction of urban spaces in *Mona Lisa* and *The Crying Game.* The story echoes two important themes that resonate throughout Neil Jordan's films: the way that experiences of violence transform the human psyche and the fact that shocking events cause people to locate the strangers, or uncanny doubles, within themselves.
Cast: Jodie Foster (Erica), Naveen Andrews (David), Terrence Howard (Mercer), Mary Steenburgen (Carol), Jane Adams (Nicole)
Color
119 min.

Bibliography

Adams, Douglas. "Three Scores Less Ordinary: The Best of 1998." *Film Score Monthly* 4.3 (March 1999): 29.

Adamson, Judith. *Graham Greene and Cinema.* Norman, Okla.: Pilgrim Books, 1984.

Agnew, Paddy. "International Critics Applaud Jordan Film on *Michael Collins.*" *Irish Times,* September 2, 1996, 5.

Anderson, Benedict. *Imagined Communities: Reflections on the Origin and Spread of Nationalism.* London: Verso, 1984.

Arata, Steven. "The Occidental Tourist: *Dracula* and the Anxiety of Reverse Colonization." In *Dracula: Bram Stoker.* Ed. Glennis Byron. 119–44. New York: St. Martin's Press, 1999.

Auty, Chris. "*Angel* in the House." *City Lights,* November 5–11, 1982, 12–13.

Backus, Margot Gayle. *The Gothic Family Romance: Heterosexuality, Child Sacrifice, and the Anglo-Irish Colonial Order.* Durham, N.C.: Duke University Press, 1999.

Barton, Ruth. *Irish National Cinema.* London: Routledge, 2004.

Baudrillard, Jean. From *Simulations.* In *Postmodernism: A Reader.* Ed. Patricia Waugh. 186–88. London: Edward Arnold, 1992.

Beardsworth, Richard. "On the Critical 'Post': Lyotard's Agitated Judgment." In *Judging Lyotard.* Ed. Andrew Benjamin. 43–80. London: Routledge, 1992.

Beckett, Samuel. "Not I." In *Ends and Odds: Eight New Dramatic Pieces.* 13–23. New York: Grove Press, 1976.

Beckett on Film. DVD. Blue Angel Films and Tyrone Productions. Ambrose Video, 2003.

Benshoff, Harry M. *Monsters in the Closet: Homosexuality and the Horror Film.* Manchester: Manchester University Press, 1997.

Belting, Hans. "The Fetish of Art in the Twentieth Century: The Case of the *Mona Lisa.*" *Diogenes* 183 (1998): 83–106.

Bew, Paul. "History It Ain't" *Daily Telegraph,* October 14, 1996. LexisNexis.

Booth, Philip. "*In Dreams;* Get Real, Please." *Sarasota Herald Tribune,* January 15, 1999, 15.

Boozer, Jack. "Bending Phallic Patriarchy in *The Crying Game." Journal of Popular Film and Television* 22.4 (Winter 1995): 172–79.

Botting, Fred. *Gothic.* London: Routledge, 1996.

Braudy, Leo. "Afterword: Rethinking Remakes." In *Play It Again Sam: Retakes on Remakes.* Ed. Andrew Horton and Stuart Y. McDougal. 327–34. Berkeley: University of California Press, 1998.

Breakfast on Pluto Home Page. Sony Pictures Classics. January 1, 2006. http://www.sonyclassics.com/breakfastonpluto/main.htm.

Bronfen, Elisabeth. *Home in Hollywood: The Imaginary Geography of Cinema.* New York: Columbia University Press, 2004.

Brophy, Philip. "Horrality—The Textuality of Contemporary Horror Films." In *The Horror Reader.* Ed. Ken Gelder. 276–84. London: Routledge, 2000.

Brown, Carolyn. "Figuring the Vampire: Death, Desire, and the Image." In *The Eight Technologies of Otherness.* Ed. Sue Golding. 117–33. London: Routledge: 1997.

Brown, Royal. *Overtones and Undertones: Reading Film Music.* Berkeley: University of California Press, 1994.

Burns, Mike. "*Michael Collins." Europe* 362 (December 1996/January 1997): 29–30. Academic Search Premier.

Byron, Glennis. "Gothic in the 1890s." In *A Companion to the Gothic.* Ed. David Punter. 132–42. Oxford: Blackwell, 2000.

Canby, Vincent. "Hoodlums Disguised as Men of the Cloth." *New York Times,* December 15, 1989, C20. LexisNexis.

———. "Red Riding Hood in *Company of Wolves." New York Times,* April 19, 1985, C8. LexisNexis.

Carr, Jay. "High Spirits." *Boston Globe,* November 18, 1988, 33. LexisNexis.

Carroll, Joe. "Conflict Flaws Collins Film, Say Critics." *Irish Times,* October 19, 1996, 8.

Carroll, Noel. *The Philosophy of Horror, or Paradoxes of the Heart.* New York: Routledge, 1990.

Carty, Ciaran. "Jordan's Journey." *(Chicago) Sunday Tribune,* January 30, 2000, 10–11.

Cassidy, Edel. "The Man behind Pluto." In *In the Can: The Essential Guide to Film in Ireland.* 2d ed. 60–62. Limerick: Cassidy Publishing, 2005.

Castle, Terry. *The Female Thermometer: Eighteenth-Century Culture and the Invention of the Uncanny.* Oxford: Oxford University Press, 1995.

———. "Phantasmagoria and Modern Reverie." In *The Horror Reader.* Ed. Ken Gelder. 29–46. London: Routledge, 2000.

Cavallero, Dani. *The Gothic Vision: Three Centuries of Horror, Terror, and Fear.* London: Continuum, 2002.

Chumo, Peter. "*The Crying Game,* Hitchcockian Romance, and the Quest for Identity." *Literature Film Quarterly* 23.4 (October 1995): 247–53.

Cixous, Hélène. "Fiction and Its Phantoms: A Reading of Freud's *Das Unheimliche* (The "Uncanny")." *New Literary History* 7.3 (Spring 1976): 525–48.
Clancy, Luke. "Ireland's Eyes" (interview with Neil Jordan). *Magill* (February 1990): 37–41.
Cleary, Joe. "'Forked-Tongued on the Border Bit': Partition and the Politics of Form in Contemporary Narratives of the Northern Irish Conflict." *South Atlantic Quarterly* 95.1 (Winter 1996): 227–76.
Collins, Jim. "Genericity in the Nineties: Eclectic Irony and the New Sincerity." In *Film Theory Goes to the Movies*. Ed. Jim Collins, Hilary Rader, and Ava Preacher Collins. 242–63. New York: Routledge, 1993.
Conrich, Ian. "Before Sound." In *The Horror Film*. Ed. Stephen Prince. 40–57. New Brunswick, N.J.: Rutgers University Press, 2004.
Coogan, Tim Pat. *The IRA: A History*. Boulder, Colo.: Rogers Rinehart, 1994.
———. *Michael Collins: The Man Who Made Ireland*. Boulder, Colo.: Rogers Rinehart, 1996.
———. *The Troubles: Ireland's Ordeal, 1966–1996, and the Search for Peace*. Boulder, Colo.: Rogers Rinehart, 1997.
Corrigan, Timothy. "*Auteurs* and the New Hollywood." In *The New American Cinema*. Ed. Jon Lewis. 38–63. Durham, N.C.: Duke University Press, 1998.
Costantini, Mariaconcetta. "Crossing Boundaries: The Revision of Gothic Paradigms in Heat and Dust." In *Empire and the Gothic: The Politics of Genre*. Ed. Andrew Smith and William Hughes. 155–71. New York: Palgrave Macmillan, 2003.
Coundouriotis, Eleni. "*Dracula* and the Idea of Europe." *Connotations* 9.2 (1999–2000): 143–59.
Craft, Christopher. "'Kiss Me with Those Red Lips': Gender and Inversion in Bram Stoker's *Dracula*." In *Dracula*. Ed. Nina Auerbach and David Skal. 444–59. New York: W. W. Norton, 1997.
Crowdus, Gary. "The Screenwriting of Irish History: Neil Jordan's *Michael Collins*." *Cineaste* 22.4 (1997): 14–19.
Crowther, Paul. "*Les Immatériaux* and the Postmodern Sublime." In *Judging Lyotard*. Ed. Andrew Benjamin. 192–205. New York: Routledge, 1992.
Cullen, Paul. "Collins Film 'Could Contain Metaphor for North.'" *Irish Times*, September 9, 1996, 1.
Cullingford, Elizabeth Butler. *Ireland's Others: Gender and Ethnicity in Irish Literature and Popular Culture*. South Bend, Ind.: Notre Dame University Press, 2001.
———. "The Reception of *Michael Collins*." *Irish Literary Supplement* 16.1 (Spring 1997): 17–18.
———. "Virgins and Mothers: Sinead O'Connor, Neil Jordan, and *The Butcher Boy*." *Yale Journal of Criticism* 15.1 (2002): 185–210.

Daly, Nicholas. "The Ferris Wheel of Identity: Gender, Race, and Nation in the Films of Neil Jordan." *New Formations* 34 (Summer 1998): 42–52.
Daoudi, Bouziane. "Algerian Rappers Sing the Blues." *UNESCO Courier* 53.7–8 (July/August 2000): 34–36. http://www.unesco.org/courier/2000_07/uk/doss23.htm.
Dare, Michael. "In the Company of Neil Jordan." *LA Weekly,* April 19, 1985. www.disinfotainmenttoday.com/emulsionalproblems/jordan.html.
Deussing, Ryan. "Berlin Stories: A Festival's High and Low Lights." *Village Voice,* March 10, 1998, 118.
Dmytryk, Edward, dir. *The End of the Affair* (1955). DVD. Columbia Tristar, 2000.
Dolan, Pamela. "An Elephant at the Altar: Religion in Contemporary Irish Cinema." In *Contemporary Irish Cinema: from* The Quiet Man *to* Dancing at Lughnasa. Ed. James MacKillop. 139–52. Syracuse, N.Y.: Syracuse University Press, 1999.
Donald, James. "The Fantastic, the Sublime, and the Popular, Or, What's at Stake in Vampire Films?" In *Fantasy and the Cinema.* Ed. James Donald. 233–51. London: British Film Institute, 1989.
Donnelly, K. J. *Pop Music in British Cinema: A Chronicle.* London: British Film Institute, 2001.
Doody, Margaret Anne. "Deserts, Ruins, and Troubled Waters: Female Dreams in Fiction and the Development of the Gothic Novel." *Genre* 10 (1977): 529–73.
———. *The True Story of the Novel.* New Brunswick, N.J.: Rutgers University Press, 1996.
Dwyer, Michael. "Are You Right There, Michael?" *Irish Times* (Weekend Supplement), November 9, 1996.
———. "Blood Simple." *Irish Times* (Weekend Supplement), January 7, 1995, 12.
———. "Dynamic, Thrilling, Epic Cinema." *Irish Times,* November 8, 1996, 13.
———. "Irish Film Received Seven Oscar Nominations." *Irish Times,* February 10, 1994, 1.
———. "Jordan's Triumph." *Irish Times* July 14, 1997, 9.
———. "On the Set." *Irish Times* (Weekend Supplement), August 5, 1995, 3.
———. "Summertime in Bray." *Irish Times,* April 12, 1991, 10.
Dyer, Richard. "Children of the Night: Vampirism as Homosexuality." In *Sweet Dreams: Sexuality, Gender, and Popular Fiction.* Ed. Susannah Radstone. 47–72. London: Lawrence and Wishart, 1988.
Eby, Douglas. "*In Dreams.*" *Cinefantastique* 31.1–2 (February 1999): 8–9.
Edelman, Lee. "At Risk in the Sublime: The Politics of Gender and Theory." In *Gender and Theory: Dialogues on Feminist Criticism.* Ed. Linda Kauffman. 213–24. Oxford: Basil Blackwell, 1989.

Edge, Sarah. "Women Are Trouble, Did You Know That, Fergus?" *Feminist Review* 50 (Summer 1995): 173–86.
Edmundson, Mark. *Nightmare on Main Street: Angels, Sadomasochism, and the Culture of the Gothic.* Cambridge, Mass.: Harvard University Press, 1997.
Estés, Clarissa Pinkola. *Women Who Run with the Wolves.* New York: Ballantine, 1996.
Falsetto, Mario. *Personal Visions: Conversations with Contemporary Film Directors.* Los Angeles: Silman James, 2000.
Farley, Fidelma. "Neil Jordan." In *Fifty Contemporary Filmmakers.* Ed. Yvonne Tasker. 186–94. London: Routledge, 2002.
Ferrante, Anthony C. "Robert Downey Jr.'s More Disturbed Than Usual in Director Neil Jordan's Psychothriller." *Fangoria* 180 (March 1999): 26–29, 82.
Finney, Angus. *The Egos Have Landed: The Rise and Fall of Palace Pictures.* London: Heinemann, 1996.
Floyd, Nigel. "The Miracle." *Monthly Film Bulletin* 58 (April 1991): 107.
Flynn, Arthur. *Irish Film: 100 Years.* Bray: Kestrel Books, 1996.
Fowkes, Katherine. *Giving Up the Ghost: Spirits, Ghosts, and Angels in Mainstream Comedy Films.* Detroit: Wayne State University Press, 1998.
Freeland, Cynthia. "Explaining the Uncanny in *The Double Life of Veronique.*" In *Horror Film and Psychoanalysis: Freud's Worst Nightmare.* Ed. Steven Schneider. 87–105. Cambridge: Cambridge University Press, 2004.
———. "Horror and Art Dread." In *The Horror Film.* Ed. Stephen Prince. 189–205. New Brunswick, N.J.: Rutgers University Press, 2004.
———. "The Sublime in Cinema." In *Passionate Views: Film, Cognition, and Emotion.* Ed. Carl Plantinga and Greg M. Smith. 65–83. Baltimore: Johns Hopkins University Press, 2000.
Freud, Sigmund. *The Standard Edition of the Complete Psychological Works of Sigmund Freud.* Ed. and trans. James Strachey. Vol. 16. London: Hogarth Press, 1953.
———. "The Uncanny" (1919). In *On Creativity and the Unconscious: Papers on the Psychology of Art, Literature, Love, Religion.* Ed. and intro. Benjamin Nelson. 122–61. New York: Harper and Row, 1958.
Gabbard, Krin. *Jammin' at the Margins: Jazz and the American Cinema.* Chicago: University of Chicago Press, 1996.
Gibbons, Luke. "Demisting the Screen: Neil Jordan's *Michael Collins.*" *Irish Literary Supplement* 16.1 (Spring 1997): 16.
———. *Edmund Burke and Ireland: Aesthetics, Politics and the Colonial Sublime.* Cambridge: Cambridge University Press, 2003.
———. "Engendering the State: Narrative, Allegory, and *Michael Collins.*" *Eire-Ireland* 31.3–4 (Fall–Winter 1996): 261–69.
———. "On the Beach: Luke Gibbons on the Other Ireland." *Artforum International* 3.2 (October 1992): 13.
Gilbert, Sandra, and Susan Gubar. *The Madwoman in the Attic: The Woman

Writer and the Literary Imagination. 2d ed. New Haven, Conn.: Yale University Press, 2000.
Giles, Jane. *The Crying Game.* London: British Film Institute, 1997.
Glicksman, Marlaine. "Irish Eyes." *Film Comment* 26.1 (1990): 9–11; 68–71.
Goddu, Teresa A. "Introduction to *American Gothic.*" In *The Horror Reader.* Ed. Ken Gelder. 265–75. London: Routledge, 2000.
Golway, Terry. "Life in the 90s." *America,* October 26, 1996, 6.
"The Good Thief." *Hollywood Reporter Online,* September 9, 2002. LexisNexis.
Gorbman, Claudia. *Unheard Melodies: Narrative Film Music.* Bloomington: Indiana University Press, 1987.
Grady, Frank. "Vampire Culture." In *Monster Theory: Reading Culture.* Ed. Jeffrey Jerome Cohen. 225–41. Minneapolis: University of Minnesota Press, 1996.
Greene, Graham. *The End of the Affair.* New York: Putnam, 1998.
Gridley, Mark C. *Jazz Styles: History and Analysis,* 3d ed. Englewood Cliffs, N.J.: Prentice Hall, 1988.
Grist, Leighton. "'It's Only a Piece of Meat': Gender Ambiguity, Sexuality, and Politics in *The Crying Game* and *M. Butterfly.*" *Cinema Journal* 42.4 (Summer 2003): 3–28.
Halberstam, Judith. *Skin Shows: Gothic Horror and the Technology of Monsters.* Durham, N.C.: Duke University Press, 1995.
Halpern, Leslie. *Dreams on Film: The Cinematic Struggle between Art and Science.* Jefferson, N.C.: MacFarland and Co., 2003.
Harris, Eoghan. "*Michael Collins:* A Tale of Bad History and Art." *Sunday Times (London),* November 10, 1996. LexisNexis.
———. "Tally Ho: Not So Funny, Mr. Jordan." *Irish Times,* October 26, 1996.
Harrison, Eric. "Nolte Carries Tale of Theft and Redemption." *Houston Chronicle,* April 18, 2003, 10.
Haslam, Richard. "'A Race Bashed in the Face': Imagining Ireland as a Damaged Child." *Jouvert: A Journal of Postcolonial Studies* 4.1 (1999). http://social.chass.ncsu.edu/jouvert.
Hawkins, Maureen S. G. "Women, 'Queers,' Love, and Politics: *The Crying Game* as a Corrective Adaptation of/Reply to *The Hostage.*" In *Representing Ireland: Gender, Class, Nationality.* Ed. Susan Shaw Sailer. 194–212. Gainesville: University Press of Florida, 1997.
Heiland, Donna. *Gothic and Gender: An Introduction.* London: Blackwell, 2004.
Hennessy, Rosemary. "Ambivalence as Alibi: On the Historical Materiality of Late Capitalist Myth in *The Crying Game* and Cultural Theory." *Genders* 24 (1996): 1–34.
Hill, John. "Crossing the Water: Hybridity and Ethics in *The Crying Game.*" *Textual Practice* 12.1 (1998): 89–100.

Hollinger, Veronica. "Fantasies of Absence: The Postmodern Vampire." In *Blood Read: The Vampire as Metaphor in Contemporary Culture.* Ed. Joan Gordon and Veronica Hollinger. 199–212. Philadelphia: University of Pennsylvania Press, 1997.

Honeycutt, Kirk. "The Good Thief." *Hollywood Reporter,* September 9, 2002. www.hollywoodreporter.com/hr/film/reviews/article_display.jsp?&rid=1887.

Hopkins, Lisa. *Screening the Gothic.* Austin: University of Texas Press, 2005.

Hopper, Keith. "'Cat-Calls from the Cheap Seats': The Third Meaning of Neil Jordan's *Michael Collins.*" *Irish Review* 21 (Autumn/Winter 1997): 1–28.

———. "Hairy on the Inside: Re-visiting Neil Jordan's *The Company of Wolves.*" *Canadian Journal of Irish Studies* 29.2 (Fall 2003): 17–26.

Horrigan, Bill. "You Are Not I." In *Image Stream.* Ed. Helen Molesworth. 67–73. Columbus: Ohio State University Wexner Center for the Arts, 2003.

Horton, Andrew. "Cinematic Makeovers and Cultural Border Crossings: Kusturica's *Time of the Gypsies* and Coppola's *Godfather* and *Godfather II.*" In *Play It Again Sam: Retakes on Remakes.* Ed. Andrew Horton and Stuart Y. McDougal. 172–90. Berkeley: University of California Press, 1998.

Huggan, Graham. "Ghost Stories, Bone Flutes, Cannibal Countermemory." In *The Horror Reader.* Ed. Ken Gelder. 352–63. London: Routledge, 2000.

Hughes, William. "A Singular Invasion: Revisiting the Postcoloniality of Bram Stoker's *Dracula.*" In *Empire and the Gothic: The Politics of Genre.* Ed. Andrew Smith and William Hughes. 88–102. New York: Palgrave Macmillan, 2003.

Hunter, Jim. "The Origin of 'Danny Boy' or 'Londonderry Air.'" www.theoriginofdannyboy.com.

Hutcheon, Linda. *The Politics of Postmodernism.* New York: Routledge, 1989.

Irving, Katrina. "EU-phoria? Irish National Identity, European Union, and *The Crying Game.*" In *Writing New Identities: Gender, Nation, and Immigration in Contemporary Europe.* Ed. Giela Brinker-Gabler and Sidonie Smith. 295–314. Minneapolis: University of Minnesota Press, 1997.

James, Caryn. "Mr. Dark's Lighter Moment." *New York Times,* April 6, 2003, AR 13.

———. "A Sinister, Sexual Fairy Tale of Transformations." *New York Times,* July 26, 1989, C17. LexisNexis.

James, Joy. "Black Femmes Fatales and Sexual Abuse in Progressive 'White' Cinema: Neil Jordan's *Mona Lisa* and *The Crying Game.*" *Camera Obscura* 33 (September 1995). RDS online database.

Jameson, Fredric. *Postmodernism, or, The Cultural Logic of Late Capitalism.* London: Verso, 1990.

Johnson, Brian D. "Tales from the Crypt." *Macleans,* November 14, 1994. Academic Search Elite.

Jones, Alan. "The Company of Wolves." *Cinefantastique* 15.1 (January 1985): 4–7.

———. "High Spirits." *Cinefantastique* 19.1–2 (January 1989): 16–20.
Jones, Stephen. *The Essential Monster Movie Guide: A Century of Creature Features on Film, TV, and Video.* New York: Billboard Books, 2000.
Jordan, Neil, dir. *Angel* (1982). DVD. Motion Picture Company of Ireland, 2003.
———, dir. *The Butcher Boy* (1997). VHS. Warner Studios, 1998.
———, dir. *The Company of Wolves* (1984). DVD. Hen's Tooth Video, 2002.
———, dir. *The Crying Game* (1992). Collector's Edition. DVD. Lion's Gate Home Entertainment, 2004.
———. *Donal McCann Remembered.* Ed. Pat Laffan and Faith O'Grady. 44–47. Dublin: New Island Press, 2000.
———. *Dream of a Beast.* London: Chatto and Windus, 1983.
———, dir. *The End of the Affair* (1999). DVD. Columbia TriStar, 2000.
———, dir. *The Good Thief* (2002). DVD. Twentieth-Century Fox/Fox Searchlight Pictures, 2003.
———. *High Spirits.* London: Faber and Faber, 1989.
———, dir. *High Spirits* (1988). DVD. MGM Home Entertainment, 2002.
———, dir. *In Dreams* (1998). DVD. Dreamworks Home Entertainment, 1999.
———, dir. *Interview with the Vampire* (1994). DVD. Warner Home Video, 2000.
———, dir. *Michael Collins* (1996). DVD. Warner Brothers Home Video, 1997.
———. *Michael Collins: Screenplay and Film Diary.* New York: Penguin, 1996.
———, dir. *The Miracle.* VHS. Palace Productions, 1990.
———, dir. *Mona Lisa* (1986). DVD. Criterion Collection, 2001.
———. *Night in Tunisia.* Dublin: Irish Writer's Cooperative, 1976.
———, dir. "Not I" (2000). *Beckett on Film.* DVD. Ambrose Video, 2003.
———. *The Past.* London: Jonathan Cape, 1980.
———. *Shade.* London: Bloomsbury Publishing, 2004.
———. *Sunrise with Sea Monster.* London: Bloomsbury, 1994.
———. "Tally Ho! Mr. Harris." *Irish Times,* October 23, 1996.
———, dir. *We're No Angels* (1989). DVD. Paramount Pictures, 2004.
Jordan, Neil, and David Leland. *Mona Lisa.* London: Faber and Faber, 1986.
"Jordan/Sheridan Partnership Launches New Cable Television Concept for Ireland." *Business Wire,* May 3, 1999, 1291. InfoTrac.
Joyce, James. *Ulysses* (1922). New York: Vintage, 1990.
Kassabian, Anahid. *Hearing Film: Tracking Identifications in Contemporary Hollywood Film Music.* New York: Routledge, 2001.
———. "The Sound of a New Film Form." In *Popular Music and Film.* Ed. Ian Inglis. 91–102. London: Wallflower Press, 2001.
Kauffmann, Stanley. "Intentions." *New Republic,* May 5, 2003, 22, 24.

Keane, John. "The Modern Democratic Revolution: Reflections on Lyotard's *Postmodern Condition.*" In *Judging Lyotard.* Ed. Andrew Benjamin. 81–90. London: Routledge, 1992.
Kearney, Richard. "Avenging *Angel:* An Analysis of Neil Jordan's First Irish Feature Film." *Studies: An Irish Quarterly Review* 71.283 (Autumn 1982): 296–303.
———. *Transitions.* Manchester: Manchester University Press, 1988.
Kemp, Stuart. "Jordan Orbits Murphy Starrer 'Pluto.'" *Hollywood Reporter,* May 13 2004. BPI Communications. LexisNexis.
Kempley, Rita. "*Interview with the Vampire.*" *Washington Post,* June 9, 1995, B7.
Kilgour, Maggie. "Dr. Frankenstein Meets Dr. Freud." In *American Gothic: New Interventions in a National Narrative.* Ed. Robert K. Martin and Eric Savoy. 40–53. Iowa City: University of Iowa Press, 1998.
Knight, Arthur. "'It Ain't Necessarily So That It Ain't Necessarily So': African American Recordings of *Porgy and Bess* as Film and Cultural Criticism." In *Soundtrack Available: Essays on Film and Popular Music.* Ed. Arthur Knight and Pamela Robertson Wojcik. 319–46. Durham, N.C.: Duke University Press, 2001.
Knight, Arthur, and Pamela Robertson Wojcik. "Overture." In *Soundtrack Available: Essays on Film and Popular Music.* Ed Arthur Knight and Pamela Robertson Wojcik. 1–15. Durham, N.C.: Duke University Press, 2001.
Kolker, Robert. "Algebraic Figures: Recalculating the Hitchcock Formula." In *Play It Again Sam: Retakes on Remakes.* Ed. Andrew Horton and Stuart Y. McDougal. 34–51. Berkeley: University of California Press, 1998.
Kotsopoulos, Aspasia, and Josephine Mills. "*The Crying Game:* Gender, Genre, and 'Postfeminism.'" *Jump Cut* 39 (June 1994): 15–24.
Lack, Russell. *Twenty-Four Frames Under: A Buried History of Film Music.* London: Quartet Books, 1997.
Landy, Marcia. "The International Cast of Irish Cinema: The Case of *Michael Collins.*" *boundary 2* 27.2 (2000): 21–44.
Lappas, Catherine. "'Seeing Is Believing, but Touching Is the Truth': Female Spectatorship and Sexuality in *The Company of Wolves.*" *Women's Studies* 25.2 (1996): 115–35.
Layden, Dervila. "Imagining the Future: Post-Troubles Comic Fiction." In *National Cinema and Beyond: Studies in Irish Film.* Ed. Kevin Rockett and John Hill. 105–14. Dublin: Four Courts Press, 2004.
Lehane, Pearse, dir. "Check the Gate: Putting Beckett on Film." *Beckett on Film.* DVD. Ambrose Video, 2003.
Lehman, Peter. "Crying over the Melodramatic Penis: Melodrama and Male Nudity in Films of the 90s." In *Masculinity: Bodies, Movies, Culture.* Ed. Peter Lehman. 25–41. London: Routledge: 2001.
Lenning, Alkeline Van, Saskia Maas, and Wendy Leeks. "Is Womanliness Noth-

ing but a Masquerade?" In *Masquerade and Identities: Essays on Gender, Sexuality, and Marginality*. Ed. Efrat Tseëlon. 83–100. London: Routledge, 2001.
Linehan, Hugh. "Greene Giant" (interview with Neil Jordan). *Irish Times*, January 27, 2000, 15–16.
———. "*Michael Collins* Breaks Irish Box Office Records." *Irish Times*, November 16, 1996, 18.
———. "A Small Country Projects Itself on the Big Screen of Quality World Cinema." *Irish Times*, February 10, 1994, 12.
London, Justin. "Leitmotifs and Musical Reference in the Classical Film Score." In *Music and Cinema*. Ed. James Buhler, Caryl Flinn, and David Neumeyer. 85–96. Hanover, N.H.: Wesleyan University Press, 2000.
Lugowski, David. "Genre Conventions and Visual Style in *The Crying Game*." *Cineaste* 20.1 (1993): 32–34.
Lurie, Susan. "Performativity in Disguise: Ideology and the Denaturalization of Identity in Theory and *The Crying Game*." *Velvet Light Trap* 43 (Spring 1999): 51–62.
Lyons, Kathleen. "Transcultural Cinema: Reading Race and Ethnicity in Neil Jordan's *The Crying Game*." *South Atlantic Review* 67.1 (Winter 2002): 92–103.
Lyotard, Jean-François. *Lessons on the Analytic of the Sublime*. Trans. Elizabeth Rottenburg. Stanford, Calif.: Stanford University Press, 1994.
———. *The Postmodern Condition: A Report on Knowledge*. Trans. Geoff Bennington and Brian Massumi. Minneapolis: University of Minnesota Press, 1984.
———. *Toward the Postmodern*. Ed. Robert Harvey and Mark S. Roberts. Amherst, N.Y.: Prometheus Books, 1999.
MacDonald, Laurence E. *The Invisible Art of Film Music: A Comprehensive History*. New York: Ardsley House, 1998.
Malcolm, Derek. "From Gentle Parable into Frantic Farce." *Manchester Guardian*, June 10, 1990, 26. LexisNexis.
———. "Hands across the Irish Sea." *Manchester Guardian Weekly*, December 18, 1988, 25. LexisNexis.
Mamet, David. *We're No Angels*. New York: Grove Weidenfeld, 1990.
Maslin, Janet. "A Ghostly Scheme to Save a Castle." *New York Times*, November 18, 1988, 10C.
———. "Rapture and Terror, Bound by Blood." *New York Times*, November 11, 1994, C1.
———. "Want to Share Dreams? Be Careful; It's Murder." *New York Times*, January 15, 1999, 14E.
———. "When Passion Turns to Poison." *New York Times*, December 3, 1999, E1. LexisNexis.
Massumi, Brian. "Realer than Real: The Simulacrum According to Deleuze

and Guattari." 1997. http://www.anu.edu.au/HRC/first_and_last/works/realer.htm.
Mazdon, Lucy. *Encore Hollywood: Remaking French Cinema.* London: British Film Institute, 2000.
McCabe, Patrick. *The Butcher Boy.* New York: Dell Publishing, 1992.
———. "On Neil Jordan." In *Writers on Directors.* Ed. Susan Gray. 153–56. New York: Watson-Guptill, 1999.
McCourt, Malachy. *Danny Boy: The Legend of the Beloved Irish Ballad.* London: Running Press, 2002.
McGowan, John. "Postmodernism." In *The Johns Hopkins Guide to Literary Theory and Criticism.* Ed. Michael Groden and Martin Kreiswirth. 768–71. Baltimore: Johns Hopkins University Press, 2005.
McIlroy, Brian. "Neil Jordan and the Anglo-Irish Gothic." In *Horror International.* Ed. Steven Jay Schneider and Tony Williams. 128–40. Detroit: Wayne State University Press, 2005.
———. *Shooting to Kill: Filmmaking and the "Troubles" in Northern Ireland.* Trowbridge: Flicks, 1998.
McLellan, Joseph. "Music for Mona Lisa." *American Record Guide* 62.1 (January/February 1999): 236.
McLoone, Martin."The Abused Child of History: Neil Jordan's *The Butcher Boy.*" *Cineaste* 23.4 (1998): 32–36.
———. *Irish Film: the Emergence of a Contemporary Cinema.* London: British Film Institute, 2000.
McSwiney, Séamas. "Trying to Take the Gun out of Irish Politics: An Interview with Neil Jordan." *Cineaste* 22.4 (1997): 20–23.
Melville, Jean-Pierre, dir. *Bob le Flambeur.* DVD. Criterion Collection, 2002.
———. "Radio Interview." *Bob le Flambeur.* DVD. Criterion Collection, 2002.
———. "Jean-Pierre Melville on *Bob le Flambeur.*" Interview with Rui Nogueira. *Bob le Flambeur.* DVD. Criterion Collection, 2002.
Metz, Christian. "Aural Objects." In *Film Theory and Criticism.* 6th ed. Ed. Leo Braudy and Marshall Cohen. 366–69. New York: Oxford University Press, 2004.
Michel, Frann. "Racial and Sexual Politics in *The Crying Game.*" *Cineaste* 20.1 (1993): 30–31.
Milligan, Hugh. "Epic Irishman Is About to Live Again." *Seattle Times,* December 17, 1995. *Irish History on the Web.* Members.cruzio.com/~sbarrett/reviews.htm.
Mishra, Vijay. *The Gothic Sublime.* Albany: State University of New York Press, 1994.
Mitchell, Elvis. "Decadence and Decay as Art Forms." *New York Times,* April 2, 2003, E3.
Moane, Geraldine. "Colonialism and the Celtic Tiger." In *Reinventing Ireland:*

Culture, Society, and the Global Economy. Ed. Peadar Kirby, Luke Gibbons, and Michael Cronin. 109–23. London: Pluto Press, 2002.

Modleski, Tania. "The Terror of Pleasure." In *The Horror Reader*. Ed. Ken Gelder. 285–93. London: Routledge, 2000.

Moore, Darrell. "Now You Can See it: The Liberal Aesthetic and Racial Representation in *The Crying Game*." *CineAction* 32 (Autumn 1993): 63–67.

Morgan, Jack. *The Biology of Horror: Gothic Literature and Film*. Carbondale: Southern Illinois University Press, 2002.

Morris, David. "Gothic Sublimity." *New Literary History* 16.2 (Winter 1985): 299–319.

Moses, Michael Valdez. "The Irish Vampire: *Dracula*, Parnell, and the Troubled Dreams of Nationhood." *Journal x* 2.1 (1997): 66–111.

Neely, Sarah. "Cultural Ventriloquism: The Voice-over in Film Adaptations of Contemporary Irish and Scottish Literature." In *National Cinema and Beyond*. Ed. Kevin Rockett and John Hill. 125–34. Dublin: Four Courts Press, 2004.

Negra, Diane. "Irishness, Innocence, and American Identity Politics before and after 11 September." In *Keeping It Real: Irish Film and Television*. Ed. Ruth Barton and Harvey O'Brien. 54–68. London: Wallflower Press, 2004.

Nesbit, Molly. "Apart without a Face: *Orlando* and *The Crying Game*." *Artforum* 31.10 (Summer 1993): 92–95.

Neumeyer, David, with Caryl Flinn and James Buhler. Introduction. to *Music and Cinema*. Ed. David Neumayer, Caryl Flinn, and James Buhler. 1–29. Hanover, N.H.: Wesleyan University Press, 2000.

Nixon, Nicola. "Making Monsters, or Serializing Killers." In *American Gothic: New Interventions in a National Narrative*. Ed. Robert K. Martin and Eric Savoy. 217–36. Iowa City: University of Iowa Press, 1998.

Nuckols, Ben. "*The Good Thief*." Associated Press. March 31, 2003. Lexis-Nexis.

O'Connor. Frank. "Guests of the Nation." In *Guests of the Nation*. 1–19. London: MacMillan and Co., 1931.

O'Dea, Tom. "Miracle Worker." *Irish Independent*, March 4, 1991.

O'Donnell, Eamonn. "*The Miracle*." *Film Base News* 24 (July/August 1991): 21–22.

O'Hehir, Andrew. "The Dying Game." *Salon.com*. January 15, 1999. www.salon.com/ent/movies/reviews/1999/01/15reviewa.html.

Olsen, Mark. "Right Place, Right Time." *Film Comment* 38.6 (November/December 2002): 62–63.

O'Rawe, Desmond. "At Home with Horror: Neil Jordan's Gothic Variations." *Irish Studies Review* 11.2 (2003): 189–98.

O'Sullivan, Charlotte. "Massacre of the Innocents." *Sight and Sound* 18.3 (March 1998): 10–13.

O'Toole, Fintan. "Diary." *New Statesman*, October 25, 1996, 6.

———. "Ireland." In *Irish Art Now: From the Poetic to the Political.* Ed. Declan McGonagle, Fintan O'Toole, and Kim Levin. 21–26. London: Merrell Holbertson Publishers and Independent Curators International, 1999.
———. "A National Cinema: Is It Possible?" *Irish Times,* November 13, 1996, 12.
Ozturk, Seyda. "Simulation Reloaded." *Cinetext: Film and Philosophy.* August 5, 2003. cinetext.philo.at/magazine/ozturk/simulation_reloaded.html.
"The Patriot Game" [1957]. *Brobdingnagian Bards: A Bard's Celtic Lyrics Directory.* www.thebards.net/music/lyrics/Patriot_Game.shtml.
Payne, Robert M. "*The Crying Game:* Crossed Lines." *Jump Cut* 39 (June 1994): 7–14.
Petrie, Duncan, ed. *Cinema and the Realms of Enchantment.* London: British Film Institute, 1993.
Piñedo, Isabel Cristina. "Postmodern Elements of the Contemporary Horror Film." In *The Horror Film.* Ed. Stephen Prince. 85–117. New Brunswick, N.J.: Rutgers University Press, 2004.
Pramaggiore, Maria. "Bullet Ridden/Star Studded History." *Jouvert: A Journal of Postcolonial Studies* 4.1 (1999). http://social.chass.ncsu.edu/jouvert.
———. "The Celtic Blue Note: Jazz in Neil Jordan's *Angel, The Miracle,* and 'Night in Tunisia.'" *Screen* 39.3 (1998): 272–88.
———. "'I Kinda Liked You as a Girl': Masculinity, Postcolonial Queens, and the Nature of Terrorism in Neil Jordan's *The Crying Game.*" In *Contemporary Irish Cinema: From* The Quiet Man *to* Dancing at Lughnasa. Ed. James MacKillop. 85–97. Syracuse, N.Y.: Syracuse University Press, 1999.
Punter, David, and Glennis Byron. *The Gothic.* Malden, Mass.: Blackwell, 2004.
Reav, Pauline. *Music in Film: Soundtracks and Synergy.* London: Wallflower Press, 2004.
Rice, Anne. *Interview with the Vampire: Book I of the Vampire Chronicles.* New York: Ballantine Books, 1976.
Robinson, Michael. "The 'Danny Boy' Trivia Collection." March 2, 2005. www.standingstones.com.
Rockett, Kevin, and Emer Rockett. *Neil Jordan: Exploring Boundaries.* Dublin: Liffey Press, 2003.
Rockett, Kevin, and Eugene Finn. *Still Irish: A Century of the Irish in Film.* Dublin: Red Mountain Press, 1995.
Rodenberg, Hans-Peter. "Bridging the Abyss: Neil Jordan, Irishman in Hollywood." *Journal for the Study of British Culture* 5.2 (1998): 155–70.
Rogers, Lori. *Feminine Nation: Performance, Gender, and Resistance in the Works of John McGahern and Neil Jordan.* Latham, Md.: University Press of America, 1998.
Romney, Jonathan. "Bad Dreams." *New Statesman,* May 3, 1999, 45.
Roth, Phyllis. "Suddenly Sexual Women in Bram Stoker's *Dracula.*" In *Drac-*

ula. Ed. Nina Auerbach and David Skal. 411–21. New York: W. W. Norton, 1997.
Royle, Nicholas. *The Uncanny.* New York: Routledge, 2003.
Russell, Hawley. "Crossing Games: Reading Black Transvestism at the Movies." *Critical Matrix* 8.12 (1994): 109–25.
Salisbury, Mark. "The New Breed of Werewolf." *Fangoria* 134 (July 1994): 20–25, 90.
Sassoon, Donald. *Becoming Mona Lisa: The Making of a Global Icon.* New York: Harcourt, 2001.
Saunders, Michael William. *Imps of the Perverse: Gay Monsters in Film.* Westport, Conn.: Praeger, 1998.
Savoy, Eric. "The Face of the Tenant: A Theory of American Gothic." In *American Gothic: New Interventions in a National Narrative.* Ed. Robert K. Martin and Eric Savoy. 3–19. Iowa City: University of Iowa Press, 1998.
Schaffer, Talia. "'A Wilde Desire Took Me': The Homoerotic History of *Dracula.*" *English Literary History* 61 (1994): 381–425.
Schmitt, Cannon. *Alien Nation: Nineteenth-Century Gothic Fictions and English Nationality.* Philadelphia: University of Pennsylvania Press, 1997.
———. "Mother Dracula: Orientalism, Degeneration, and Anglo-Irish National Subjectivity in the *Fin de Siècle.*" *Bucknell Review* 38 (1994): 25–43.
Schruers, Fred. "Neil Jordan." *Rolling Stone,* November 14, 1996, 82. Academic Search Premier.
Schwartz, Ronald. *Noir, Now and Then: Film Noir Originals and Remakes, 1944–1999.* Westport, Conn.: Greenwood Press, 2001.
Sedgwick, Eve Kosofsky. *The Coherence of Gothic Conventions.* New York: Methuen, 1986.
Seltzer, Mark. *Serial Killers: Death and Life in America's Wound Culture.* New York: Routledge, 1998.
Sheehy, Ted. "*The Butcher Boy.*" *Film Ireland* 63 (February/March 1998): 14–15.
———. "A Look over Jordan." *Film Ireland* 74 (February/March 2000): 16–18.
Shields, Paula. "2 Way Mirror." *Film Ireland* 91 (March/April 2003): 16–18.
Silverman, Kaja. *The Acoustic Mirror: The Female Voice in Psychoanalysis and Cinema.* Bloomington: Indiana University Press, 1988.
Simon, John. "Not So Jocund." *National Review,* July 18, 1986, 56, 58–59.
Skal, David. *The Monster Show: A Cultural History of Horror.* New York: Faber and Faber, 2001.
Smith, Jeff. "Movie Music as Moving Music: Emotion, Cognition, and the Film Score." In *Passionate Views: Film, Cognition, and Emotion.* Ed. Carl Plantinga and Greg M. Smith. 147–67. Baltimore: Johns Hopkins University Press, 2000.
———. "Popular Music and Comic Allusion in Contemporary Cinema." In

Soundtrack Available: Essays on Film and Popular Music. Ed. Pamela Robertson Wojcik and Arthur Knight. 407–30. Durham, N.C.: Duke University Press, 2001.

Smith, Webster. "Observations on the *Mona Lisa* Landscape." *Art Bulletin* 67.2 (1985): 183–99.

Smyth, Gerry. "*The Crying Game:* Postcolonial or Postmodern?" *Paragraph* 20.2 (1997): 154–73.

"The South Bank Show: *Michael Collins.*" London Weekend Television, 1996. *Michael Collins* DVD. Warner Home Video, 1997.

Staunton, Dennis. "Neil Jordan's New Film a Hit in Berlin." *Irish Times,* February 22, 1991, 10.

Stoddart, Helen. "Horror, Circus, and Orientalism." In *Empire and the Gothic: The Politics of Genre.* Ed. Andrew Smith and William Hughes. 118–35. New York: Palgrave Macmillan, 2003.

Studlar, Gaylyn. *In the Realm of Pleasure: Von Sternberg, Dietrich, and the Masochistic Aesthetic.* Urbana: University of Illinois Press, 1988.

Sweeny, Ellen E. "'Pigs!': Polluting Bodies and Knowledge in Neil Jordan's *The Butcher Boy.*" In *National Cinema and Beyond.* Ed. Kevin Rockett and John Hill. 77–88. Dublin: Four Courts Press, 2004.

Taubin, Amy. "Fierce Creatures: *The Butcher Boy* and *The Spanish Prisoner.*" *Village Voice,* April 7, 1998. Academic Search Elite.

Taylor, Charles. "*The Good Thief.*" *Salon.com.* April 2, 2003. LexisNexis.

Taylor, Paul. "*Angel.*" *Monthly Film Bulletin* 49.586 (November 1982): 257–58.

———. "*The Company of Wolves.*" *Monthly Film Bulletin* 51.608 (September 1984): 264–65.

Taylor, Paul, and Steve Jenkins. "Wolf at the Door." *Monthly Film Bulletin* 51.608 (September 1984): 265–66.

Telotte, J. P. "Through a Pumpkin's Eye: The Reflexive Nature of Horror." In *American Horrors: Essays on the Modern American Horror Film.* Ed. Gregory A. Waller. 114–28. Urbana: University of Illinois Press, 1987.

Todorov, Tsvetan. *The Fantastic.* Trans. Richard Howard. Ithaca, N.Y.: Cornell University Press, 1990.

Toibin, Colm. "The *In Dublin* Interview: Neil Jordan." *In Dublin,* April 29, 1982.

Travers, Peter. "Irish Shocker: *The Butcher Boy.*" *Rolling Stone,* April 16, 1998. Academic Search Elite.

Tybjerg, Casper. "Shadow-Souls and Strange Adventures: Horror and the Supernatural in European Silent Film." In *The Horror Film.* Ed. Stephen Prince. 15–39. New Brunswick, N.J.: Rutgers University Press, 2004.

Valente, Joseph. *Dracula's Crypt: Bram Stoker, Irishness, and the Question of Blood.* Urbana: University of Illinois Press, 2002.

Veeder, William. "The Nurture of the Gothic, or How Can a Text Be Both

Popular and Subversive?" In *American Gothic: New Interventions in a National Narrative.* Ed. Robert K. Martin and Eric Savoy. 20–39. Iowa City: University of Iowa Press, 1998.
Vineberg, Steven. "*The End of the Affair:* Neil Jordan's Comeback." *Chronicle of Higher Education,* January 28, 2000. Academic Search Elite.
Williams, Linda. *Hard Core: Power, Pleasure, and "The Frenzy of the Visible."* Berkeley: University of California Press, 1999.
———. "When the Woman Looks." In *Re-Vision: Essays in Feminist Criticism.* Ed. Mary Ann Doane, Patricia Mellencamp, and Linda Williams. 83–99. Frederick, Md.: American Film Institute, 1984.
Winarski, Kathleen Gallagher. "Neil Jordan's *The Miracle:* From Fiction to Film." In *Contemporary Irish Cinema: From* The Quiet Man *to* Dancing at Lughnasa. Ed. James MacKillop. 98–109. Syracuse, N.Y.: Syracuse University Press, 1999.
Wolfreys, Julian. *Victorian Hauntings: Spectrality, Gothic, the Uncanny, and Literature.* London: Palgrave Macmillan, 2002.
Wood, Robin. *Hollywood from Vietnam to Reagan.* New York: Columbia University Press, 1986.
———. "What Lies Beneath?" Foreword to *Horror Film and Psychoanalysis: Freud's Worst Nightmare.* Ed. Steven Jay Schneider. xiii–xviii. Cambridge: Cambridge University Press, 2004.
Woodworth, Paddy. "Jordan: Taking Comedy Seriously." *Irish Times,* November 2, 1988, 12.
Woolley, Stephen. "When Is a Film Not a Film? When British Journalists Don't See It." *New Statesman,* November 8, 1996, 38. Academic Search Elite.
Wynne, Catherine. "Crossing the Border: Post-Colonial Carnival in Neil Jordan's *The Crying Game.*" In *Moving Pictures, Migrating Identities.* Ed. Eva Rueschmann. 139–58. Jackson: University Press of Mississippi, 2003.
Yaeger, Patricia. "Toward a Female Sublime." In *Gender and Theory.* Ed. Linda Kauffman. 191–212. Oxford: Basil Blackwell, 1989.
Zanger, Jules. "Metaphor into Metonymy: The Vampire Next Door." In *Blood Read: The Vampire as Metaphor in Contemporary Culture.* Ed. Joan Gordon and Veronica Hollinger. 17–26. Philadelphia: University of Pennsylvania Press, 1997.
Zillax, Amy. "The Scorpion and the Frog: Agency and Identity in Neil Jordan's *The Crying Game.*" *Camera Obscura* 25 (May 1995). RDS online database.
Zipes, Jack, ed. *The Oxford Companion to Fairy Tales.* Oxford: Oxford University Press, 2000.
Zizek, Slavoj. "From Courtly Love to *The Crying Game.*" *New Left Review* 202 (November/December 1993): 95–108.
Zucker, Carole. "The Poetics of Point of View: Neil Jordan's *The Butcher Boy.*" *Literature Film Quarterly* 31.3 (2003): 203–8.

———. "'Sweetest Tongue Has Sharpest Tooth': The Dangers of Dreaming in Neil Jordan's *The Company of Wolves*." *Literature Film Quarterly* 28.1 (2000): 66–71.

Zylinka, Joanna. *On Spiders, Cyborgs, and Being Scared.* Manchester: Manchester University Press, 2001.

Index

Maria Pramaggiore is a professor of film studies at North Carolina State University in Raleigh. She was a Fulbright Fellow at University College Cork in 2007 and is the author of *Identifying Others and Performing Identities: Irish and African-American Cinema, 1980–2000*. She coauthored *Film: A Critical Introduction* with Tom Wallis and coedited *Re-presenting Bisexualities: Subjects and Cultures of Fluid Desire* with Donald E. Hall.

Books in the series Contemporary Film Directors

Nelson Pereira dos Santos
Darlene J. Sadlier

Abbas Kiarostami
Mehrnaz Saeed-Vafa and Jonathan Rosenbaum

Joel and Ethan Coen
R. Barton Palmer

Claire Denis
Judith Mayne

Wong Kar-wai
Peter Brunette

Edward Yang
John Anderson

Pedro Almodóvar
Marvin D'Lugo

Chris Marker
Nora Alter

Abel Ferrara
Nicole Brenez, translated by Adrian Martin

Jane Campion
Kathleen McHugh

Jim Jarmusch
Juan Suárez

Roman Polanski
James Morrison

Manoel de Oliveira
John Randal Johnson

Neil Jordan
Maria Pramaggiore

Paul Schrader
George Kouvaros

The University of Illinois Press
is a founding member of the
Association of American University Presses.

Composed in 10/13 New Caledonia
with Helvetica Neue display
by Jim Proefrock
at the University of Illinois Press
Manufactured by Cushing-Malloy, Inc.

University of Illinois Press
1325 South Oak Street
Champaign, IL 61820-6903
www.press.uillinois.edu